OXFORD RESEARCH STUDIES IN GEOGRAPHY

General Editors
J. Gottmann   J.A. Steers
F.V. Emery   C.D. Harris

Arroyos and Environmental Change in the American South-West

Ronald U. Cooke
Bedford College, University of London

and

Richard W. Reeves
University of Arizona, Tucson

CLARENDON PRESS · OXFORD
1976

Oxford University Press, Ely House, London W. 1

GLASGOW NEW YORK TORONTO MELBOURNE WELLINGTON
CAPE TOWN IBADAN NAIROBI DAR ES SALAAM LUSAKA ADDIS ABABA
DELHI BOMBAY CALCUTTA MADRAS KARACHI LAHORE DACCA
KUALA LUMPUR SINGAPORE HONG KONG TOKYO

ISBN 0 19 823213 6

© *Oxford University Press 1976*

*Printed in Great Britain by
Fletcher & Son Ltd, Norwich*

EDITORIAL PREFACE

The word arroyo, according to the *O.E.D.* is found as early as 775 in Old Spanish, but is of uncertain origin. It was usually translated into English as a small stream, water-course or similar feature but is now used to describe gullies characterised by steeply sloping or vertical walls in cohesive, fine sediments and by flat and generally sandy floors. Arroyos are found in several arid or semi-arid parts of the world, including the south-western United States, parts of India, South Africa and around the Mediterranean. Their occurrence and development are sometimes spectacular and have often received comment.

The authors have worked mainly in Arizona and California, and they have been able to obtain and assess a great deal of field evidence. In several places they have also been able to correlate this with early surveys made when the first farmers and pastoralists settled in the region. Perhaps the most interesting feature of their study is that they have shown how physiography and geology, archaeology, climatology, and land management have had to be taken into account in explaining arroyos. Those in the United States have possibly all developed since 1850. Many were started by white settlers in their transformation of the original landscape into one considered, at the time, more suitable for agriculture or pastoral use. The destruction of the original vegetation often led to the cutting of small runnels in storms; it was only a matter of time before these became true arroyos. The Indians, too, may well have played a similar, but less effective, part. On the other hand, some may well have originated from natural causes.

Whatever their origin arroyos are now a major feature in many landscapes and the authors of this volume are to be congratulated on studying them so comprehensively in two major regions. They have not only made an important contribution to geomorphology, but have also given both the student and the general reader a convincing account of the development of these channels.

Oxford, Spring 1975   J.G.   J.A.S.
                                                     F.V.E.   C.D.H.

PREFACE

The folklore of the American South-West is dominated by conflicts, such as the familiar struggles between cowboys and Indians, and farmers and pastoralists. Behind these dramas lies the more persistent struggle between the inhabitants and their natural environment. It was fought by groups as diverse as Mormons, Texans, and Papago Indians, using barbed wire, windmills, irrigation ditches, and other weapons against forces that included fire, flood, and drought. In this study we examine an important aspect of environmental transformation that arose during the struggle since about 1850: the formation of arroyos in some of the major alluvial valley floors in southern Arizona and coastal California.

The nature and causes of arroyo formation have been a matter of concern and debate for many years among interested individuals in such disparate fields as geology, range management, archaeology, and climatology. Much of the interest lies in the related possibilities of explaining arroyos in terms of contemporaneous environmental changes, and of controlling arroyo cutting and the soil erosion accompanying it. We would hesitate to enter the debate if it were not for two rather surprising facts. In the first place, although many studies imply the widespread occurrence of arroyos and many explanations invoke regional environmental changes, there have been remarkably few attempts to study arroyo distribution. Thus we find that arroyos are much more numerous in California than previous observers have indicated, and arroyos are not quite as common in southern Arizona as we had been led to believe. A second, even more important fact is that in southern Arizona and coastal California much of the extensive body of historical evidence relevant to a study of arroyos and environmental change has not previously been analysed.

Our approach has been to create a generalized explanatory model of arroyo formation and to test a number of hypotheses within it in the context of a wide range of field and historical evidence. Our inquiry leads us into the under-developed, but potentially fertile, territory on the frontiers between historical research and scientific analysis of environmental change. We recognise at the outset that the fragmentary historical record makes impossible a perfect explanation of arroyos and the environmental changes related to them: the best that we can hope to do is to narrow the area of speculation and uncertainty, and to make progress towards identifying the most probable explanations. We hope that this attempt to join the equation with the archive contributes to the environmental debate in the American South-West, and that the results are also relevant to the discussion of similar problems in semi-arid lands elsewhere.

We are pleased to acknowledge the encouragement and assistance of many friends. In the field we have been helped by J. Haskell, D. Houston, D. Josif,

W. Miller, and W. Sigleo. Archival research was facilitated by the generous co-operation of many organizations, especially the Arizona Historical Society (Tucson), the Bureau of Land Management (Phoenix, Sacramento, and Riverside), the Southern Pacific Transportation Company (San Francisco), the U.S. Geological Survey (Tucson), the National Archives (Washington), the universities of California (Los Angeles) and Arizona (Tucson), and the National Oceanic and Atmospheric Administration (Asheville). Much of the research in southern Arizona was undertaken when Cooke was a Visiting Professor in the Department of Geography and Area Development of the University of Arizona (Tucson). Dr. G.E. Hollis, Dr. R. Bennett, Dr. A. Lavell, and K. Hughes contributed to the task of data analysis, and Valerie Cawley expertly drew the diagrams in the Department of Geography, University College London. Finally, we are grateful to Professor A.H. Clark, Dr. D.R. Harris, Professor L.B. Leopold, and others who have kindly read and commented upon parts of the manuscript. Although they do not necessarily subscribe to our views, they have helped to eliminate errors and clarify our presentation. We are responsible for any remaining shortcomings.

Ronald U. Cooke
Richard W. Reeves

January 1974

ACKNOWLEDGEMENTS

The authors and publishers wish to express their thanks to the following for permission to reproduce copyright material: L.T. Burcham and the California Division of Forestry for Figure III.2 and data in Figures III.24 and III.25; R.M. Turner, W.D. Sellers, and the University of Arizona Press for Figure II.13; A.A. Nichol and the University of Arizona College of Agriculture for Figure II.19; and W.B. Bull and the *American Journal of Science* for data on Figure III.13.

CONTENTS

LIST OF FIGURES

PART I

The Arroyo Problem

DIMENSIONS OF THE PROBLEM

During the past hundred years many debris-filled valleys throughout the South-Western United States have experienced rapid and pronounced erosion. Gentle swales and broad, undissected plains that occasionally carried shallow floods became deeply incised with arroyos — valley bottom gullies characterized by steeply sloping or vertical walls in cohesive, fine sediments and by flat and generally sandy floors. Valley floors once covered by grass and sedge and adorned with occasional clumps of trees and bushes were transformed into desiccated alluvial terraces that have been periodically diminished by losses to encroaching arroyos. The bed of one rather insignificant stream in California was lowered more than 65 feet in one place, and now courses for several miles through a trench hundreds of feet wide. Most changes, however, were somewhat less spectacular.

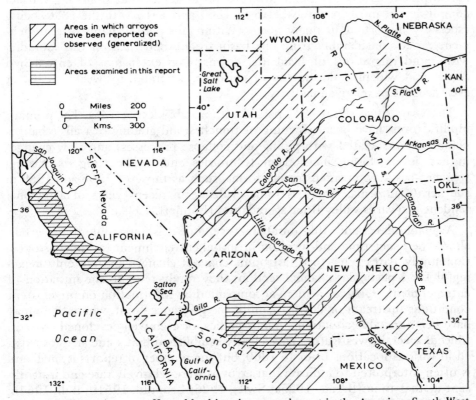

Figure I.1 The main areas affected by historic entrenchment in the American South-West

The full magnitude and areal extent of this modern entrenchment can only be generally deduced. The scientific and popular literature of the South-West contains scores of references to arroyos and arroyo cutting, but incomplete and often vague reporting, definitional problems, and the effects of conservation measures in intensively used areas make precise location of arroyos rather difficult.

Figure I.1 represents a highly generalized picture — based on both published accounts and personal observations — of the main areas affected by entrenchment in the South-West. Only in southern Arizona (Part II) and coastal California (Part III) has the precise distribution of arroyos been studied. Hundreds of arroyos, with an aggregate length of thousands of miles and involving several hundred thousand square miles of land, occur in several states and many major drainage basins, and under a wide variety of environmental conditions. Yet many alluviated valleys — perhaps a majority — do not appear to have been incised at all.

There is remarkable agreement on the general period in which arroyo cutting was most active, although precise, reliable dates for specific valleys are surprisingly few. Available information indicates that trenching was accomplished in most localities between 1865 and 1915 with the 1880s being especially important in many places. Within this period, dates of entrenchment varied considerably from one basin to another. Incision was sporadic, with rapid migrations of headcuts, downstream extensions of entrenched zones, and widening during runoff episodes, separated by weeks, years, or even decades of relative inactivity.

The years since about 1915 passed with notably less activity. The primary modifications have been widening of trenches and grading of walls (changes commonly associated with piping and collapse processes) and slow changes in bed levels. Some incision of tributaries and head-cutting of existing trenches has accompanied major storms, such as those of 1938 and 1969 in southern California. There is some evidence in recent years of a regional tendency towards valley-floor aggradation (Emmett, 1974).

Available dates are often unsatisfactory, and it is impossible to be certain about the exact time and location of initial entrenchment for most arroyos. Commonly dates refer to catastrophic channel changes and are only meaningful for a particular channel section; they rarely refer to the initiation of entrenchment. They are seldom accompanied by information on pre-existent conditions upstream or downstream of the reference point, where there may have been unstable situations, minor gullies, or even well-developed arroyos. Indeed, several investigators have clearly established that some arroyos existed in various locations prior to 1860, but the number of reports is small and is often interpreted to indicate that arroyos were relatively rare and insignificant at that time (Bryan, 1925a; Swift, 1926; Leopold, 1951b; Bull, 1964b; Denevan, 1967).

INTEREST IN THE PROBLEM

The episode of erosional activity that affected the South-West is not unique. Pronounced soil erosion, gullying, and related sedimentation problems are well known in other parts of the world during historical times, and they have often accompanied pioneer settlement and significant land-use changes. But several aspects of the South-Western episode have tended to focus attention on it. The great size of some arroyos has tended to set them apart from similar but smaller features elsewhere. The early adoption of a special and exotic-sounding name, first proposed by Dodge (1902) and later popularized by Bryan in numerous articles, has tended to suggest their distinctiveness. Also important was the coincidence that arroyos happened to be forming at a time when the South-West was developing its reputation as a principal field laboratory for many natural sciences.

But two additional reasons were mainly responsible for focusing attention on South-Western arroyos. In the first place, arroyo cutting had a rapid and detrimental effect on the flat, fertile, and easily irrigated valley floors, the most desirable sites for settlement and economic activity within an otherwise harsh, dry environment. Secondly, some alluvial deposits which had been entrenched were found to contain conclusive evidence of previous cutting and filling episodes, suggesting to some a continuity of causation from geological to historical times.

Since the discovery of arroyos by the scientific community at the turn of the century, arroyo cutting has generated a significant body of research and a literature which includes more than a hundred pertinent articles. There are two cardinal foci of interest in this material. Firstly, many practical aspects of arroyo cutting have been considered. Most investigators refer to the undesirable consequences of arroyo formation, and a few studies have recommended management practices that might help to stabilize or heal existing trenches and prevent entrenchment of unaffected valleys (Thornthwaite, Sharpe, and Dosch, 1942; Peterson, 1950; Schumm and Hadley, 1957). Secondly, many studies have emphasized a more academic aspect of arroyo cutting: its importance in the attempt to understand the nature of a complex environment and the changes it experiences.

Practical Aspects: The Effects of Arroyo Cutting

Arroyo cutting had several effects on South-Western environments. Major consequences included loss of land, increased sediment production, altered hydrological relationships, changes in vegetation, and some significant effects on settlements. Nothing approaching a reliable estimate of these consequences is possible for the South-West as a whole, but some historical sources provide instructive local details and general observations.

In many valleys substantial proportions of floodplain — often exceeding 25 per cent — have been removed by arroyo cutting. In one unusual but well-documented case (Kennan, 1917) — cutting of the arroyos along the

New and Alamo rivers in the Imperial Valley (California) during 1906 — over 15,000 acres of land were converted into deep channels, and between 400 and 450 million cubic yards of material were removed in nine months. According to Kennan (1917, p.59)" . . . the channels thus formed during the floods of 1906 had an aggregate length of more than forty miles, and . . . the solid matter scoured out of them and carried down into the Salton Sea was nearly four times as great as the whole amount excavated in the digging of the Panama Canal."

The effect of increased sediment loads on lands and drainage systems downstream of arroyos is unknown, but it must have been considerable, especially during the period of incision. Hydrological changes were certainly significant. Before entrenchment, the valley bottoms provided inefficient and hydraulically rough channels which acted to retard and spread floods, to promote infiltration, and to moderate peak discharges. The alluvial fills served important water-storage and flow-regulatory functions by absorbing runoff and providing a source of water for riparian vegetation and for base-flow in dry periods.

Cutting of arroyos at once produced narrow, deep, and relatively smooth drains for the efficient removal of water from drainage systems, and initiated rapid draining of alluvial deposits. Discharge characteristics of flows must have altered drastically, becoming relatively more 'peaked' and of shorter duration. Dense grass cover and lush stands of riparian vegetation — dependent either on overflow or reliable supplies of near-surface water — dwindled, and were replaced by increasingly xeric plant communities and their attendant wildlife (Bryan, 1928b; Cottam and Stewart, 1940).

Consequences of arroyo cutting for human settlement are frequently mentioned in the literature but rarely chronicled in detail. Loss of land to expanding arroyos, and consequent lowering of water-tables and desiccation of newly formed terraces greatly reduced productivity and provided new, costly problems, such as the need for canal deepening. Agriculture, often recently established and mostly of a semi-subsistence nature in the late nineteenth century, was seriously restricted by the diminution of suitably watered arable land in valley bottoms. Where cropping had depended on irrigation, problems of increasingly fluctuating and decreasingly reliable water sources, and difficulties of transferring water to fields, succeeded in driving out farmers or increasing their emphasis on livestock (Gregory and Moore, 1931).

But livestock production — the basis of the rural economy in many areas affected by entrenchment from as early as 1880 — also suffered. Valley floors, often containing cienegas — meadows of grass and sedge nourished by high water tables — had provided the best and most dependable forage and supplies of stock water during the dry season. Indeed, they were often the only significant locations of these necessities during prolonged droughts. Loss or decline of these resources with entrenchment and contemporaneous overgrazing permanently affected livestock-carrying capacities. On the other hand, near to viable settlements at places where highly capitalized and productive irrigation agriculture was developing based on well water, these problems were less significant, and in some instances arroyos actually alleviated flooding by providing useful, low-cost storm drains. Nevertheless, arroyo floods often carried expense with them: railroads and roads were damaged, and bridges, land fills, culverts, and channel-stabilization structures had to be provided. Watershed conservation practices were also expensive, and occasionally of dubious value (Peterson and Branson, 1962; Peterson and Hadley, 1955).

Academic Aspects: Arroyos and Environmental Change

Despite the often costly effects of arroyo cutting, a dominant interest of many investigators has been in the possible significance of arroyos with respect to other environmental changes. Arroyos have often been taken to be indicators of environmental change. Behind this role lies the assumption that stream erosion and deposition, and the resulting channel morphology, are more or less reliable indicators of prevailing, or at least recent, watershed conditions. Notable alterations in these indicators are taken to represent significant changes in one or more environmental variables within a water-shed. Some environmental variables have been viewed traditionally as being relatively unchanging (e.g. geology), whereas others, especially land use, vegetation, and climate, are believed both to have changed rapidly in recent times and to impose direct and indirect controls on steamflow and related phenomena.

The cutting of arroyos — spectacular and irrefutable — is thus seen as evidence of environmental change over a huge area and within a fairly well-defined period of time. Attempts to identify the environmental changes, to determine the relative importance of land use and climate, and to establish links between the changes and stream activity have become the central area of inquiry in the study of arroyos.

A diversity of fringe interests surrounds this focus. Some have worked towards improving the understanding of geomorphological processes in dry environments (Leopold and Miller, 1956; Schumm and Hadley, 1957; Melton, 1965). To a few others, arroyo cutting has been useful in developing arguments in the protracted controversy concerning man-environment relations, both in support of geographical determinism (Huntington, 1914; Bryan, 1929; 1940; 1941) and in opposition to it (Reagan, 1924a; Thornthwaite, Sharpe, and Dosch, 1942). And since the 1920s, several authors have considered the possible significance of modern arroyo cutting in the interpretation of past environments. Hypothesized relationships between environmental change and contemporary arroyos have been used to interpret geological evidence of cutting and filling in several South-Western valleys, and to construct Quaternary chronologies of environmental change (Albritton and Bryan, 1939; Sayles and Antevs, 1941; Martin, 1964). These chronologies have been used in the study of South-Western archaeology (Hack, 1939; Bryan, 1941; Miller and Wendorf, 1958).

REVIEW: HYPOTHESES OF ARROYO ORIGIN

Knowledge of the causes of arroyo cutting during the last hundred years is essential to developing strategies for erosion control, and to understanding the role of arroyos in changing environments. If, as has been widely argued, man's activities are alone responsible, appropriate conservation practices should prevent erosion worsening, and perhaps aid the recovery of damaged land. Conclusive proof of the relationship between man and arroyos would tend to cast doubt on the role of possible contemporary changes in natural phenomena, and would certainly limit the value of contemporary evidence in the interpretation of prehistoric periods of arroyo cutting. Alternatively, if certain natural phenomena, such as climate, have changed significantly and can be causally related to entrenchment, many conservation strategies could be futile.

It is worth noting in advance that there is a certain correlation between the professional interests of investigators and the conclusions they reach on the causes of arroyo cutting. Agriculturalists, foresters, and conservationists commonly indict man for his excesses. In contrast, some geologists, palaeobotanists, and archaeologists have sought and found 'natural' explanations. Such partiality is, perhaps, a measure of the luxury permitted by incomplete historical evidence.

There have been several previous reviews of arroyo studies (Bryan, 1925a; Antevs, 1952; Schumm and Hadley, 1957; Hastings and Turner, 1965; Tuan, 1966). These articles provide some order to a large and often confusing literature, as well as valuable insights into the historical development of concepts and controversies. Most studies include explanatory hypotheses which fall generally into one of three categories based on: (a) human landuse changes, (b) secular climatic changes, and (c) random environmental variations.

Human Land-Use Changes

The earliest students of arroyos considered, without doubt, that thoughtless human actions caused entrenchment. The apparent coincidence of white settlement and arroyo formation provided powerful underpinning to their interpretations. Dodge (1902; 1910) pointed to several detrimental aspects of settlement. The introduction of livestock and consequent depletion of vegetation were seen as the prime causes of entrenchment, with the removal of vegetation and soil compaction along trails playing a secondary role. These changes would reduce infiltration of rainfall, and thus increase runoff, floods in valley bottoms, and erosion of stream beds. Trails along the valleys would provide incipient channels and loci for entrenchment. Dodge considered that arroyo cutting was progressing when he wrote, at least in the San Juan drainage (Colorado, New Mexico, Utah), and he predicted the imminent dissection of several alluvial valley floors.

Hough (1906), the first to assign a single date (1875) to the initiation of

arroyos throughout the South-West, stressed the effects of introduced livestock in the southern Colorado Plateau. Similarly, Thornber (1910) emphasized overgrazing by huge numbers of livestock in his assessment of
rangeland conditions in southern Arizona.

Rich (1911), a geologist working in western New Mexico, drew attention
to the importance of vegetation cover in regulating runoff and the balance
between erosion and deposition by streams. He contemplated and rejected
several explanatory hypotheses, such as those relating to climatic change. His
preferred argument, which describes the mechanics for much subsequent
work linking arroyos, vegetation, and human factors, was as follows (Rich,
1911, pp. 241—2):

If we have a semi-arid climate favorable to the formation of a fairly efficient vegetation
cover, and the balance between erosion and deposition is so adjusted that the streams are
silting up with fine material; with considerable rainfall at certain times of the year,
prevented, however, by the vegetation cover from forming heavy floods, and if by some
means we remove the vegetation cover without changing the amount or distribution of
the rainfall, marked results of a different nature will follow. The rain, still as heavy as
before, will fall on a bare surface unprotected by vegetation and with little capacity to
hold in reserve the excess precipitation. A rapid runoff in the form of floods must result.
These floods, rushing down the valleys, will have power to cut where before deposition
was in progress. Good sized boulders will be carried down and strewn along the stream
courses and over the flats. The result of such floods would be manifest in the trenching of
the valley bottoms and the spreading out over the flats of boulders larger than those in
the valley fill itself.

Emphasizing the correlation between dates of settlement and trenching, Rich
attributed disruption of vegetation to man alone. He mentioned timber
felling in mountains, overgrazing on slopes and in valleys, cutting of grass for
hay in valley bottoms, and compaction along well-travelled routes.

Rich's arguments depend on gross assumptions and circumstantial evidence, but he was sufficiently confident to extend them beyond western
New Mexico (Rich, 1911, p.245):

. . . it is evident that, since the trenching is the result of the removal of vegetation cover,
we will be likely to find it only in those regions whose normal climate is such that the
normal vegetation would be luxuriant enough to become an important factor in the
conservation of the rainfall, and in the protection of the valley bottoms from direct
erosion. In such regions the overstocking, to which the west has been subjected, will have
so reduced the cover as to cause increased floods with accompanying stream trenching. In
regions normally too arid for the formation of an efficient vegetation cover the trenching
should not be apparent.

Such statements form the tenuous basis of many hypotheses of arroyo
formation. Whether the ultimate control of vegetation is human, climatic,
biological, or a combination of these, or whether trenching is induced or
inhibited by plant cover, almost all investigators have made an assumed
relationship between vegetation and runoff the corner-stone underlying their
respective hypotheses.

Duce (1918) found man and his livestock responsible for arroyos in southern Colorado, where he dated incision between 1860 and 1865 in the south-

east and during the 1870s in valleys of south-western Colorado. Olmstead (1919) identified cultural causes of entrenchment in the upper basin of the Gila River. The forester and naturalist, Aldo Leopold (1921) suggested that trails, roads, farming, and grazing (especially of valley-bottom watering-places) caused trenching in twenty-four valleys within fourteen South-Western National Forests. Swift (1926) collected accounts of entrenchment for several South-Western drainage basins and came to similar conclusions, as did Wynne (1926) for the West Fork of the Gila River.

Two original explanations of trenching brought about by human activities in the Colorado Plateau region were suggested in short notes by Reagan. The first (1924a) associated modern down-cutting in areas south and south-east of the Colorado River with the disappearance of irrigation societies. According to Reagan, retention of water by check dams and spreading of water on fields by ancient agricultural peoples (unnamed, but presumably Pueblo) promoted aggradation of valley bottoms. After these peoples left the region it remained in a 'state of equilibrium' for hundreds of years. The coming of the Navajo with his livestock and the white man with his roads and trails permitted increased runoff to rush down slopes and into valley bottoms, where trenches were formed. Reagan's second explanation (1924b, p.284) attributed trenches to overgrazing, either 'by domestic stock of civilized man or by the increasing and incoming of herds of wild beasts'. He indicated that wild animal populations were controlled by peoples who used such animals for food and clothing. This left ' . . . rather rank vegetation to dominate any part of the region not under cultivation' (Reagan, 1924b, p.284) and pro-tected these areas from erosion. To account for cutting of deep channels in the past for which there was growing evidence, Reagan hypothesized that a series of 'good' years led to over-population followed in 'bad' years by serious depletion of vegetation and propensity toward erosion. Reduction of livestock populations through starvation, disease, and migration eventually allowed vegetation to recover and streams to aggrade.

Bailey (1935; Bailey, Craddock, and Croft, 1947), in attempting to ascer-tain whether the modern cycle of arroyo cutting had resulted from climatic change or from human destruction of vegetation, reasoned that if climate had varied sufficiently to produce incision of streams throughout the Colorado Plateau, naturally barren areas, as well as those having more continuous cover at the time of white settlement, would exhibit modifications in gra-dational processes. He studied two naturally barren areas near Bryce Canyon and found no such modifications, and thus concluded that ' . . . utilization of the region by man and the consequent reduction and modification in the plant cover are major factors in starting the new epicycles of erosion' (Bailey, 1935, p.337).

Cooperrider and Hendricks (1937), examining soil erosion and channelling in the upper Rio Grande system of New Mexico and Colorado with respect to possible climatic, tectonic, and human causes of entrenchment, concluded that theories relating accelerated erosion and runoff to climatic and geologic changes are untenable. They argued that misuse and abuse of land by man through introduction of cattle and sheep, timber cutting, man-caused fires, dry farming, and wagon trailing were responsible for entrenchment. Colton (1937) also found settlement and overgrazing responsible for floods and down-cutting on the little Colorado in the 1890s, and Cottam and Stewart (1940) used the same explanation for entrenchment at Mountain Meadow, Utah, in 1884.

Thornthwaite, Sharpe, and Dosch (1942) studied the relations between climate and accelerated erosion, first examining climate and concepts of climatic change, then reviewing normal and accelerated erosion in selected drainage basins of north-eastern Arizona, and finally describing the history of erosion since settlement in that area. Four possible causes of accelerated erosion were discussed at length — diastrophism, native agriculture, climate, and grazing. They concluded that modern trenching of valleys in their study area and probably elsewhere was due to human interference, primarily through overgrazing, in the critical balance between climate and vegetation that exists in that region.

Antevs, an eminent Quaternary scholar who published several articles relating Quaternary climate and archaeology in the South-West (1954; 1955a; 1955b; Sayles and Antevs, 1941) summarized most arroyo literature in 1952. He concluded that 'the main ultimate causes of arroyo cutting in the South-West were drought in the past and overgrazing since about 1875. The cause of past arroyo-filling was a moderate increase in moisture' (Antevs, 1952, p. 384).

In a refreshingly perspicacious analysis of cienega entrenchment in south-eastern Arizona, the geomorphologist Melton (1965) asserted that the environmental changes responsible for historic entrenchment of cienegas undoubtedly acted through a reduction of grass cover by grazing and the re-establishment of distinct channels. He significantly advanced arroyo discussion with original observations on hydraulic changes, which he supported by quantitative estimates. Melton argued that, in addition to increasing runoff, grazing of hillsides by livestock resulted in large contributions of sand and fine gravel which are now commonly found masking finer cinega deposits. These deposits tended to reduce the originally high vegetational retardance of the cienegas, and to increase *transverse* gradients across the valley floors (thus increasing flow depths). Such changes promoted increased flow velocities which caused erosion during times of high rainfall and runoff. Once the sod-covered surface was breached, deep trenches were readily excavated from the easily eroded cienega deposits.

Secular Climatic Changes

Many investigators have been impressed by the fact that arroyo cutting and filling occurred in prehistoric times — before man could have caused the necessary changes — and have found climatic changes adequate to move the erosion-sedimentation seesaw. Some of these investigators have sought to attribute all *modern* trenching to the same cause, whereas others have argued that climatic variations acted in conjunction with human interference. But the precise nature of climatic changes in historical times, whatever their role in initiating arroyos, is a matter of controversy. There are those who argue, for instance, that secular climatic changes are not perceptible in the climatic record. Three major categories of proposed climatic change require review: those involving (a) increases in available moisture, (b) decreases in available moisture, and (c) variations in rainfall intensity.

(a) Increases in available moisture In his influential book *The Climatic Factor as Illustrated in Arid America*, Huntington (1914) persuasively argued on a slender factual foundation the case for a climatic interpretation of alternating periods of erosion and deposition and of terrace formation. In the light of conditions in the Santa Cruz Valley (Arizona) and his observations in many other arid areas, Huntington explained the accumulation of valley-bottom fills by a change to generally arid conditions — brought about by decreasing rainfall, increasing temperatures, or both — that would cause desiccation of vegetation, promote rapid removal of soil from de-vegetated mountain slopes during storms, and overload streams. He argued that a shift towards more humid conditions would have opposite effects, because increasing density of vegetation on slopes would hold soil in place, giving rise to 'clear-flowing' streams 'ready to become erosive agents at the first opportunity' (Huntington, 1914, p.32). In short, trenching would occur with a change to a more humid climate. The argument is similar in essence to Dutton's (1882) speculations many years earlier in the Grand Canyon region. Otherwise 'changes towards humidity' have not been popular in arroyo studies, although some authors have viewed them with cautious approval in explaining past 'epicycles of erosion' (Gregory and Moore, 1932; Bryan, 1922; Quinn, 1957).

Referring specifically to changes in the Santa Cruz Valley, Huntington tempered his climatic argument with an important and apposite Western metaphor:

Here, on a small scale, we have an example of the entire process of terrace making. First slow deposition lasting 200 years, next a rapid cutting of a channel with a marked shifting downstream of the area of deposition and finally a slight and possibly temporary resumption of the process of deposition in the old areas. Man, to be sure, has played some part in the matter, but he has simply served as the means, so to speak, of pulling the trigger which allowed certain natural forces to come into play.

This is the first statement of the 'trigger-pull' explanation used by so many later investigators who saw a link between entrenchment and climatic change.

(b) Decreases in available moisture In 1928 Bryan, a versatile field geologist,

published a climatic model that he was to develop and defend in several works during the following quarter-century. In contrast to Huntington's views, Bryan (1928a) said that a slight shift towards drier conditions, by causing a depletion of vegetation cover and reducing water infiltration into soil would produce significant increases in storm runoff. Floods through valley bottoms would be greater than previously experienced, possessing increased power to erode and to transport debris and thus being able to initiate gullies in certain reaches. Once gullies were initiated, subsequent floods would cause headcuts to migrate upstream, leading eventually to the integration of the separate gullies to form a continous arroyo. Bryan associated alluviation of valley floors with wetter conditions, attendant improvements in vegetation cover, and less flashy runoff. Like Huntington, Bryan considered 'overgrazing' and other effects of settlement to be the 'trigger pull' that precipitated the impending change.

This climatic model was reiterated by Bryan in several later works, including a paper describing ecological changes accompanying entrenchment (1928b); a popular discussion of modern and prehistoric erosion in the South-West (1940); a discussion of palaeo-Indian floodplain agriculture and migrations (1941); interpretations of alluvial fills in western Texas (Albritton and Bryan, 1939) and in central Mexico (1948); and two archaeological site studies (1950; 1954) in which he examined his earlier suggestion that an erosion cycle similar to that in the latter half of the nineteenth century 'may easily have been the cause that brought the Great Pueblo period to an end' (Bryan, 1929, p.455).

Bryan's model has been adopted in several studies dealing with alluvial stratigraphy and interpretations of prehistoric environmental conditions in South-Western valleys, and in attempts to establish chronologies of South-Western events spanning the last several thousand years. Some of these studies also suggested that climatic desiccation was primarily responsible for modern arroyos, although human actions were given a role (Hack, 1939; Leopold and Snyder, 1951; Judson, 1952). Antevs (1955a; 1955b; 1962; Sayles and Antevs, 1941) embraced Bryan's model for explaining prehistoric erosion cycles, and even elaborated on its possible operation, but he viewed modern arroyos as a direct response to human land-use changes (Antevs, 1952).

Richardson (1945) discussed the significance of climatic oscillations in terrace formation, and offered a suggestion that could be used to reconcile the views of Huntington and Bryan. He hypothesized a level of minimum erosion under a climate just sufficiently humid to produce a closed vegetation cover. In these circumstances, increased erosion and thus entrenchment and terrace formation might accompany a change to either drier or wetter conditions.

(c) Variations in rainfall intensity   In recent years, a number of workers

have recognized the grossness and vagueness of hypotheses which seek to explain arroyos in terms of general shifts of climate to more humid or more arid conditions, and some have attempted to develop more sophisticated notions of climatic change based on analysis of climatic data.

Leopold (1951a), a noted earth scientist and conservationist, disputing a claim by Thornthwaite, Sharpe, and Dosch (1942) that the precipitation and temperature records in the South-West contain no significant trends, attempted to establish that climate had indeed undergone slow change in parts of the South-West between 1850 and 1930. From an analysis of daily rainfall data from four New Mexican locations, he concluded that frequency of light rains (smaller than 0·5 inch per day) had progressively increased during this period and that the change had partially been compensated for by a decrease in rainfall of higher intensities, so that annual totals showed little change. Leopold suggested that these trends were regional rather than local, and that they were more likely to explain arroyo cutting and filling than secular changes in annual rainfall totals. He suggested that reduced frequency of 'light' rains in the early part of the period weakened protective vegetation cover, and increased frequency of 'heavy' rains at the same time increased the incidence of erosion. Erosion in this context may have been 'triggered' by overgrazing.

Since Leopold's pioneering work in 1951, he has developed ideas concerning the significance and causes of variations in rainfall intensity (Leopold and Miller, 1954) and restated his early views in the conclusions to an important monograph (Leopold, Emmett, and Myrick, 1966). It is interesting to note, however, that in two co-authored articles on entrenchment (Leopold and Snyder, 1951; Leopold and Miller, 1956), the latter proposing a comprehensive system of arroyo evolution, fluctuations in rainfall intensity are ignored. Miller and Wendorf (1958), and Cooley (1962) expressed a preference for subtle climatic fluctuations of the type proposed by Leopold in their interpretations of alluvial stratigraphy in valleys of northern New Mexico and the Colorado River drainage respectively.

Two other investigators, Martin and Schoenwetter, working together (Martin, Schoenwetter, and Arms, 1961) and separately (Martin, 1964; Schoenwetter, 1962) have suggested a climatic model for past episodes of cutting and filling similar to that of Leopold. Drawing their evidence largely from palynological interpretation of valley-floor deposits, they concluded that prehistoric trenching is associated with periods of intense summer rainfall, and one of Martin's diagrams suggests that this conclusion could be extended to modern arroyo cutting. They do not recognize a decrease of light-rain frequency in prehistoric times, but Martin (1964) has indicated that erosion periods may have been wetter than usual, and he has intimated (personal communication, 1970) that the role of vegetation away from the floodplain environment in controlling runoff may have been negligible in semi-arid south-eastern Arizona.

Tuan (1966) reached no definite conclusions about climatic changes in his study of New Mexican arroyos, but he implied a preference for the ideas of Martin and Schoenwetter over those of Bryan.

Random Frequency-Magnitude Variations

A few South-Western investigators have sought to explain arroyos outside of the conventional framework of 'human' or 'climatic' changes. They have stressed the peculiarities of the semi-arid environment, the mechanics of trenching and filling, or the randomness of meteorological and geomorphological events. For the most part, they have tended to view cutting and filling in South-Western valleys as part of a natural sequence of events which before the 1880s was not generally synchronized throughout the region and since then has merely been accelerated. The principle mechanisms envisaged in this context are: (a) unusual flood or rainfall events, (b) differential flows through the drainage net, (c) inherent disadjustments in stream profiles, and (d) lateral shifts in channel positions.

(a) Floods, unusual storms, and wet periods Gregory (1917), a geologist writing on the Navajo country, concluded that arroyos were cut by floods and that streams aggraded during periods of 'low water'. He envisaged a fine balance between aggradation and degradation in dry regions with steep gradients, and observed that slight changes in 'amount of rain, its distribution, or the character of storms and changes in the amount and nature of flora result in significant modifications in stream habit' (Gregory, 1917, p.130). He conceded that human factors influenced modern entrenchment, but considered them not to be entirely responsible. Similarly, Gregory noted that whereas 'the hypothesis of climatic fluctuation' (evidently Huntington's) best explained past episodes of alluviation and terrace cutting, he implied ' . . . nothing as regards cyclical conditions of aridity and humidity' (Gregory, 1917, p.131). These views were restated in a later study of southern Utah (Gregory and Moore, 1931).

In 1938 Woolley and Alter struck at the bases of most cultural *and* climatic hypotheses on entrenchment — depletion of vegetation and increased peak runoff. Working with historical accounts in the South-West since 1540, they concluded that (Woolley and Alter, 1938, pp. 606—7):

. . . no extreme phase of the precipitation cycle, whether upward and comparatively wet, or downward and relatively dry — nor the practices of man in substituting domestic livestock for wild game and diverting irrigation water onto two per cent of the land — have ever been sufficient to produce a material change of a permanent character in the general aspect of the native vegetation.

Later Woolley (1946), describing the history of cloudburst floods and associated erosion in Utah between 1850 and 1938, found these major floods were basically random in location and time and certainly no less frequent before modern settlement and land-use changes than at present.

The conclusions of Thornthwaite, Sharpe, and Dosch (1942) on the human role in modern entrenchment (summarized above) should also be viewed in the light of the more general ideas of these authors concerning climate, climatic change, and erosion and sedimentation processes in a semi-arid environment. In the Polacca Wash drainage they found evidence of several erosion and deposition episodes, but the deposits could not be meaningfully correlated. The apparent spatial and temporal randomness of past and present erosion and sedimentation led the authors to identify and stress the delicate balance between erosion and sedimentation under semi-arid conditions. In their view, modern entrenchment simply represented an intensification of a normal gullying sequence initiated by rapid runoff and rare-but-expectable intense storms. They stated (Thornthwaite, Sharpe, and Dosch, 1942, p.124):

Large storms have always occurred. Before overgrazing lowered the resistance of the surface only the greatest rains could carve arroyos and enlarge wash channels. The land recovered rapidly, moreover, and discontinuous channels had little opportunity to join with others to form long continuous waterways. Perhaps only the 100-year rain cut new channels on the naturally vegetated surface, perhaps only the 500-year rain. Big rains have been and always will be unpredictable. None may occur for many years, or two or more may take place a few days apart. Big storms, especially if grouped and if coming at a dry season or after a long drought, have always been able to cut channels and start a sub-cycle of accelerated erosion.

In studying arroyos of western Fresno County (California), Bull (1964b) established that the two main periods of entrenchment — 1875–95 and 1935–45 — coincided with periods when rainfall was unusually great in amount and in frequency of large daily rainfalls. He concluded that high runoff and channel discharges arising from these climatic circumstances were primarily responsible for entrenchment. But he did not regard the climatic circumstances as part of any secular climatic change.

(b) Differential flows through the drainage net Dellenbaugh (1912), in responding to Rich (1911), was the first to assume a somewhat uniform-itarian position on the causes of arroyo cutting. He stated (Dellenbaugh, 1912, p.656):

. . . it seemed to me Mr. Rich presented only one phase of the subject. While the stated factor, 'removal of vegetation cover' may in some localities accelerate the retrograding [trenching] of stream-beds, it is not, in my opinion, the cause of retrograding. I noted the same characteristics (and others probably also noted) years ago in places where there were no cattle and never had been any.

The 'trenching', Mr. Rich says, 'is still in progress', which is true, for it has always been and always will be in progress, cattle or no cattle, vegetation or no vegetation, not only in semi-arid regions but everywhere. There are differences in degree and rate — that is all — and in arid regions the rate is conspicuous.

He then went on to suggest that localized 'cloudbursts' within a drainage system would result in differential erosion of stream beds which would occasionally cut across the mouths of tributary channels leaving 'hanging valleys'. Subsequent tributary flow would result in incision at their mouths and arroyo elongation through upstream migration of headcuts.

(c) Disadjustments in longitudinal profiles Although Schumm and Hadley (1957) admitted the possible influence of climatic change and recognized that overgrazing accelerated trenching in historic times, they stressed another important aspect of arroyo formation. Their examination of longitudinal profiles of small discontinuously entrenched valleys in Wyoming and New Mexico showed that trenching of valley fills is commonly associated with a steepening of the gradient on the valley fill. They suggested that in small ephemeral-drainage basins (those studied did not exceed 19 square miles in area) localized deposition might arise from flow dissipation (caused by infiltration, evaporation, etc.). Such deposition might build up the slope of valley fills to critical values at certain points, where entrenchment might be triggered. Schumm and Hadley went on to generalize about these changes in terms of semi-arid cycles of erosion and deposition in small drainage basins. The importance of their study is that it draws attention to a mechanism which is essentially independent of environmental change, and which satisfactorily explains the commonly observed phenomenon of discontinuous trenching.

(d) Lateral shifts in channel position LaMarche (1966) documented an 800-year history of entrenchment along a tributary of Red Creek in Utah with an analysis of variations in growth rings of trees growing along the channel. He concluded that lateral shifting of Red Creek on its floodplain, rather than cyclic episodes of regional extent, was responsible for controlling gully erosion. This notion is not entirely original, but its careful substantiation is a definite step forward.

SUMMARY: A MODEL OF ARROYO FORMATION

A reader of the prodigious arroyo literature may be justifiably perplexed by the shifting currents of conflicting arguments, the discharge of unsubstantiated assertions, the pools of controversy, and the shoals of abandoned hypotheses. In this section an attempt is made to create some order from the apparent confusion. As a summary of relevant ideas, an aid to memory and discussion, and a prospectus of working hypotheses, a deductive model of arroyo formation is useful (Figure I.2). This model portrays the general types of environmental changes and the links between them that may be related to arroyo formation in the American South-West since the beginning of the nineteenth century. It includes, with little discrimination, changes and links that may be powerful or ineffectual, serious or inconsequential, testable or untestable, possible or probable. And it is unequivocally based on two assumptions.

In the first place, it is assumed that arroyos arise from changes in fluvial systems that lead to increased erosion of valley floors by running water. This assumption allows the model to be developed on sound hydraulic principles. The second assumption is that similar landforms (in this instance, arroyos) can be produced from different initial conditions and in different ways. This notion of *equifinality* directs attention away from the search for a single, universal explanatory hypothesis, and encourages the pursuit of multiple working hypotheses.

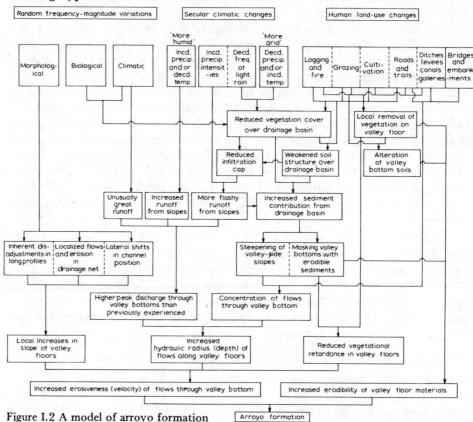

Figure I.2 A model of arroyo formation

Prior to arroyo formation, the relevant sections of valley floors were evidently either relatively stable or aggrading. Many apparently possessed no channels at all. There are two fundamental changes that — together or individually — could have led to localized erosion and arroyo initiation: increased erodibility of valley-floor materials, and increased erosiveness of flows through valley bottoms.[1]

Erodibility of Materials

Erodibility, a measure of the ability of sediment and soil to withstand erosion forces, is largely determined by particulate and structural properties of the material (cohesiveness, permeability, and particle shape, size and density, etc.) and by the extent to which material is protected from the direct attack of erosion processes. In the valley floors of the South-West, increased erodibility is likely to result from one or more of three changes.

Vegetation changes — reduction, removal, or replacement — might increase the extent to which materials are directly exposed to the action of running water. Weakening of soil structure could result directly from cultivation, from the trampling of animals and passage of vehicles, or indirectly from vegetation changes. Those activities causing compaction of soil could also lead to the reduction of infiltration capacity in the soil, thus increasing in certain circumstances the availability of surface water. Finally, the masking of valley-floor vegetation and soil by flood sediments, as suggested by Melton (1965), could provide more erodible surface conditions, thus facilitating entrenchment.

It is extremely difficult to estimate precisely the extent to which erodibility might be increased as a result of such changes, but data in Chow (1959, e.g. Tables 7.3 and 7.6, and Figures 7.3 and 7.4) provide a general indication. For example, grass-lined channels with slopes between 0 and 5 per cent formed in easily eroded soils may be able to withstand flow velocities of 6 f.p.s. with a Bermuda-grass cover or 5 f.p.s. with a cover of Buffalo grass or blue grama. In contrast, unvegetated surfaces where silts or fine sands predominate may be unable to withstand velocities less than 2·0 f.p.s., although particle-size distribution, cohesiveness, and compaction of the soil, as well as depth of flow and fluid density, significantly affect permissible velocities.

Erosiveness of Flows

Erosiveness, the propensity for flows to detach and remove materials from a given reach more rapidly than they are replaced from upstream, is a function of numerous interrelated hydraulic, channel-form, and sediment-load variables, and is exceedingly difficult to evaluate precisely. However, several relevant approaches to measuring erosiveness have been devised over the years by engineers in their attempts to design stable channels in alluvial materials (Albertson and Simons, 1964). One of the oldest and most easily comprehended of these, *the method of permissible velocity*, uses mean velocity of flow as a surrogate for erosiveness. Mean velocity is a useful specific measure and, furthermore, is definable in terms of three variables that provide insights into the way increases in erosiveness may occur. The empirically derived Manning equation, the most popular means of estimating the mean velocity of turbulent, uniform flow in open channels, defines the relationship:

$$\bar{V} = \frac{1 \cdot 5 \, S^{1/2} \, R^{2/3}}{n}$$

where $\bar{V}$ = mean velocity of flow in feet per second
     S = gradient of water surface
     R = hydraulic radius in feet
and n = the Manning roughness coefficient.

Increased erosiveness of flows through valley bottoms could therefore be achieved by one or more of three related changes: increase of slope, increase of hydraulic radius, and reduction of surface roughness (i.e. resistance to flow).

(a) Increase of slope Locally increased water-surface gradients would accompany increases in valley-floor slopes, and these in turn could arise from several morphological changes. Firstly, significant disadjustments in the longitudinal profiles of valley floors might develop and, indeed, may be inherent in ephemeral alluvial drainage systems of semi-arid environments. Because a point is reached in most ephemeral flows where discharge of water begins to decline downstream due to infiltration losses and evaporation, and sediment concentration begins to increase, recurrent deposition may occur in particular areas and cause critical increases of valley-floor slopes (Schumm and Hadley, 1957). Secondly, tributary valleys could be left 'hanging' following localized flows and erosions in major valleys; and the newly increased slopes at the mouths of tributaries could provide the loci for entrenchment by subsequent tributary flows (Dellenbaugh, 1912). Finally, lateral shifts in flow during floods, or the normal progression of meanders in large valleys, could likewise undercut and steepen the gradients of tributaries (LaMarche, 1966); and other changes in flow positions such as those that lead to a straightening or shortening of channels would also raise flow gradients. All such slope changes might occur under a relatively stable set of environmental conditions, or they could be promoted by atypical weather sequences, secular climatic changes, or human regulation.

(b) Increase of hydraulic radius Hydraulic radius is a measure of the independence of flow from resistance imposed by boundary conditions and is defined as the cross-sectional area of flow divided by its wetted perimeter. In wide, shallow channels such as those previously situated in (or represented by) the smooth floors of many South-Western valleys, hydraulic radius may be taken as approximately equal to flow depth. Two essentially independent changes could produce significant increases in hydraulic radius and thus increase velocity: (i) over-all *increases of discharge* through the valleys and (ii) *concentration of flows* within the valley floors.

(i) Increase of discharge. Discharge is a product of mean width and mean depth of flow, and mean flow velocity, and an increase in discharge could be reflected in an upward adjustment of one or more of these variables.

Because hydraulic radius (flow depth) normally increases with the magnitude of floods, environmental changes that lead to increases of discharge could also raise the erosiveness of valley-floor flows, although an unpredictable and possibly substantial portion of the increased energy in such flows is likely to be used in transporting increased sediment contributions from slopes.

The range of possible reasons for increased discharge is broad. Storms of great intensity have direct effects on runoff from slopes and flood flows. Particularly great intensity or relative abundance of such storms, representing either 'chance' occurrences (Woolley and Altev, 1938) or secular trends (Martin, 1964), might produce floods of sufficient magnitude or frequency to accomplish valley-floor entrenchment. Similarly, it is conceivable that occasional wet periods (Gregory, 1917) or a definite trend towards humid conditions, characterized by increased amounts of precipitation and/or reduced temperature (Huntington, 1914), might cause an increase in runoff, provided the surplus of moisture is not consumed by the growth of more luxuriant vegetation.

Vegetation acts as an important regulator of runoff, and appropriate modifications of watershed vegetation might lead to higher 'peak' discharges (i.e. increased 'flashiness' of runoff). One set of modifications could arise from random biological (Reagan, 1924b) or climatic-frequency variations (Thornthwaite, Sharpe, and Dosch, 1942), such as prolonged droughts, which reduce vegetation cover and lead — through reduced interception and infiltration capacity — to more 'flashy' runoff. Similar effects could be produced by human land-use changes such as clearing of forests for timber, deliberate or accidental burning, vegetation clearance for farming, or overgrazing by cattle and sheep (e.g. Dodge, 1902; Rich, 1911). Secular changes of climate which might reduce the availability of water for plant growth could also lead to increased peak discharge during storms. A trend either towards generally drier conditions (Bryan, 1928a) or towards reduced frequency of light-or moderate-intensity storms that promote plant growth (Leopold, 1951a) might produce this response.

(ii) Concentration of flows. Concentration of flows is achieved by restricting the width of flows which, in order to maintain normally experienced discharges, requires increased flow depth and, for most channel shapes found in nature or built by man, results in increased hydraulic radius and increased velocity.

Concentration of flows in valley floors could happen naturally. For example, deposition of sediment eroded from valley-side slopes or alluvial fans at the mouths of tributary valleys might increase the *transverse* gradients of the valley floors and thus concentrate flow along their longitudinal axes (Melton, 1965). The changes necessary to promote erosion of valley-side slopes could include modification of soil structure, vegetation, runoff, and climatic conditions. More probable, rapid, and effective concentration of flow could be accomplished by accidental or deliberate human actions, amongst which the creation of embankments, bridges, ditches, canals, infiltration galleries, roads, and trails in valley floors are the most important (Dodge, 1902; Rich, 1911).

(c) Reduction of surface roughness Flow velocity can also be increased if

surface roughness (n in Manning's equation) is reduced. The main roughness element in valley floors of the South-West, the principle resistance to flow, is undoubtedly vegetation. Removal of riparian vegetation could lead to a reduction of surface roughness and thus increase the erosiveness of valley-floor flows. The possible causes of valley-floor vegetation change have been described above, but it is unlikely that short-term or secular variations in general climate would greatly affect the valley-floor environment with its store of subsurface water. Removal of riparian vegetation by man is likely to be the most important change in directly reducing surface roughness. Inundation of vegetation by sediments supplied during floods or from erosion of slopes may also have some effects on surface roughness (Melton, 1965). It is not at all clear that certain other valley-floor vegetation changes — such as colonization by *mesquite* — would actually reduce resistance to flow.

A point of general importance emerges from this discussion. It is clear that increased erosiveness of flows can be achieved by changes in significant hydraulic variables (notably slope, hydraulic radius, and surface roughness). Such changes could be accomplished without any increase in the amount of water available by internal adjustments to a given discharge, *or* by an increase of discharge (which is likely to increase hydraulic radius). This dual possibility is commonly ignored in arroyo studies.

Values of Hydraulic Variables

Manning's equation conveniently describes the relative importance of changes to slope, hydraulic radius, and surface roughness in altering mean velocity of flow. In examining hydraulic changes leading to valley-floor entrenchment during historical times, it would be very useful to know precise values for the different variables before and during entrenchment. Such data are scarce

But some relevant estimates are possible. Melton (1965), in an exploration of the potential of precise hydraulic arguments in explaining entrenchment, made estimates of the conditions associated with cienega entrenchment in southern Arizona. Recognizing that the Manning equation is not applicable under conditions in which a large retardance coefficient is provided by high, dense cienega grass, Melton argued as follows. Prior to entrenchment, reasonable

figures for the hydraulic radius (R) would be 0·5 feet and for the gradient (S) 0·02, in the upstream reaches. Then taking VR from Chow (1959, p. 182) we can construct the following table of velocity (V) in relation to roughness (n), which applies to *grassy channels*:

n	VR	V (f.p.s.)
0·08	6·8	13·6
0·1	4·2	8·4
0·15	2·5	5·0
0·2	1·6	3·2
0·4	0·6	1·2

Note that the gradient does not enter into these figures. For easily eroded soils such as the cienega deposits, a maximum stream velocity of about 6 feet per second is permissible, and, as the actual values were probably much below that, the roughness was necessarily greater than 0·1. If we assume that under new conditions immediately prior to entrenchment, the roughness coefficient was reduced to a value comparable to modern sandy arroyos, for example, 0·02, and the hydraulic radius increased to 1·5 feet, then Manning's formula becomes applicable:

$$\overline{V} = \frac{(1 \cdot 49)(1 \cdot 5)^{0 \cdot 667}(0 \cdot 02)^{0 \cdot 5}}{0 \cdot 02} = 13 \cdot 7 \text{ f.p.s.}$$

This would put the velocity above the critical value . . . (Melton, 1965, p.33).

Figures I.3 and I.4 summarize some effects on flow velocity of changing separately depth (d), hydraulic radius (R), width (w), and discharge. To change only one variable at a time is, of course, rather unrealistic, but the graphs do

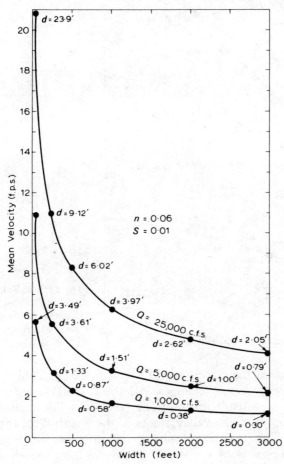

Figure I.3 Relations between flow width and mean flow velocity for various depths and discharges

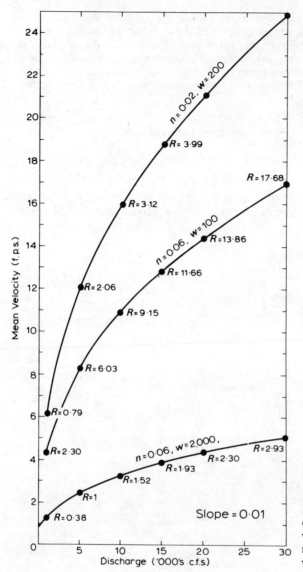

Figure I.4 Relations between discharge and mean flow velocity for various hydraulic radii, Manning n values and widths of flow.

give an impression of the direction and magnitude of erodibility changes that could accompany hydraulic changes. All the calculations are based on the Manning equation, and on assumptions concerning the values of variables likely to be encountered in valley floors of the South-West at present and in the recent past. For instance, discharges of up to as much as 25,000 c.f.s. with a recurrence interval of about 100 years are conceivable in certain Arizonan valleys (see Figure II.12) under present conditions, although peak discharges before entrenchment may have been much smaller. The slope of

0·01 is representative of valley-floor slopes in many areas and occurs, for example, along the Santa Cruz Valley near Tucson. The range of flow-width values is based on estimates from major southern Arizonan and Californian valleys. It is to be hoped that the values of n and R are reasonable guesses.

EVALUATING THE MODEL

The model demonstrates the multitude of ways in which arroyos could have been formed and displays some of the complexity of links between explanatory mechanisms. It serves to emphasize the absurdity of invoking a single mechanism to explain arroyos unless there is sound evidence for it. And it opens to question the factual foundations of widely accepted explanatory panaceas such as hypotheses of 'climatic change' and 'overgrazing'.

But for these reasons, and because many hypotheses are untestable in the light of an incomplete historical record, perfect explanation of arroyo initiation is impossible. The most satisfactory way to proceed is to examine testable hypotheses in the context of available evidence, in the hope of narrowing the area of uncertainty and speculation, and of working logically towards a recognition of the most effective and plausible causes of arroyo formation.

This path is followed in the succeeding pages. In examining the nature and causes of arroyo formation in southern Arizona and coastal California, attention is focused on two groups of hypotheses in each area. The first includes *regional* hypotheses, such as those related to changes of climate, vegetation, and discharge, which presumably brought changes throughout entire drainage basins. The second encompasses *local* hypotheses of valley-floor change, in which modifications of flow characteristics (such as drainage concentration) are important. The evaluation of hypotheses is preceded by descriptions of each arroyo and pertinent contemporary and historical information.

The questions asked and the hypotheses tested are similar in the two study areas, but approaches to them inevitably differ in detail because of the constraints imposed by the nature of field and historical evidence, and environmental differences between the two areas. It must be emphasized that the concern is only with the most recent of several entrenchment episodes in which, because of human activity, circumstances differ fundamentally from those prevailing during previous prehistoric episodes. Within this latest episode, attention is concentrated on the major arroyos, for minor gullies are not normally associated with relevant historical evidence.

PART II

Arroyos in Southern Arizona

INTRODUCTION

Context

Southern Arizona — the area of the state south of the Gila River — is classic, dry, basin-and-range country. The scenic panorama is dominated by north- to north-west-trending isolated mountain ranges rising several thousand feet above the broad intervening basins. In general the mountains become lower and smaller and the basins become more extensive from east to west. The floors of the larger basins provide the principal drainage-ways for ephemeral runoff. Drainage in most of the eastern basins extends, with varying degrees of success, north towards the Gila River; that in some of the western basins moves towards Mexico.

The arid and semi-arid climates of the area are dominated by a biseasonal precipitation regime. Winter precipitation, arising largely from storm centres in the westerlies, contrasts with the more intense, more localized storms of the summer months associated with the moist, tropical air from the south-east. The pattern of precipitation and temperature is controlled by marked altitudinal and longitudinal gradients. For example, precipitation tends to increase and temperatures tend to decline with altitude; and winter precipitation becomes relatively more important westwards as total precipitation declines in that direction (Green and Sellers, 1964; McDonald, 1956).

The pattern of vegetation reflects the altitudinal and longitudinal constraints imposed by topography and climate. The major vegetation zones of desert-shrub, desert-grassland, oak-woodland, and conifer communities are arranged altitudinally, with the lower, warmer, and drier areas dominated by desert vegetation, and the mountain peaks clothed in places with coniferous forests. Spatially, the desert shrub dominates the plains of the South-West, and the desert grassland is pre-eminent on the higher, cooler plains of the east (Nichol, 1952).

Imposed upon these varied patterns of the natural environment is an equally complex palimpsest of culture (Hastings and Turner, 1965). The whole area has been the territory of Indian groups, notably including the mobile Apache, the irrigating Sobaipuri, and the hunting-gathering-irrigating Papago. More than two centuries of conversion, harassment, infestation, and patronage by Spaniards, Mexicans, and Anglo-Americans have reduced Indian influence, until today (apart from exclaves such as that of San Xavier) only the land west of the Baboquivari Mountains is an exclusive Indian reserve. The impact of the Spanish, and later the Mexicans, has been considerable. Concern with Christendom, colonization, and cattle, together with the search for minerals, fundamentally altered patterns of Indian activity and promoted the development of the valley floors. Descendants of Spanish settlers are still to be found in the area, especially in the San Pedro and Santa Cruz valleys.

It was only after the Gadsden Purchase of 1853 that Anglo-Americans began to assert their hegemony over the area. They came with diverse motives. Some of the earliest settlers were Mormons who penetrated southwards in the 1870s, extending the frontiers of Deseret, and established peaceful irrigation communities in an alien, Indian-controlled countryside. There were those who came to mine copper, gold, lead, and silver, and many others followed to sustain them. In particular, livestock were brought into the area in large numbers and irrigation agriculture was important in some valleys. The railroad, and to a lesser extent the windmill and removal of the Indian menace, were vital factors in opening up the grasslands to range cattle after 1880. Each cultural group has to some extent modified the natural environment.

Towards the end of the nineteenth century the floors of some of the major basin floors of southern Arizona were entrenched, and arroyos were created. The problems of when, where, and why these arroyos were formed, and how they were developed, provide the focus of this essay. Its novelty, if it has one, lies in the aerial and field survey of arroyos, the analysis of historical data, and the testing of some new hypotheses and the reappraisal of old ones.

The Pattern of Arroyos

It is rather surprising that in the long history of arroyo research in Arizona there has apparently been no full survey of the features. In order to rectify this omission, this study began with an aerial reconnaissance of the basin floors in southern Arizona. The pattern of major arroyos within them derived from this survey is shown in Figure II.1. On the diagram, major arroyos with two vertical alluvial banks separating the channel bottom from a smooth alluvial terrace above are shown by a solid line; where one bank is degraded or simply not present, or where a clearly defined channel is not bounded by vertical walls, a dashed line is used. Undissected basin floors — washes — are marked by dotted lines.

Two important observations emerged from this survey. Firstly, not all basin floors are entrenched. This is particularly so in the west of the state, but it is also true along parts of the Altar, Santa Cruz, Sulphur Spring, and Sulphur Springs valleys. One frequently gains the impression from previous studies of arroyos that entrenchment is universal; it is not. Secondly, within the entrenched valleys, entrenchment is often intermittent. In the Santa Cruz Valley, for instance, there are two zones of pronounced entrenchment. Intermittent entrenchment is also a feature of valley floors on the Papago Reservation, such as Vamori Wash. Field examination of arroyos confirms this observation. These two findings alone might justify a re-examination of

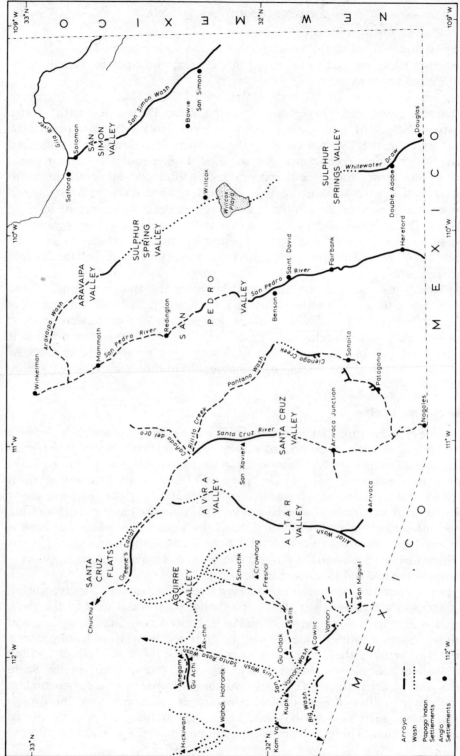

Figure II.1 The pattern of major arroyos in southern Arizona

those explanatory hypotheses of entrenchment that invoke regional environmental changes.

Field study of arroyos yields further useful generalizations. Although the
erosional and sedimentary history of valley floors in southern Arizona is
complex, as many have explained (e.g. Haynes, 1968), a simple pattern is
evident in most valleys. Following a period of pedimentation and complementary alluviation a soil was formed over much of the surface of the plains.
This soil, which varies in detail from valley to valley, is characterized by a
distinctive reddish-brown B-horizon and pronounced bands of caliche. After
the relatively stable period this palaeosol represents, the valley floors were
entrenched in places and then alluviated with grey-buff-coloured clays and
silts, and relatively flat 'inner valley' floors were created. Almost without
exception, arroyos were initiated in this younger, fine-grained deposit. In
some cases they have been cut down through it to expose the palaeosol and
the older alluvium. A distinctive feature of this younger alluvium is that it is
easily erodible by water and yet it is able to sustain vertical banks. It is in
these respects similar to loess deposits east of the Rocky Mountains, and it is
these qualities, amongst others, which give arroyos their distinctive form.
Another distinctive feature of arroyos is that, although most of them have
been progressively enlarged since their initiation, the enlargement has been in
the context of cutting and filling, as revealed by the terraces and terrace
deposits within the arroyos.

Sources of Data

Sources of data for the study of arroyo initiation and development are
numerous. Those which have been most used in previous studies include
photographs, newspapers, legal documents, explorers' and travellers' accounts, and the reminiscences of pioneers. Such material relevant to the
study of arroyos in Arizona, including old maps, is to be found largely in the
archives of the University of Arizona, Tucson, and the Arizona Historical
Society, Tucson, and it has been used extensively here. Government
documents comprise another important source. These include surveys of the
suitability of terrain for railroad routes, reports of Territory, State, and
Indian Bureau officials, the results of scientific surveys and research at
experiment stations, and numerous water-supply and related studies spon-
sored by the U.S. Geological Survey.

One major untapped source pertinent to arroyo problems is the field
notebooks that were prepared during the first land surveys and their
subsequent revisions by the U.S. General Land Office. These legal documents
provide much information on topographic, soil, and vegetation conditions of
valley floors along section-line traverses. Copies are kept by the Bureau of
Land Management, Phoenix. As a historical source they have been widely
used elsewhere in the United States (e.g. Buffington and Herbel, 1965;
Pattison, 1957), and in view of their apparent accuracy and value in Arizona

one is rather surprised that Bryan (1954) found similar documents for the Chaco Canyon area of New Mexico contained such gross errors as to make them useless. Another source of precisely surveyed data that has proved useful in studying certain locations is the archive of the Southern Pacific Transportation Company, San Francisco.

In piecing together one hundred years of daily rainfall records for several stations in southern Arizona in order to test certain notions of climatic change, records were gathered from several archives, notably those of the Meteorological Office, Bracknell (England), the National Archives, Washington, and the Environmental Data Service, Asheville (N.C.).

Armed with information collected from archives and the field, three principal themes are examined in the following pages. Firstly, evidence relating to the nature of arroyo initiation and development is reviewed for each of the major entrenched valleys. In the second section, hypotheses of regional environmental change are explored, especially those relating to modifications of climate and vegetation and the change of water discharge. And thirdly, hypotheses of valley-floor change that incorporate notions of slope alteration, drainage concentration, and localized modification of vegetation and soils are evaluated.

EVIDENCE FROM THE MAJOR VALLEYS

Arroyos along the San Simon Valley[2]

The axis of the 2,300-square-mile San Simon Basin extends over 100 miles from south-west New Mexico, through south-east Arizona to the Gila River. The basin is fringed by mountains, but the area is dominated by extensive alluvial plains. The valley axis is, like many others in Arizona, composed of fluvial and lacustrine sediments which are dominated by clays, silts, and fine sands and include lenses of coarser sands and gravels. Sections through these sediments reveal that the recent alluvial history of the area has been marked by phases of erosion and deposition. These valley-floor sediments have been entrenched in much of the area between Safford and San Simon, and the entrenchment has attracted more attention than most in Arizona.

The vegetation along the valley floor and adjacent slopes today consists mainly of creosote bush and mesquite, ephedra and tarbush, a few cotton-wood and salt cedar trees, and various grasses including tobosa, and certain gramas. The basin as a whole is regarded as a seriously disturbed environment, characterized by extensive soil and arroyo erosion, impoverished vegetation, and a high annual sediment yield of approximately 0·3 acre feet per square mile (Jordan and Maynard, 1970). For this reason it has been the focus of land management and conservation effort for over thirty years. The arroyos have been described and discussed for even longer, and several scientists have deplored the environmental changes in historic times. Olmstead (1919, p. 79) was provoked to proclaim: 'Oh, Liberty, how many crimes are committed in thy name! ' More recently, Peterson (1950, p. 410) declared: 'Today's picture of the valley, from both the conservation and the range-use viewpoint, is one of devastation.' These are undoubtedly somewhat exaggerated sentiments. Nevertheless, it is clear that the lower areas of the San Simon Valley have been transformed during the last century.

Descriptions of the valley around 1880, and their representation in subsequent literature, emphasize two themes: vegetation and other conditions were ideally suited for cattle; and water was readily available along the valley floor. Hinton (1878), an early topographer of the state, described much fine grazing land and some agricultural land along the valley, emphasizing the cover of sacaton and nutritious gramas. To Barnes (1936), the valley in 1882 was composed of meadows covered with two-foot lush grasses, more-open areas dominated by luxuriantly growing gramas, and stirrup-touching sacaton along the washes. Swift (1926) reported that Mr. Prina ('a reliable, level-headed man of honor') described the country north of Solomonville[3] as 'consisting of fields of waving grass in 1884'. Peterson (1950) reconstructed a picture of 'pristine beauty' from the accounts of early settlers describing large areas of grass thick and tall enough to be harvested for hay. Olmstead (1919) recounted similar sentiments and Bryan (1925a) repeated them.

Certainly the original vegetation was different from today's, and certainly it was better for cattle, because it was sufficiently attractive to bring an estimated 50,000 cattle into the area during the 1880s and early 1890s[4] (Thornber, 1910). But the eloquence of rustic reminiscences can easily lead to an exaggerated impression of the differences. It is not always clear when the observations were made: then, as now, there were 'good' and 'bad' years; and even today grass could be harvested in certain areas when rainfall is above average. Equally, old-timers tend to remember particular places and better times, and it is dangerous to extend such observations to the whole of the valley. More important from the point of view of arroyo development, it is not clear how far such vegetation changes led to increased erosion in the valley floor: it is by no means inevitable that they should have done so. For example, localized runoff from valley slopes of seriously deteriorated grassland could have transported more debris and deposited it in the valley floor, or the flows — most of which are generated in the mountainous part of the watershed — might not have reached the valley axis but may have disappeared in the permeable alluvial deposits adjacent to it.

There clearly were watering-places along the valley floor in the pre-arroyo period; and there still are. Peterson (1950) spoke of a perennial stream flowing through most of the valley floor and meandering across it in a shallow, tree-lined channel. Barnes (1936) recalled that in 1882 there were practically no banks to the stream, 'it simply flowed softly and quietly on the top of the ground, except at its lower end where it entered the Gila', and here there was a channel some 20 feet wide and no more than 3 feet deep. Barnes (1936; 1960) also spoke of intermittent flow along the valley, and of a 'living stream' north of San Simon that was known in the 1840s as the Rio San Domingo or the Rio De Sauz (River of Willows) to the Spanish-speaking residents, and became known as San Simon River to the early white settlers. The Butterfield Stage Line, established in 1859, used the permanent water at San Simon. Examination of aerial photographs shows a pattern of riparian vegetation that strongly suggests meandering flow lines, a pattern that clearly preceded the arroyo cut across it.

It seems unlikely that the perennial flow ever extended throughout the valley to the Gila, for two reasons. Firstly, the General Land Office surveyors' books[5] relating to the first survey of the valley between 1875 and 1885 (Figure II.2) only mention a 'wash' or 'creek' in the *southern* part of the area. The surveyors usually mentioned flowing water and, indeed, dry washes, together with other linear features such as roads. Here they may have been lax; more likely, there was no flow at the time the northern part of the valley was surveyed. Secondly, there is a sound hydrological reason why perennial flow only occurred in part of the valley. San Simon lies in a small artesian basin which was roughly coincident with a 1,200—1,600-acre cienega from which perennial flow extended downstream (e.g. Hutton, in Leopold, 1951b). In 1952 the discharge was of approximately 8,000 a.f.p.a. (De Cook, 1952). But this flow did not reach the Gila in 1917 because the creek "some distance downstream' was then normally dry (Schwennesen, 1917). There is no reason to believe it was not normally dry before and indeed the surveyors' books and Barnes's description (1936) suggest that it was. Schwennesen (1917) added that at San Simon a small continuous flow was maintained by waste water from flowing wells and that downstream the creek had by 1917 cut nearly to the water-table. Although much of the valley floor below San Simon was normally dry, there is no doubt that floods from time to time extended down the valley to the Gila River.

The historical record provides interesting evidence of the origin and development of arroyos from the Gila River south to San Simon. There is no record of entrenchment in the northern part of the valley in 1875 (Figure II.2). The first entrenchment is said to have occurred in about 1883, when settlers near Solomonville, distressed by detritus being deposited on their land during floods following heavy rains, excavated a channel some 4 feet deep and 20 feet wide in order to concentrate flow from the San Simon Valley and discharge it more efficiently to the Gila River. Funnelling levees were also said to have been built upstream of the canal to promote drainage concentration. Olmstead (1919) first described these facts, and he argued that the channel acted as a locus for arroyo initiation. The channel may first have been severely eroded in the floods of 1890, as the description in the *Graham County Bulletin* for Friday 11 July 1890 suggests, in its characteristic vernacular:

In the vicinity of Solomonville, and between here and Safford, there was more water on last Sunday night than has been recorded since old Noah floated his ark over the corpses of the first settlers . . . .

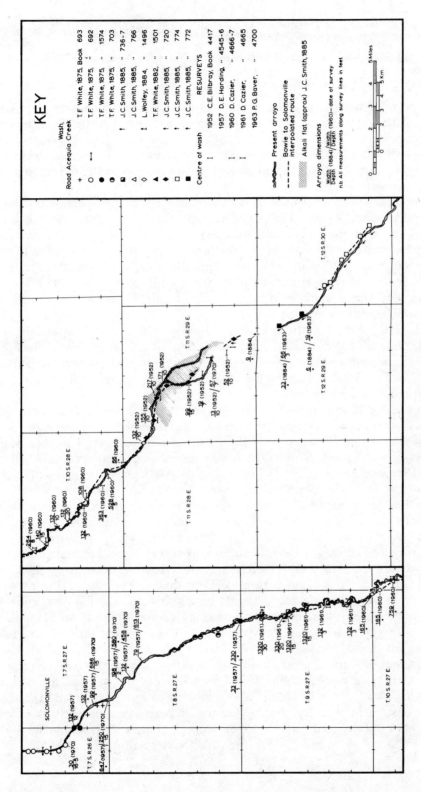

Figure II.2 San Simon Valley: historical data

The rain must have been much heavier south of here for the waters of the San Simon was what eclipsed all former records and done the damage . . . .

The San Simon was over a mile wide and running strong between here and Safford . . . .

In the same issue, a headline reads: 'Floods Galore. Much damage in Gila Valley. Ditches wrecked. The San Simon cuts a swath to the Gila, leaving destruction in its wake.' On 15 August 1890, the same paper declares: 'On Tuesday there was an immense rainfall in the vicinity of Whitelock's cienega, and the water came down in a body just east of Solomonville, inundating the valley for over a mile.'

Three asides arise from these and similar accounts that are pertinent to later arguments. Firstly, the 1890 floods were large, in the eyes of local inhabitants, and they probably occurred at about the time that damage caused by cattle could have been pronounced. Secondly, because the floods are usually compared with previous events, flooding can be assumed to have been no new phenomenon. Thirdly, the floods probably caused arroyo cutting, but there is no evidence of arroyo cutting far to the south of Solomonville in these reports.

Today, the arroyo in the vicinity of Solomonville is relatively straight and has an unusually low width—depth ratio (e.g. 30 : 16·5 in T.7 S., R.26 E.) and these two observations could both be interpreted to support Olmstead's story. (Swift (1926) did not think that the flood channel, if it existed, had been greatly enlarged by 1900.)

Subsequent development of entrenchment is less clear. Olmstead, and several later authors (some of whom may simply have derived their information from Olmstead) speak of the arroyo extending by headward erosion over 60 miles. This extension seems to have been accomplished by 1917 (Schwennesen, 1917).[6] Today, there has been entrenchment along most of the valley between Solomonville and San Simon (except where the arroyo has been buried by reservoir sedimentation); but the arroyo varies greatly in dimensions (Figure II.2) and the entrenchment is not continuous.

The historical record provides two clues to the timing of entrenchment. Firstly, data from the surveyors' notebooks reveal beyond reasonable doubt that between 1875 and 1885 there was no arroyo at least as far south as T.11 S., R.29 E. The same data also show that the course of the present arroyo was then followed fairly closely by a wagon road which was probably used to carry 'ore wagons from the mining camps' (Jordan and Maynard, 1970) along a route where 'stock, feed and water were readily available' (Bureau of Land Management, no date). Secondly, a Bureau of Land Management document (no date) suggests that excessive channel erosion began during heavy rains in 1905–6, following the serious drought of 1902–5.[7] Heavy rains in 1916,[8] also following an extended drought, caused further entrenchment. By the 1930s, the arroyo was apparently over 200 feet wide in places and up to 30 feet deep (Barnes, 1936), and generally it was some 9 feet deep and 75–90 feet wide (Sayles and Antevs, 1941).

There is little doubt that the entrenchment closely followed the line of the old wagon road: the surveyors' notebook data strongly suggest it, and independent witnesses (e.g. Knechtel, 1938) corroborate this view. It might be speculated that (a) the road had the effect of concentrating flow, (b) traffic stripped vegetation and thus reduced surface roughness, (c) traffic destroyed soil structure, created ruts, reduced infiltration capacity, and promoted runoff, and (d) vegetation removal and traffic together made exposed sediment more vulnerable to erosion.

Cattle trails, which are similar in many respects to wagon roads, also acted as loci of gully development along the San Simon Valley, according to Swift (1926) and Knechtel (1938). It seems probable that the greatest density of trails would be along the valley floor where water was most readily available, and the trails may have had the effect of further concentrating flow. The cattle also probably caused the destruction of riparian vegetation.

Because the road acted as the line along which most entrenchment occurred, there is no reason to imagine that entrenchment proceeded by headward erosion from the flood-control channel near Solomonville. It is probable that entrenchment occurred from place to place along the line as local conditions dictated. Once initiated, subsequent floods would modify the arroyos. The tendency has been towards widening and deepening (Figure II.2), lengthening and the creation of a sinuous trench, and all these changes can be seen as reflecting adjustments in the fluvial system to increasingly concentrated flow. In addition, erosion *and* deposition have alternated from time to time along the valley, as field evidence and the historical record occasionally show (e.g. T.11 S., R.29 E., Figure II.2, cf. 1952 and 1970 measurements).

It has been argued that the flood-control channel and the wagon road served to concentrate flow, increase erosion velocities, and promote arroyo development. There is another possibility. In 1884, the Gila, Globe, and Northern Railway was extended through the area, and for over twenty miles it closely followed the valley floor (Figure II.3) along a course that reflected a compromise between the undesirable dissected alluvial plains and the flood-prone valley flats. In fact, the railroad was largely built on low embankments across the flood zone.[9] The unintentional effect of the railroad embankment in certain stretches of the valley could have been to concentrate flow and to further erosion. It is possible, for example, that flood width could have been reduced by as much as 40 per cent in places. Certainly the embankment was eroded by floods, for the line had to be relocated in two areas, and construction of several protective barriers was necessary. Certainly, too, tributary erosion was encouraged where flow was deliberately concentrated through trestle passes in the embankment (Figure II.3).

Much discussion of soil erosion in the San Simon Valley identifies three main causes: (a) vegetation depletion and resulting increased runoff associ-

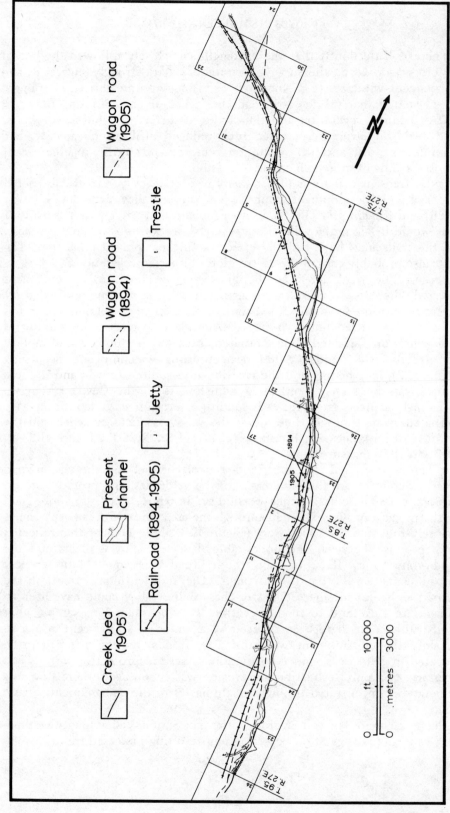

Figure II.3 San Simon Valley: the relations between the valley floor and transportation routes

ated with overgrazing by cattle, (b) heavy rains following the droughts in the early part of the century, and (c) undesirable homesteading and dry farming. Undoubtedly these phenomena may have contributed towards general soil erosion, but it is not clear that they were individually or collectively responsible for arroyo initiation. It is quite possible that new features created along the valley floor, such as canals, embankments, and roads, were equally, if not more important; at the very least they determined the location of the entrenchment.

Concern with arroyo cutting and soil erosion has given rise to a series of conservation measures. Between 1935 and 1942 the Civilian Conservation Corps attempted to stop arroyo development by creating numerous small structures designed to restrict slope runoff and improve vegetation. These structures included low spreaders built of brush and loose rocks, contour furrows, and small gully plugs. It is significant that these 'upslope' measures failed to control the main channel. The C.C.C. and subsequently the Soil Conservation Service and the Bureau of Land Management have built at least ten structures across the main arroyos to retard flow, capture sediment, and prevent erosion. These structures have been more successful. At the same time, shrub control, revegetation, and range management programmes have been pursued, and the quality of the range has been improved. Today there are about 5,000 cattle in the valley, compared with ten times that number in the boom years of the 1880s (Jordan and Maynard, 1970).

The Aravaipa Arroyo

The geomorphology of the Aravaipa Valley is somewhat different from that of other major entrenched valleys in southern Arizona. It extends from the northern end of Sulphur Spring Valley to the San Pedro River, first passing between the north-westerly-trending Galiuro-Winchester and Pinaleño mountains and then changing direction abruptly to cross the Galiuro Mountains. The gradient of the valley floor is significantly steeper than those of the other major valleys.

Near its headwaters, the valley floor is characterized by a narrow alluvial floodplain created by deposition in the deeply dissected pediment and alluvial-fan topography flanking the mountain ranges. (The contrast is most pronounced between the dissected piedmont plains of the upper Aravaipa and the largely undissected plains of the adjacent Sulphur Springs Valley.) In the headwater area, the alluvial floodplain is similar to those elsewhere in southern Arizona where arroyos have been formed — comprising recent sediments resting in places on a reddish palaeosol; the only significant difference is that here the alluvium has a relatively higher proportion of gravels.

Downvalley, the topography changes. The alluvial floodplain becomes narrower, the dissection of piedmont surfaces is greater, and the relatively open landscape is replaced by bedrock plateaux and canyons. The main canyon, reminiscent of the 'goosenecks' of the San Juan River, results from downcutting of the Aravaipa drainage as the Galiuro Mountains were uplifted across its path.

Today the remote and lightly populated floor of the Aravaipa Valley has an arroyo in the headwater area and, downstream in the canyon, a relatively wide and shallow, vegetation-free channel with intermittent, perennial flow. The former floodplain is cultivated in places and grazed in others, but the dominant impression is of mesquite thickets and abandoned land, punctuated by patches of poor grass and isolated cottonwood trees.

There appears to be relatively little evidence of changing occupance and valley-floor conditions in the Aravaipa Valley. The headwater arroyo appears not to have been previously described. Folklore and general descriptions suggest that Indians were a problem in the area, and that nearby Fort Grant provided protection. More significantly, hay for the cavalry at Fort Grant in the 1870s and 1880s used to be cut in the Aravaipa Valley, by mowing

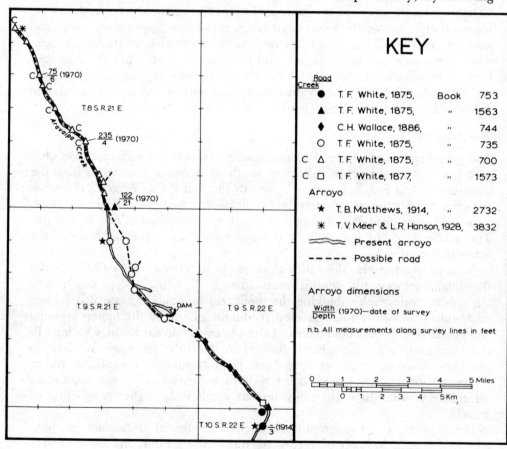

Figure II.4 Aravaipa Valley: historical data

machines in wet years, and with heavy hoes in drier years (Hastings, 1959). As Hastings observed, this evidence from a government report on hygiene indicates that grass quality was variable, but it does not indicate any significant difference between 1880 and the present: in wet years, a mower could still be used to crop hay in some areas near Fort Grant.

The only precise evidence of valley-floor changes comes from General Land Office surveyors' notebooks[10] and field observations covering the area south of T.7 S. The surveyors' notebooks indicate two important features along the valley in 1875–7. Firstly, there was a 'creek', but it is only mentioned *to the north of* section line 21./28, T.8 S., R.21 E., although the surveyor (T.F. White) also traversed the land south to the watershed (Figure II.4). No depths were given for the creek, but it was between 66 and 132 feet wide at section lines. Secondly, there were several wagon roads on the valley floor, including one which in 1875–7 was adjacent to and occasionally crossed the creek (where it existed). This road headed southeast across the divide towards Willcox. In 1886 it was called the 'Globe to Willcox' road. By 1914 the situation had changed. The area south of the creek, which was apparently undissected in 1875–7, had become entrenched. And the line of entrenchment precisely followed the line of the former road. Two observations in 1914 indicate depths for the arroyo of 6 and 3 feet. Today the arroyo is up to approximately 250 feet wide and 21 feet deep (Figure II.4). Its continuity has been interrupted by the accumulation of water and sediment behind earth dams across the valley floor.

Although the evidence is not entirely conclusive, it seems clear that an arroyo was formed along the line of the old wagon road near the watershed of the Aravaipa drainage between 1886 and 1914. The argument concerning the effect of the road and its traffic on runoff and erosion could be the same as that used in the San Simon Valley.

Whitewater Draw

Douglas Basin is the southern drainage unit within Sulphur Springs Valley and its 1,023 square miles are drained by Whitewater Draw, a tributary of the Yaqui River in Mexico. The basin is flanked by mountains, but over 70 per cent of the area comprises broad, largely undissected alluvial plains that slope gently southward at approximately 10 feet per mile. The Quaternary history of these plains has been marked by alternating phases of erosion and deposition that are revealed by sections along Whitewater Draw (Antevs, 1941), and by the patterns of palaeosols and palaeochannels clearly evident from the air. Whitewater Draw itself is developed in a sequence of alluvial deposits similar to that found elsewhere in valley floors of southern Arizona.

Only the broad outline of land use in the Douglas Basin is clear. The favourable ground-water conditions in the valley were appreciated as early as 1873, but their development did not begin until the 1880s when Indian problems had been solved (White and Childers, 1967). Then, cattle and

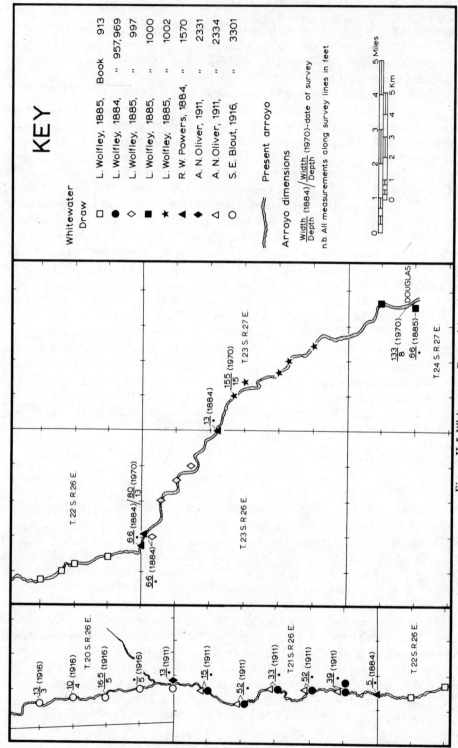

Figure II.5 Whitewater Draw: historical data

windmills came to characterize the scene, as indeed they still do in some areas today. Since about 1910, well water has sustained irrigation agriculture. In 1940 some 4,000 acres were irrigated; by 1951, over 14,000 acres were in use; and in 1965 the figure had grown greatly to 40,000—50,000 acres. As a result of this increase in ground-water use, ground-water levels have been declining (White and Childers, 1967).

Today, the major axis of the Douglas Basin is entrenched along much of its length. From near Elfrida to the basin headwaters north of the Swisselm Mountains there is a channel which seems to be similar to those found near the heads of many alluvial fans (Cooke and Warren, 1973), and there is no evidence that this has been produced or developed in historic times.

Whitewater Draw — an arroyo named after the outcrops of (white) caliche along its banks — extends southward from what appears to be a cienega south-south-west of Elfrida to the Mexican border and beyond. This arroyo has certainly developed in historic times. It is today a meandering feature (Figure II.5), with a width/depth ratio generally less than 10, and with a distinct inner channel that could be a recent artificial excavation. Entrenchment is confined to the arroyo and to a narrow zone adjacent to it — many long, tributary drainage lines are not significantly entrenched.

The arroyo is unusual because there is flow for much of the time in a short reach north-west of Douglas. For 41 years of record at a gauging station near Douglas, average runoff is 7,610 a.f.p.a., and the maximum recorded flow is 5,060 c.f.s. (on 7 August 1955).[11] Data between 1933 and 1965 indicate that mean annual baseflow has been gradually depleted, probably as the result of a declining water-table associated with well-water irrigation (White and Childers, 1967).

Much has been written on the erosional history of Whitewater Draw. The evidence is summarized below.

(a) The first surveyors (1884—5)[12] refer to a 'creek' or 'river' along the line of the present arroyo south of T.19 S., but they say little of its nature. One reference mentions a creek being five feet wide along a section line in 1884.

(b) A map of Cochise County[13] shows that by about 1900 there were properties along the whole length of the present arroyo and — perhaps as important — there were apparently few 'sites' away from it. The line was clearly a source of surface or well water.

(c) By 1910 a freshly cut channel with an average width of 60 feet and an average depth of 10 feet (and a depth nowhere greater than 25 feet) extended through T.22 S., T.23 S., and T.24 S. In the fall of 1910 the head of the arroyo was approximately at the south line of T.21 S. and according to F.J. Randell, a local resident, it was eroded headward fully one-quarter of a mile during the rainy season of 1910 (Meinzer and Kelton, 1913).

In T.21 S. and the southern part of T.20 S. (the cienega area) there was an interrupted channel that was narrower and shallower than the main arroyo;

in places it tapped groundwater, in others it was filled with impounded water (Meinzer and Kelton, 1913). There were also levees, apparently natural in origin, along some of the channels. William Cowan, a pioneer ranchman, is reported to have said that the entire arroyo north of the Mexican border had been cut since 1884 (Meinzer and Kelton, 1913).

(d) Certainly by 1911 there was a distinct channel in T.21 S., and it was up to 52 feet wide (Figure II.5). And it is clear that by 1916 the arroyo was present in the next township north (T.20 S.), where it was up to 16·5 feet wide and 5 feet deep (Figure II.5).

(e) After 1916 there seems to have been little further headward erosion of the arroyo, for it terminates today in T.20 S. Other changes since 1916 do not seem to have been very pronounced. In 1941 Antevs estimated that the arroyo had an average width of about 90 feet, and an average depth of about 12 feet (Antevs, 1941). In 1955 the maximum reported depth of 25 feet was no greater than an estimate in 1910 (Coates and Cushman, 1955). Today measurements at randomly selected sites suggest that the arroyo is up to 15 feet deep and 155 feet wide. The most marked change since 1916 seems to be that of channel widening, although there is local evidence of 'cutting and filling' in the channel. A persistent inner channel within the arroyo is not mentioned in the literature.

Most of these data are generalized and they are probably not very precise. But they indicate beyond reasonable doubt that Whitewater Creek was transformed into an arroyo after 1884 and largely before 1910. Subsequently there was slight headward extension into the cienega, and some widening of the feature. The reasons for the entrenchment are less clear.

Both overgrazing and climatic change have been championed in the Douglas Basin, as elsewhere, as a cause of entrenchment (Coates and Cushman, 1955). Antevs (1941), for example, stated categorically that the erosion was largely caused by overgrazing, vegetation change, and consequent increase in runoff. Local evidence for this attractive hypothesis is frail: the widespread establishment of mesquite between 1900 and 1910 (Coates and Cushman, 1955) seems certain, and cattle may have been responsible for the change. The effect of such change on surface-flow conditions is less clear, and the fact that numerous, long drainage lines tributary to the Draw across the rangelands are not significantly entrenched could be used to argue against this 'regional' hypothesis. On the other hand, cattle would undoubtedly have concentrated along the line of the creek, created trails, and destroyed riparian vegetation: these changes alone could have been responsible for the localized incision. This idea fits the observation that entrenchment is rather localized, and the fact that the arroyo is downstream of what seems to be a cienega — a possible source of water — might be used to support it further. There is no convincing evidence of drainage concentration — but Meinzer and Kelton's mention of levees is intriguing; and waste water from irrigation ditches is directed into the Draw in places today.

Entrenchment along the San Pedro Valley

The San Pedro River basin is one of the largest tributary to the Gila River, covering over 4,720 square miles. The major valley is some 180 miles long, extending from south of the Mexican border north-north-west to the Gila River at Winkelman. The valley is dominated by a series of dissected piedmont plains (Tuan, 1962) similar to, but more extensive than, those in the Aravaipa Valley. Dissection of the plains created a trough within the valley that has subsequently been partly filled by alluvial sediments. Today this 'inner valley' is flanked by bluffs and its floor has been the location of all recent entrenchment.

The inner valley fill is distinctive in two ways: it is neither uniform in thickness nor uniform in surface slope. Firstly, there is a series of alluvial basins along the valley that are separated by narrow zones where bedrock outcrops at the surface and restricts the valley width — near Charleston, at 'The Narrows', at Redington, and near the Gila River. Some of the basins supply artesian water (for example, near St. David). Secondly, the longitudinal profile of the floor of the inner valley reflects the partitioning, because it becomes significantly *steeper* in each successive basin downstream.

Today the inner valley floor is trenched for most, but not all, of its length. The present river path varies from a sandy wash over 800 feet wide with banks as low as 2 feet high to a relatively narrow arroyo over 30 feet deep. Flow along this path is intermittent, being fairly regular for most of the year in some places; occasionally floods sweep along much of the valley.

There is evidence that the hydrological conditions have changed somewhat in historic times. Hastings and Turner (1965) reported two accounts from the 1850s that described intermittent flow along the valley and ephemeral flow at a particular point and this is basically the situation today. But there are numerous reports of perennial flow at certain localities in the past and it seems that overall flow may have been reduced. W.T. Lee (1905) said that 'the San Pedro has a continuous surface flow, although the volume is small during the dry season.' There is a tendency towards more frequent mention of intermittent flow after about 1915, perhaps suggesting a decline in surface flow (Rodgers, 1965), but possibly reflecting an increase in water abstraction for irrigation purposes. Certainly old-timers believe that flow has declined [14] (see also Rodgers, 1965). A more certain hydrological change has been the drying-up of the several important cienegas (e.g. at St. David, between Benson and Tres Alamos, and near the San Pedro/Babocomari junction), due in part to deliberate draining, as at St. David (McClintock, 1921), and in part to entrenchment and consequent lowering of the water-table.

The history of land use in the valley has been described by Rodgers (1965) and it is sufficient here to list the principal phases: (a) before about 1870, the main activity was associated with the Apaches and, before them, irrigating Sobaipuri Indians, and with the pastoralists connected with Spanish land grants along the river (e.g. the grants of San Juan de las

Boquillas and San Rafael del Valle, south of Charleston); (b) early Mormon and other 'white' settlement from 1877 which involved irrigation; (c) following the construction of railroads, the extensive cattle boom of the last years of the nineteenth century, and the mining boom of the 1880s (at Tombstone and elsewhere); (d) progressive decline in pastoral, and agricultural activity during the twentieth century. From all the evidence of this occupation, one thing is clear: the valley floor has been a focus of human activity for well over a century.

Entrenchment along the San Pedro Valley is well documented, although the evidence is often patchy and ambiguous. In his often quoted paper on arroyos, Bryan (1925a) stated: 'The trench of the San Pedro River was cut progressively headward between the years 1883, when the arroyo first formed at the mouth of the river, and 1892 when the head water fall cut through the boundaries of the Boquillas Grant 125 miles upstream.'

From the available evidence it seems that these assertions are almost wholly incorrect. The dates are not substantiated, and the notion of headward erosion seems to be derived more from the contemporary geomorphological 'conventional wisdom' related to drainage rejuvenation than from historical data. All available sources point towards a more complex history, of which the main features are summarized below.

(a) At the time of the first land surveys (1873—81)[15] the 'San Pedro River' was recorded along the whole length of the valley, and it is clear that in some places it flowed in a channel and in others it flowed in a well-defined 'wash' zone. The meandering pattern of the river was not greatly different from that of today. Normally surveyors did not record depth of the channel before the 1890s, but they did record widths (Figure II.6).

Early evidence of entrenchment — or perhaps of a river well-established in its channel — comes from several sources. For instance, in the early 1870s, the first Mormon settlers at St. David found the river was 'usually in a deep gully, in places over 20 feet deep below the surface of silty ground' (McClintock, 1921). Hastings (1958—9) and Leopold (1951b) recorded even earlier evidence: John Russell Bartlett, writing about the river near the present site of St. David in 1851, described it as having banks not less than 8 to 10 feet high; N.H. Hutton mentioned in 1857 that the river was flowing between banks 10 to 12 feet high near Tres Alamos; and the builders of a wagon road also reported in 1859 that the river flowed between banks 10 to 12 feet high at one place.

Other evidence makes it clear that not all areas were entrenched. The early land surveys record numerous *acequias* and irrigation ditches adjacent to the river (Figure II.6), and it is unlikely that they would have been constructed where the main river was entrenched. (Some of the *acequias* could have been natural distributaries on the floodplain that were used for irrigation purposes.) In addition, there are records of several marshy, cienega areas, and beaver ponds, which served as water-storage areas. Such areas would not have

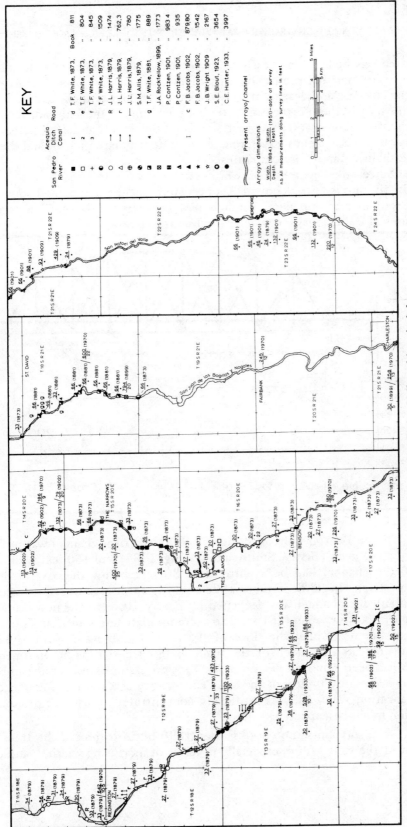

Figure II.6 San Pedro Valley: historical data

been entrenched. In the early days of settlement these areas of standing water were malarial, presenting a problem that was only overcome by draining the cienegas and destroying beaver dams (e.g. McClintock, 1921).

One fact is therefore clear. Before the coming of the railroad, the cattle boom, the miners, and the great floods of the 1880s and 1890s, the inner valley of the San Pedro River was discontinuously entrenched, and the river was established in its present course.

(b) Since the beginning of white settlement in the 1870s, the pattern of discontinuous entrenchment has persisted, but the entrenched zones have increased in size and new entrenchment has been initiated. The principal features of the extensive evidence are discussed below.

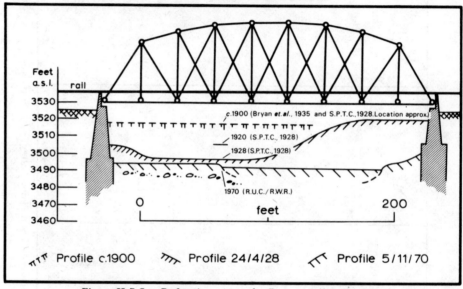

Figure II.7 San Pedro Arroyo at the Benson railroad bridge

(i) At the Benson railroad bridge in 1900, the river channel was probably only 3 feet deep (Bryan, Smith, and Waring, 1934) and 160 feet wide.[16] By 1920 the channel had been entrenched 30 feet below the base of the rail (Figure II.7). On 28 September 1926 the original bridge was destroyed by a flood and the channel was deepened by nearly 10 feet. The new bridge was built with a wider span (261 feet) to accommodate larger discharges between the abutments. Today the floor of the arroyo at Benson is up to 42 feet below the rail and much of the bank material between the abutments in 1928 has been removed (Figure II.7). Erosion at the Benson railroad bridge is not necessarily typical of the San Pedro Valley as a whole, of course, for it is a location where flow is artificially concentrated and where pronounced erosion might be expected.

(ii) The surveyors' notebooks after 1890 begin to record the transformation of the valley floor, especially in terms of increasing width[17] and depth of entrenched areas (Figure II.6). Although these data are probably very reliable, they are unfortunately inadequate for the sequence of change along the river to be fully chronicled. Several points deserve emphasis. Firstly, the depth of entrenchment at any one time varies considerably along the river, as it does today. Secondly, entrenchment seems to have been most pronounced in the Benson and Redington basins, although it was by no means confined to these areas. Thirdly, arroyo enlargement did not always simply involve continuous widening and/or deepening of the channel. In places, for example, present arroyo depth is less than that recorded previously (e.g. secs. 28/29, T.14 S., R.20 E.). And a study of present-day cross-sections reveals several small terraces and three or four distinct stratigraphic units containing bottle-glass and other artifacts which point to cutting and filling episodes within the general phase of arroyo development. Fourthly, as Rodgers (1965) has said, the evidence from notebooks, interviews with old residents, and other sources related to the valley south of Benson points to rather slow development of arroyos in some areas only (not to rapid headward erosion) and perhaps this was a reflection of gradual adjustment within the drainage network to changed conditions. Finally, entrenchment is reported to have been initiated north of Benson — between The Narrows and Hot Springs Canyon — as late as 1926–7 (Melton, 1965, quoting an oral communication with a rancher, Charles Gillespie).

(iii) Hastings and Turner (1965) presented an outstanding photographic record of vegetation changes along the San Pedro Valley since the beginning of white settlement. Although the authors were not primarily concerned with the arroyos, several interesting facts are evident from the photographs. For example, the San Pedro and Babocomari rivers were not entrenched about 1890 near Fairbank (Hastings and Turner, 1965, Plates 57a, b). Yet only a few miles further upstream, the San Pedro River seems to have been flowing in a channel with eroded banks in 1891 (Hastings and Turner, 1965, Plates 48a, b). Similarly, the river flowed in a channel at Charleston in 1883 (Hastings and Turner, 1965, Plates 51a, b). In an earlier article, Hastings (1959) recorded incision of 12 feet near Tres Alamos between 1885 and 1889, erosion at Dudleyville (near the junction of the San Pedro and the Gila rivers) in 1890, and probable channelling near Mammoth in 1886.

(iv) In most entrenched valleys there is evidence of artificial drainage concentration that may have promoted erosion. The San Pedro Valley is no exception, but the evidence is circumstantial and less convincing. The railroad bridge at Benson has been mentioned. The embankment of the branch line south of Benson — especially near St. David, and between Charleston and Hereford — may also have concentrated flow.[18] All the early surveys show a tracery of roads and ditches on the plain of the river. Some of these lines may have acted as loci for entrenchment. Such is certainly the case at Redington, where a former section-line road is now a deep tributary arroyo of the main trench. Bryan *et al.* (1934) described several more recent irrigation ditches along the river, and they also recorded that floods frequently destroyed diversion dams and canals, and that as entrenchment progressed some canals had to be abandoned or deepened (see also Newell, 1905). Unfortunately it is not clear whether any of these canals acted as loci for entrenchment. Also in some areas dikes were constructed to protect fields, canal intakes, and railroad embankments and these may have served to concentrate flow.

In attempting to explain the discontinuous trenching along the San Pedro Valley it is necessary to distinguish between entrenchment that occurred before 'white' settlement and that which followed it. It is unlikely that the early entrenchment was caused by human activity, except in so far as Sobaipuri irrigation or cattle on the Spanish land-grant areas may have caused some damage. Alternative explanations are therefore necessary. Perhaps the most likely is that channels were formed at morphologically or hydrologically appropriate locations in the system — in steeper reaches or downstream of cienegas, for example. These possibilities are considered in more detail below (pages 90–94). Alternatively, early entrenchment could have been the result of climatic-vegetation-runoff changes. The first hypothesis does not require environmental *change* to cause channelling, the second does.

After about 1880 the possible causes of entrenchment multiply. Drainage concentration could have been a factor. Climatic change might have played a role. There were severe floods during the last two decades of the century, and these may have initiated entrenchment. Finally, there is a strong possibility that vegetation changes resulting from overgrazing within the watershed (especially south of Benson), cattle damage along trails and the river, and deforestation of some catchment areas for mining timber may have promoted entrenchment.

Evidence of vegetation change is extensive and conclusive.[19] It is recorded on numerous photographs reproduced in Hastings and Turner (1965). Rodgers (1965) reviewed the evidence in the southern San Pedro Valley. He argued that, as there appears (in his view) to be no evidence of a climatic change before or after 1885 and yet there was significant alteration of the drainage system after that time, vegetation disturbance is the most probable cause of increased runoff and erosion. Perhaps the most important alteration was the exploitation of woodlands in the higher, wetter areas of the Dragoon, Mule, Whetstone, and Huachuca mountains, for this change may have very significantly augmented runoff. In addition, the rangelands were also being transformed. Between 1885 and 1900 much of the range was given over to cattle, and Rodgers (1965) estimated that the range was overstocked for all but three of these years; and there had been 'drought' conditions for ten of these fifteen years. Another event that may have been of importance was a major brush fire that followed the earthquake of 1887. Destruction of the grasslands was reported to have been very extensive,[20] and as it coincided with a time of great grazing pressure, grassland recovery may have been impossible.

This combination of environmental changes led to disasters and to further changes. In 1893, for instance, 40—60 per cent of all cattle in the area died. Grazing capacity was seriously reduced. Grass and woodland were succeeded by shrub vegetation. Floods may have increased in size and frequency, and entrenchment may have been associated with them.

Arroyos along the Santa Cruz Valley

The Santa Cruz River rises in Arizona, flows south into Mexico, and then flows north across the border. The river valley covers over 8,600 square miles and may be divided into two main sections. In the southern section, which extends north to the neighbourhood of Redrock, landforms are similar in general to those in the San Pedro Valley — the river runs in an 'inner valley' created within broad, dissected pediments and alluvial plains and flanked by mountains — and it is fed by several major tributaries (Bryan, 1925b; Tuan, 1959). Terraces flank the inner valley in places, and their variability in number and altitude probably reflects local tectonic activity in this basin-range country. North of Redrock the topography changes abruptly: the river flows into a broad plain, uninterrupted by mountains, that extends to the Gila River and is confluent with plains emerging from the Altar and Aguirre valleys. This contrast may be seen as reflecting a fundamental distinction within the system between the headwater zone where erosion is predominant and the downstream zone where deposition is dominant.

Entrenchment within the valley is confined to the southern section except for an arroyo west of Redrock (see below), and a 5-6-mile-long trench that extends south from the Gila River and probably resulted from headward erosion following downcutting of the main river (Bryan, 1925b). Entrenchment in the southern zone is not continuous, and indeed it never has been. It is most pronounced between San Xavier and Tucson. Elsewhere the course of the river is marked by a broad, vegetation-free channel with low or poorly developed banks. And there are still places where the course of the river is ill-defined as it is, for example, south of the Papago Reservation at San Xavier.

Today, as in the past, there are areas where water is near to the surface. Early records refer to several cienegas including those near Arivaca Junction, at San Xavier and Tucson, and north of Rillito, but today most of them have been trenched and drained. The water-table is still relatively near the surface at these places, but it has fallen in recent years due to pumping (Arizona Bureau of Mines, 1969; Clyma and Shaw, 1968; De la Torre, 1970). Flow along the valley is largely ephemeral, although there is perennial baseflow near Nogales, in Sonoita Creek, and in Pantano Wash (De la Torre, 1970). It appears that flow was normally ephemeral in the past, too, because the earliest surveyors' notebooks[21] often refer to the 'dry bed of the Santa Cruz River'. Floods, especially those in July, August, and September, are a regular feature of the hydrological history of the Santa Cruz River. They are usually recorded in the local newspapers (Grove, 1962), in reports concerning the Indian Reservations (e.g. Berger, 1898, 1901), and in most other records of activity on the valley floor. It is interesting to note from such records that, although the summer floods were certainly responsible — and were seen to be responsible — for arroyo cutting, floods were not universally regarded as a bad thing. For example, the *Arizona Weekly Citizen* stated on 5 August 1893: 'The floods in the Santa Cruz will do immense good in developing the big flows of water a little below the surface. The floods cut down and developed good flows for the Allison brothers, Sam Hughes and Buckalow's ranch. The good done by the waters more than compensates the damage.'[22] Similarly, Berger (1898) said of San Xavier Reservation: 'The land is generally overflooded every year in the rainy season, and the floods are continually causing damage to irrigating ditches and to roads and bridges, and in many locations also prevent the planting for the so-called second crop; but otherwise these floods do much good, as the considerable amount of sediment they bring is considered to be, and, as a matter of fact, is, a great fertilizer, and land so overflowed does not need any artificial fertilizing.'

Two other features of the floods are important. Firstly, their lengths of flow along the valley vary greatly, and infiltration into the bed is high: by no means all floods flow the whole length of the valley. Secondly, the percentage of rainfall reaching the stream is extremely small. For example, the average ratio of streamflow to rainfall (in per cent) is only 3·0 at Nogales and 0·6 at Tucson. Ninety-three per cent of flood peaks above a selected base discharge coincide with the summer months when high-intensity rainstorms occur (De la Torre, 1970).

The land-use history of the southern Santa Cruz Valley differs in many ways from that in the topographically similar San Pedro Valley. The Santa Cruz Valley had no Mormon settlements. The Indian settlement along the Santa Cruz was more stable and more persistent. Irrigation has been practised more or less continuously by Indians living near the Spanish missions at Tubac and San Xavier at least since Kino visited the area in 1689 (Bolton, 1936; Dobyns, 1962). Irrigation development by white settlers has also been more extensive, especially near Eloy, than in the San Pedro Valley. The urban development at Tucson, which may have significantly altered runoff into the Santa Cruz and Rillito, has no counterpart in the neighbouring valley. Cattle and sheep were introduced early into the Santa Cruz Valley, by Father Espinoza in 1763 (Dobyns, 1962). (There were Spanish land grants, similar to those in the San Pedro Valley, such as that of San Ignacio de la Cañoa, and descendents of original grantees still live in the area.) Finally, the floor of the Santa Cruz Valley has been a historical routeway for many generations. The major difference between the Santa Cruz and San Pedro valleys, therefore, is that man has used the former more intensively and more successfully. As a result, the documentary evidence

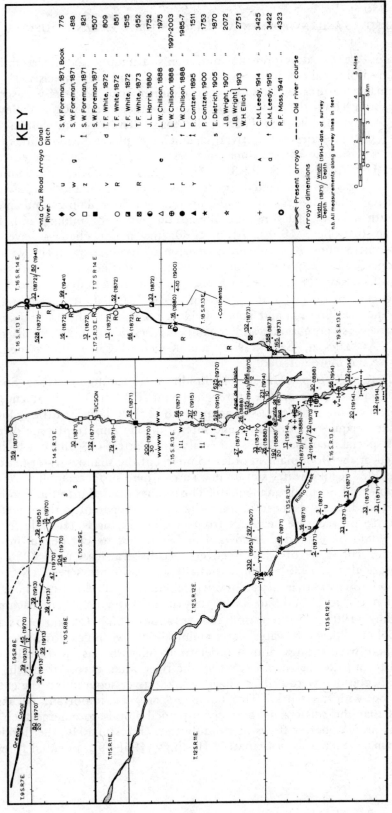

Figure II.8 Santa Cruz Valley: historical data

concerning arroyo development and man's attempts to understand and control hydrological conditions is more extensive and more precise.

The main features of floodplain development can be briefly described. Before about 1880, the valley floor of the southern Santa Cruz Valley was similar to that of the San Pedro. The early surveyors' notebooks often describe the presence of a river channel, in places 'wide and sandy', sometimes with low banks, sometimes without. There was some entrenchment by 1871 (e.g. T.15 S., R.13 E., Figure II.8). In addition, unchannelled, marshy cienegas are mentioned for example near Tucson and San Xavier. In 1857 Silver Lake was created on the untrenched floodplain behind an earth dam south-west of Tucson, and served the needs of milling and, later, recreation (Cusolich, 1953). After 1880, the major changes have been localized entrenchment, headward extension of some arroyos, and widening and deepening of all; the establishment of a continuous vegetation-free, sandy swath along the line of flow, and the draining and drying of cienegas.

Entrenchment occurred at the site of Greene's Canal, at Tucson and San Xavier, and near Sonoita and Tubac. Evidence relating to the last two areas is from surveyors' notebooks, and it confirms Bryan's (1922, 1925b) observations. At Tucson, San Xavier, and Greene's Canal the evidence is conclusive and more detailed.

(a) *Tucson* The pattern of landholdings (reflecting a strong Spanish heritage) and acequias on the untrenched Santa Cruz floodplain at Tucson is clearly shown on the Fergusson map of 1862.[23] Relatively little is known about the acequias at this time and later, but one important type of ditch deserves special mention. This is the infiltration 'ditch' or 'gallery' which was excavated in the floodplain in order to intercept the shallow water-table and thus provide a regular water supply in an area where surface supplies were unpredictable and normally inadequate. The ditches headed into the floodplain upstream and were deepest at their headings. Apparently there were no attempts to protect the headings from erosion. If the water-table fell, the gallery would be extended headward and it would be cut deeper into the floodplain. This type of water recovery was used at least until 1938 (U.S. Dept. Agriculture, 1939). Unintentionally these ditches served to concentrate flood flows and to increase flow depths and erosion velocities. There is no doubt that at Tucson and San Xavier they acted as the loci of entrenchment.

Spalding (1909, p.9) reported that in about 1889 'Certain old settlers undertook to "develop water" at a point about two miles down the river, where there were springs, and in order to accomplish this most easily, cut a channel for a little distance, expecting the river when it rose to do the rest. Their expectations were fully realized, for the river scoured out the cut and carried on with its work.' This comment may be important because it suggests that the settlers *deliberately* intended floods to enlarge their cuts and thus provide better flows of groundwater. Unfortunately, the floods did more damage than was anticipated. Hastings (1958–9) collected from the

Arizona Daily Star of 1890 the contemporary descriptions of arroyo initiation and rapid development in the irrigation ditch at Tucson dug by Sam Hughes: [24]

5 August 1890. The flood yesterday washed a deep cut across the hospital road, so that the road now is not only impassable but extremely dangerous for teams or travel as the embankment of the cut is perpendicular and the water below deep, and pedestrians might easily endanger their lives.

6 August. Another flood . . . It is thought that the washout in the Santa Cruz, opposite this city, will reach Stevens Avenue this morning.

7 August. The channel or cut being made by the overflow of the Santa Cruz river, is now one mile and a half long, by from one to two hundred yards wide — in other words — it extends from the smelter to about two hundred yards this side of Judge Satterwhite's place.

8 August. More than fifty acres of land which has formerly been under cultivation in the Santa Cruz bottom, has been rendered worthless by being washed out so as to form an arroyo.

9 August. The single channel which was being washed out through the fields of the Santa Cruz by the floods, resulted in considerable damage but this damage has been greatly increased from the fact that the wash or channel has forked at the head, and there are now several channels being cut by the flood, all of which run into the main channel. If the flood keeps up a few days longer there will be hundreds of acres of land lost to agriculture. As these new channels or washes are spreading out over the valley, they will cut through and greatly damage the irrigating canals.

13 August. The raging Santa Cruz continues to wash out a channel and the head of it is now opposite town. It may reach Silver Lake before the rainy season is over.

On 15 August 1890 the *Graham County Bulletin* reported that the arroyo was 5—20 feet deep, up to 150 feet wide, and over a mile long. Clearly the major damage was done in 1890, although there are suggestions of an arroyo in the vicinity of Tucson before this time (e.g. *Arizona Weekly Citizen*, 5 August 1893; the *Arizona Daily Star*, 10 September 1887 refers to 'the arroyo'). Floods along the river in 1890, 1891 and 1892 (Cusolich, 1953; Turner *et al.*, 1943) breached the dam of Silver Lake and soon the arroyo extended into the drained floor of the lake. As Warren Allison (Odom, no date) explained: 'The summer of 1890 was a very wet summer and there were many big floods. The Santa Cruz didn't have a channel before that; this channel that is down there now was made in 1890 and those floods took lake out, fish and all.'

According to Olberg and Schanck (1913) the arroyo was 18 miles long by 1912, having been extended by numerous floods (Figures II.8, II.9). It is possible that the railroad, which crosses part of the floodplain on an embankment near Tucson, also served to concentrate floods; certainly it was washed out from time to time (e.g. in 1887).

Drainage from tributary channels was recognized as being an important contributor to the floods. A trench was therefore cut along the west side of the floodplain to trap tributary flow and keep it away from the growing arroyo. Flood also transformed this trench into an arroyo.

(b) San Xavier del Bac The long and complex history of irrigation and

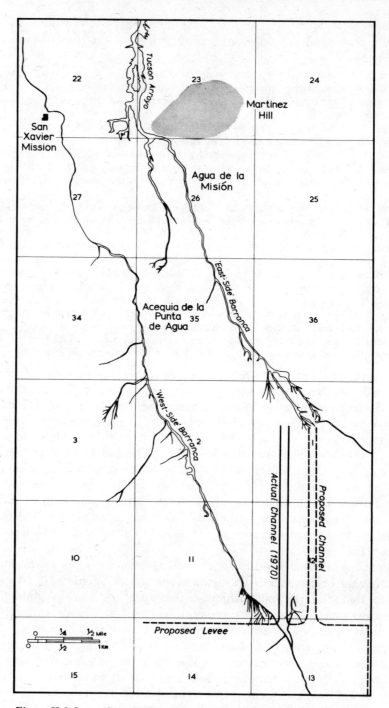

Figure II.9 Santa Cruz Valley: data from Olberg and Schanck (1913)

erosion on the Papago Reservation at San Xavier has been reported in detail by Olberg and Schanck (1913) in a perceptive government document, and it has been reviewed by Castetter and Bell (1942). The Sobaipuri and subsequently the Papago irrigated by flood water (which was diverted in historical times by dikes and brush dams) and by spring water.

There were two main sources of spring water: the *Agua de la Misión* and the *Acequia de la Punta de Agua* (Figure II.9). Springs at the Agua de la Misión were destroyed by an earthquake in 1883 and flow was forced to the surface higher up the valley. Development of this water led to the formation of the East-side *Barranca*, a channel 100–200 feet wide, 15–20 feet deep, and over 2 miles long. The acequia de la Punta de Agua is first mentioned in a Mexican grant of 1851 and is shown on a map of San Xavier dated 1871.[25] Construction of the infiltration gallery resulted in a channel 60–100 feet wide and 6–20 feet deep that came to be known as the West-side Barranca and by 1912 it was approximately 2 miles long. Certainly both arroyos are shown on the Roskruge Map of 1882. The ditches dried up from time to time, and it was necessary to deepen and extend them artificially (Berger, 1901). Thus the two arroyos on the San Xavier Reservation were initiated and extended as infiltration galleries by man, and were exploited by floods.

Meanwhile the Tucson arroyo was being extended by headward erosion during floods (Figure II.8) and by bank caving and piping during low-flow or times of drought. Development of this arroyo was probably helped by concentration of flow *within* it in order to recover water more efficiently for irrigation. Canal irrigation became progressively more difficult as the channel became deeper (Olberg and Schanck, 1913), and flow-concentrating structures such as those for the Farmers' Ditch were frequently washed out. By 1912 the arroyo had reached the Papago Reservation and was about to merge with the arroyo of the Agua de la Misión.

So serious was the threat of erosion on the reservation that a flood-control plan became necessary. Olberg and Schanck (1913) proposed to concentrate flow into a single channel, the East-side Barranca, by diverting flood water eastwards along a dike at the head of the West-side Barranca and directing flow northwards along an artificial channel (Figure II.9). These proposals were accepted, and the new structures effectively prevented further headward extension of the East-side Barranca (although it became much wider and deeper), and stabilized the West-side Barranca. The new flood-control channel has not been seriously eroded. Olberg and Schanck's report marks a turning-point: their successful plan seems to have been the first to be based on a critical evaluation of all available hydrological information.

(c) Green's Canal The only arroyo on the Santa Cruz Plains has been created entirely from the ill-fated Greene's Canal (Figure II.8, T.9 S., T.10 S.). Plans[26] were drawn in 1909 of a canal and reservoir for the Santa Cruz Reservoir Land Co. The plans were changed somewhat, but the enterprise was completed in 1910. The intention was to concentrate flood

water from the Santa Cruz River into the canal (using dikes, brush dams, and embankments), transfer the water along the canal to the reservoir, and distribute it for the irrigation of farm land on the Santa Cruz Plains near Toltec. Unfortunately, the major flood of 1914 destroyed the enterprise (Aguirre, pers. comm., 1970) by breaking the dam, and by damaging the canal and eroding it to a depth of about 12 feet (Turner *et al.*, 1943). Colonel William C. Greene and his colleagues had made the common error of underestimating the size of floods and the erosional effects of drainage concentration. Since 1914, floods have tended to follow the canal, at least for part of its length, and the arroyo has become sinuous, deeper, and wider (Figure II.8). In 1962, for example, flood discharge was estimated at between 17,000 c.f.s. (Rainer, pers. comm., 1970) and 24,100 c.f.s. (Lewis, 1963), the canal overflowed, dikes were breached, and large areas were eroded and flooded (Eloy Soil Conservation District, 1969). Since 1916, lands in the district have been irrigated by well water.

(d) Rillito arroyo The Rillito is a major tributary of the Santa Cruz that was significantly altered between 1858 and 1910. Unlike most other historical arroyos in the Santa Cruz Valley, this arroyo is not associated with conclusive evidence of drainage concentration being responsible for channel erosion although there were acequias (including infiltration ditches) in the valley floor. The only detailed description of the changes is by Smith (1910), who appears to attribute the changes to overgrazing and haymaking. He stated (1910, p. 98):

[In 1858] The entire valley was . . . an unbroken forest, principally of mesquite, with a good growth of gramma and other grasses between the trees. The river course was indefinite, — a continuous grove of tall cottonwood, ash, willow and walnut trees with underbrush and sacaton and galleta grass, and it was further obstructed by beaver dams. The vegetative covering on mountain slopes, on foothills and plains held the rainfall, causing a large proportion of it to be absorbed into the soil. Such portion as found its way to the river channel was retarded and controlled in its flow, and perhaps not oftener than once in a century did a master flood erode and sweep the river channel.

In the fall of 1872 the United States Army post was moved from the military plaza in Tucson to the junction of the Pantano Wash and the Rillito. There was a great demand for hay and the grass was cut off with hoes to supply the post on large contracts. A few years of such cropping of the grass sufficed to kill it. Cattle were brought in to the country during the seventies and roamed the valley and hills, destroying the root grasses and wearing trails which later became rivulets in time of rain, increasing the runoff of water to the river. New and unusual[27] floods cut out a wide channel . . .

. . . the first real flood to reach the Rillito occurred in 1881, but it was much spread out over the valley and not until the nineties was the present deep broad wash with vertical banks eroded.

Conclusion. The detailed evidence from the three loci of entrenchment along the Santa Cruz Valley point to several important conclusions. Firstly, all three loci are unquestionably characterized by man-made drainage-concentration features. Secondly, entrenchment was initiated at different times in the three areas and, in each case, it was initiated shortly after the drainage-concentration features were established. These two conclusions provide strong support, in these areas, for the 'drainage-concentration' hypothesis of arroyo development. Thirdly, although no direct evidence of drainage concentration has been discovered in other areas of entrenchment in the basin, there has been much activity on the floodplain in such areas for many years, and the possibility remains that roads, acequias, and cattle trails etc. concentrated flow. Fourthly, entrenchment was initially discontinuous, and it still is. Fifthly, it is clear that man, often working in an alien semi-arid environment, persistently tried to control the effects of drought and flood and, in so doing, took measures that frequently failed to accommodate the floods. The history of floodplain management demonstrates an increasing awareness of the hydrological environment, but adequate perception unfortunately only came after damage had been done. Finally, it remains to determine whether the floods between 1870 and 1914 which actually did the eroding were in any way unusual and, if so, whether they arose from climatic and/or vegetational changes in the watershed. This problem is considered in a later section.

Arroyos in Avra and Altar Valleys

The Altar-Avra Basin, which is tributary to the Santa Cruz and lies to the west of it, extends from near the Mexican border northwards to the Santa Cruz Plains. Locally residents usually divide the basin into two parts — the Altar Valley in the south and the Avra Valley in the north, with the division lying along the line between T.14 S. and T.15 S. Altar Valley has most of the features described in other valleys: mountains flanked by pediments and alluvial plains, an inner valley that widens northwards, and an arroyo along much of its length. In Altar Valley pediments form an unusually large portion of the plains and this fact may be of some importance because groundwater aquifers in alluvium are rather restricted, and the proportion of precipitation that runs off may be relatively high. In Avra Valley the plains are broader, pediments are restricted, the groundwater reservoir is extensive, and there is only one short entrenched section.

Land-use history in the region has been rather simple. Andrews (1937) commented that the area was sparsely settled and had been of slight economic interest except for grazing. This seems to have been true for many years mainly because the area has been the western frontier of white settlement and has been relatively remote from the main centres of activity. Cattle grazing certainly was the chief interest in 1886, and in Altar Valley it still is. It was not until 1950 that the groundwater aquifer in Avra Valley was seriously exploited for irrigation, although there was a little irrigation based on imported water before that time (White, Matlock, and Schwalen, 1966).

Entrenchment in Altar Valley has resulted in a well-developed arroyo, known as Altar Wash in the south and Brawley Wash in the north. Although the entrenchment varies in magnitude along the valley, the arroyo is a relatively continuous, meandering feature that is up to 20 feet deep and up to 1,300 feet wide (Figure II.10). The only precise evidence concerning the arroyo in this very poorly documented area comes from the notes of the first survey made by a well-known local surveyor, George Roskruge, in 1886.[28]

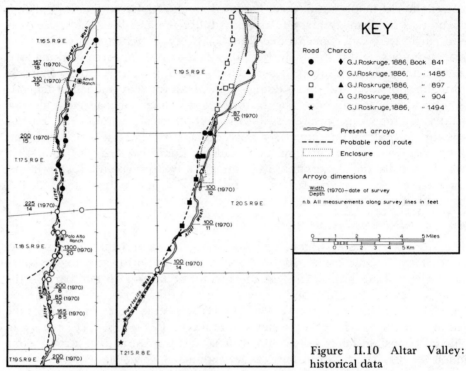

Figure II.10 Altar Valley: historical data

It is quite clear that there was no entrenchment in 1886 (Figure II.10). But there is evidence of three features on the narrow, grassy floodplain that may have been loci for subsequent erosion.

Firstly, there were several roads on the valley floor, including the main wagon road from Tucson to Altar (Mexico). The present arroyo follows the lines of these roads in several places, especially along Puertocito Wash (Figure II.10, T.21 S., R.8 E.) and near Palo Alto Ranch (T.18 S., R.9 E.).[29] There are places where the 1886 road and the present arroyo are not coincident. Field investigations revealed traces of the old road in locations given by Roskruge: the old road is relatively free of vegetation and is incised into the floodplain by several feet. These two observations confirm previous deductions (in the San Simon Valley, for instance).

A second feature of the 1886 record is two enclosures along the valley floor (Figure II.10). Both enclosures are now entrenched. A possible clue to the cause of entrenchment in the southern of these two enclosures is contained in a note by Roskruge (Book 904, T.20 S., R.9 E., 1886):

Through the center of this Township running N & S there is a large body of fine bottom land, susceptible of raising almost any kind of crop, if properly watered. In secs 4,5,8,9,

& 17 there is a post and wire fence enclosing about 600 acres of this land, the fence being the property of A. Hemme. I am informed that Mr. Hemme intends to conduct water on to this land by iron-pipes laid from Arivaca Creek a distance of 7 or 8 miles.

It is not known if this irrigation scheme materialized but if it did it probably would have provided a concentrated supply of water along the axis of the enclosure. Equally, grazing of animals or even cultivation of crops within the enclosed area might have promoted erosion.

A third feature of interest is the *charco*, of which nine are mentioned (Figure II.10). Charcos are hollows in generally undissected floodplains that contain water from time to time (Bryan, 1920). The origins of these features are varied, but mainly they are either natural depressions eroded, for example, by scour on the outside of meander bends, or they have been excavated by man. In either case they contain pools of water after a rainfall or flood and provide watering-places for cattle and horses. Bryan, who studied the features throughout the Papago country (1920 and 1925b), made several pertinent comments on them.

in places where the [flood] current is exceptionally swift, part of the mud laid down by past floods is removed and a relatively large channel is formed. It is characteristic of these channels that they begin with a series of little cliffs, 6 inches to 18 inches high, which lead down to numerous small channels and rill marks which collect together into a single channel which pursues a somewhat sinuous course in the direction of the drainage, and finally ends more or less abruptly. In many instances the channel ends in a vertical wall 3 to 5 feet high. It is evident that concentration of the current of a flood normally spreads in broad sheets over the flat, digs the original channel, and movement of water into this channel toward the end of the flood or during minor floods causes erosion of the fan-like set of miniature canyons at the upper end.

In this passage (Bryan, 1920, p.204) a natural origin is envisaged, but the current could be 'exceptionally swift' or 'concentration' could be increased due to irregularities created by man. In either case, the result is a depression below the level of the floodplain in which water collects.

Speaking of smaller charcos in grassy flats, Bryan (1920, p.205) continued:

Channel cutting of the kind previously described sometimes takes place in these flats, and many of the smaller charcos seem to be due to a breaking of the grass cover which allows erosion to take place over a very small area. Other holes seem to be due almost wholly to the activities of animals, both wild and domestic, which come to feed in the flat immediately after the rain. Very shallow pools of water attract them: they drink the muddy water, roll in the mud, and trample and compact the bottom. Thus a somewhat deeper hole is formed ... The maximum depth below the surface attained by this process seems to be about two feet.

Whatever the origin of charcos they could have served to concentrate floodwater flow and promote erosion. In Altar Valley nearly all the charcos of 1886 were sites of subsequent entrenchment.

Thus entrenchment in Altar Valley coincides in part with the lines of old roads, the location of charcos, and the area of two enclosures. It is not clear whether these features merely acted as loci of erosion that was certain to occur somewhere, or whether the changes of hydraulic conditions associated with them caused erosion where there would otherwise have been none. The arroyo was formed after 1886. By 1923 it had banks 2—6 feet high and extended almost to Anvil Ranch (Bryan, 1925b). By 1937 it was up to 20 feet deep and 600 feet wide (Andrews, 1937). And today it extends as far as T.14 S., is up to 1,300 feet wide, and is still no more than 20 feet deep.

There is no doubt about the origin of the arroyo in Avra Valley. When the land was sub-divided in the 1950s for irrigation, the fields were protected

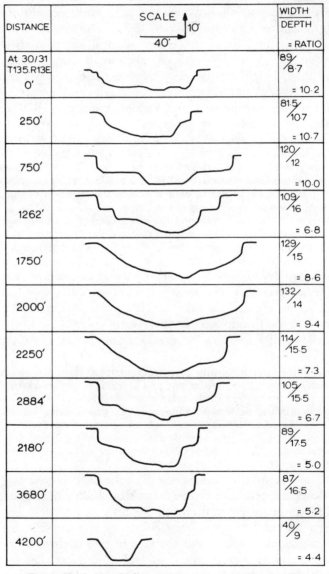

Figure II.11 Avra Valley arroyo: cross-sections, 1970

from occasional flooding by dikes, and floodwater was diverted into flood channels. One of these channels, that in the south of the area and nearest to major floods coming down the valley, was too small to accommodate large floods, such as that of 1962.(Lewis, 1963), and it has been seriously eroded. The dimensions of this arroyo are shown in Figure II.11. It is interesting to note that in places the terrace remnants in this valley are structurally controlled by the resistant B or caliche horizons of the palaeosol referred to elsewhere. The Avra arroyo is unquestionably the result of artificial drainage concentration.

Arroyos in the Papago Country: a Speculation

Beyond the Baboquivari divide lies the Papago ('Bean People') Indian Reservation — a different cultural and natural environment.

The Papago country differs in many ways from the basin-and-range lands to the east. It is dominated by broad, gently sloping alluvial plains and poorly integrated drainage systems. Mountains are fewer and the relief smaller. The area is also drier, although the precipitation regime is still dominated by summer storms. Despite the greater aridity and many years of vegetation modification by man, there remain grassy plains, and broad swaths of riparian vegetation still characterize most valley floors. A further contrast with the basins to the east is that valley-floor entrenchment is less frequent and less spectacular. Nevertheless, there are several arroyos within the reservation (Figure II.1).

It is within this harsh environment that the Papago Indians live. The tribe is generally regarded as an environmentally differentiated group of the Pima Indians (Hackenberg, 1962). Their traditional society was characterized by small groups of peaceful, industrious, and skilled agriculturalists, meagre in equipment, and informal and decentralized in organization (Castetter and Bell, 1942). Traditionally, the Papago response to the harsh desert environment has been a semi-nomadic existence in which kinship groups move between winter and summer occupation sites.The winter settlement ('The Well') was usually in the mountains or their foothills at a permanent source of water; this settlement was the base for hunting by the men and gathering by the women.

The summer village ('The Field') was on the alluvial plains some miles away from the winter settlement. According to Castetter and Bell (1942, p.44): 'Papago agriculture, involving no storage of water, was characteristically of the primitive but efficient *de temporal* "thunderstorm" type; that is, flood-water farming in which seed was planted in moist ground at the mouth of a wash after the first rains, which came in summer.' This agricultural system was reported as early as 1694 and it persists today.[30] Field and documentary evidence indicates that the Papago skilfully directed flood water from the wash on to prepared land by means of canals and dikes. Together with planting, weeding, and harvesting crops such as corn, beans, and squashes, preparation of irrigation structures was an important feature of summer activity.

Maintenance of the summer settlement depended on a supply of drinking-water. *Charcos* — of either natural or artificial origin — provided temporary storage along flood-water channels and elsewhere, and dikes, dams, and ditches were often constructed to promote water storage (McDowell, 1920; Hoover, 1929; Castetter and Bell, 1942).[31] But the charcos dried up in the fall, and the farmers then moved back to the hills; it was only with the development of wells that some 'Field' settlements became permanent. In the context of arroyos the important features of flood-water farming are that it depends on floods, their concentration at certain points, and the creation of distribution structures and drinking-water storage facilities.

The location of arroyos in the Papago country was determined from an aerial reconnaissance, examination of aerial photographs and field traverses (Figure II.1). As far as it is possible to judge from this preliminary evidence, entrenchment in valley floors is confined to two types of position, both of which are related to 'The Field' settlements. Some summer settlements are at the downstream end of the larger arroyos, notably Gu Oidak ('Big Field'), Schuchk, Gu Achi ('Big narrow ridge'), Anegam ('Slender tree'), Cowlic ('Corner'), and Ak-chin ('Arroyo mouth').[32] Other summer settlements are immediately upstream of entrenchment, as at Kom Vo ('Hackberry charco'), Hickiwan ('Zig zag'), Vamori ('Swamp'), and Wahak Hotrontk (Figure II.1). By the standards of arroyos in eastern basins, none of the arroyos is long or large. The entrenchment at Sells is perhaps the most pronounced, and here the arroyo is several miles long, and up to about 250 feet wide and 10 feet deep.

The dates of entrenchment are unknown. It is clear, however, that many of the present arroyos had been formed by the first decade of this century.[33] The causes of entrenchment can only be a matter of speculation because precise evidence is absent. But three hypotheses seem to deserve further investigation.

The first is that entrenchment is the result of natural conditions in the drainage systems, arising where discharges and flow are greatest or as a response to changing slope conditions along the valley floor which arise from sedimentation by ephemeral flow.[34] Such explanations would seem reasonable for the Gu Oidak, Gu Achi, and Ak-chin arroyos, all of which occur where drainage is naturally concentrated in high-order drainage lines along clearly defined axes of alluvial plains. The hypothesis cannot be applied to all arroyos in the reservation because some of the most likely natural locations are without arroyos.

A possible explanation of these arroyos downstream of 'Field' settlements might be that vegetation removal — in the preparation of fields or, more recently, with the grazing of livestock around villages — might have caused increased runoff from these areas. And the creation and continued development of charcos near settlements could have provided local concentration of flow. No precise evidence is to hand to support this hypothesis.

A third hypothesis is that arroyos are related to deliberate concentration of runoff in order to direct and increase water-supply to fields or to improve drinking-water supplies. The fundamental, unsolved problem here is whether the Papago selected the mouths of established arroyos for flood farming, or whether the arroyos were created slowly by flood flows as the flood-farming system was developed on originally untrenched plains.

Many authors have stated that the Papago selected arroyo mouths for the location of summer villages because floodwaters were naturally concentrated at such sites (e.g. Bryan, 1929; Dobyns, 1951; Underhill, 1939). The alternative view — that the arroyos were in part created as the result of irrigation practices — is novel, and there is some slender evidence that might be interpreted as supporting it.

Firstly, not all flood-farming sites are associated with arroyos, and therefore the existence of an arroyo was not necessary for the location of a summer settlement. Secondly, it is clear that the Papago took elaborate measures to divert floodwater from washes to fields; one might contend that the action of concentrating flow into a single channel in order to increase and improve supplies is but a logical extension of the distributional practices. Old Papago farmers at Crowhang were interviewed in order to test this notion.[35] Two old-timers in this community, which is within the basin of the Schuchk arroyo, emphasized the job of canal digging to facilitate movement of water from the 'river' to the fields, work that was done at the turn of the nineteenth century with plough and shovel. Both stated, however, that ditches and dikes were also constructed in order to direct water *into* the 'river', especially when water was short.[36] This work was said to have been done with shovels and wooden hoes and usually just before the summer rains, although some ditching was done in winter. Joaquin Ochoa added that the position of catchment ditches and dikes was altered from time to time, and that the main channel was periodically deepened by horse-drawn fresnos. (It should be noted that the residents of Crowhang were speaking only of small flood-farming systems, involving a few acres of land and relatively short channels.)

A third source of evidence is the field. At Fresnol, near the head of Sells Wash, and between Fresnol and Sells, there are several channels leading to or from the wash — channels clearly created by man. The age of these features is unknown, but some undoubtedly serve, intentionally or unintentionally, to concentrate runoff into the wash. In addition, long, straight 'canals' are evident from the air in some localities, and these also concentrate flow.

Fourthly, support for the concentration hypothesis comes from the archaeological record. Castetter and Bell (1942) described traces of irrigation canals on the reservation which date from A.D. 1200 to 1400. 'One such canal runs in a straight line for seventeen miles in a west by southwest direction from Baboquivari Mountain to the vicinity of Vamori' (Castetter and Bell, 1942, p.36). In his account of the excavations at Ventana Cave, on the north-west margin of the reservation, Haury (1950) mentioned the possibility of canals gathering runoff from gently sloping terrain and providing water for irrigation in the 'Sells Phase' (A.D. 1250—1400).

Such scanty evidence justifies no definite conclusions. But the possibility of drainage concentration leading to entrenchment in some areas of the reservation certainly deserves fuller investigation.

These speculations prompt another. The late nineteenth century was not the first period in which man-made hydraulic alterations occurred in South-Western valley floors. The spread of irrigation techniques through much of the area is closely associated with the development and diffusion of Pueblo cultures — Hohokam, Anasasi, Mogollon, Sinagua. These cultures were particularly active between about the tenth and fourteenth centuries A.D., at a time when arroyo cutting was proceeding in several South-Western valleys. Is this a coincidence?

HYPOTHESES OF REGIONAL CHANGE

Introduction

In Part I it was established that increased flow velocity could be accomplished either by an increase of discharge or by a change of flow characteristics within a given discharge. In this section the first possibility is examined in the context of explanatory hypotheses that require regional or general environmental changes. The second possibility is considered in the following section, where hypotheses of localized, valley-floor changes are reviewed.

The discharge of water in a drainage system — an isolated event in a system characterized by ephemeral flow — is governed by several independent and semi-dependent variables. The more important of these are climate, vegetation, the dimensions of the basin, and ground materials. As the last two can be regarded as constant in southern Arizona during the last hundred years, significant changes of valley-floor discharge, if they occurred, must be explained in terms of climatic or vegetational change. To be specific, increased magnitude, frequency, or 'flashiness' of discharge could result from increased precipitation, or from increased runoff from the same amount of precipitation due to vegetation alteration and accompanying changes, or from both.

Conventional wisdom, propounded by numerous authors, has for many years alleged that both types of changes occurred contemporaneously towards the end of the nineteenth century and created a situation admirably suited to the generation of more erosive flows. Bryan (1928b, p.477), for example, succinctly stated the argument as follows:

The cause of the deepening of stream channels also involves a botanical factor. With the settlement of the area by white men, domestic grazing animals were introduced in such numbers that the native vegetation was in places completely destroyed. This loss of the vegetative cover by overgrazing resulted in a more rapid run-off after rain and increased the erosive power of streams. In so far as the cutting of the deep continuous channels was coincident with overgrazing the increase in erosive power of streams seems an adequate cause of the formation of arroyos. However, some arroyos appear to have been cut before overgrazing began, and there is geologic and archaeological evidence that on some streams a similar arroyo was formed and filled up in the time of the pre-historic Indians. Thus there is reason for believing that the fundamental cause of arroyo formation is a change to a drier climate. In this theory, overgrazing becomes a mere accessory which sets the date when cutting might begin.

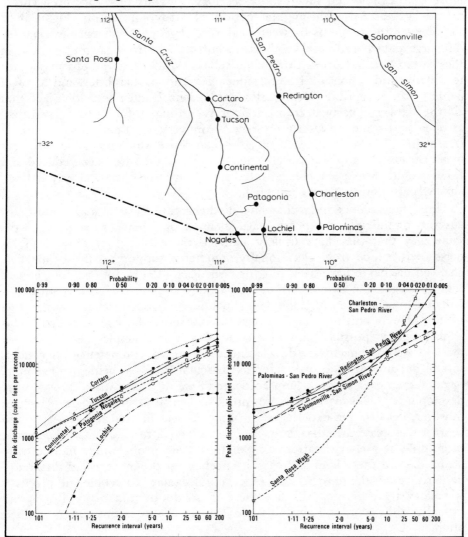

Figure II.12 Relations between peak discharge and recurrence interval for selected gauging stations in southern Arizona. For explanation, see text. Based on U.S. Geological Survey (1971) data

In this section an attempt is made to evaluate the evidence upon which the various threads of this explanatory hypothesis are based. Critical to the hypothesis of course, is the notion that discharge changed significantly in the major valleys at the times when arroyos were initiated. It would be desirable to present at the outset of this discussion evidence of such changes. But no conclusive evidence is available. A search for appropriate discharge records has been unsuccessful. No gauging stations were operational before 1900 and most were established much more recently.[37] Thus there are no accurate records of discharge during the period of arroyo initiation. Figure II.12 summarizes the relations between peak discharge and recurrence interval for discharge data over relatively short, recent periods from gauging stations in the Santa Cruz and other entrenched valleys. While these graphs may give a reasonable indication of flood frequencies and probabilities and a rough guide to the magnitude of peak flows at present, it must be emphasized that all the data are derived from stations recording flows within established arroyos, and some curves are projected from very short periods of record. It is probable that such flows are greater than those which preceded entrench-ment because floodplain and channel storage would have been reduced and flows would have been concentrated in relatively efficient, clearly defined channels after arroyos were initiated.

Three facts concerning changing discharge are clear. Firstly, most dis-cussants of the arroyo problem have assumed that changes occurred, in the same way that they have usually assumed the explanatory hypothesis, or parts of it, to be true. Occasionally arguments supporting the concept of changed discharge have been put forward. Rich (1911), for example, argued that because some arroyo beds in New Mexico contain coarse debris which is absent from the adjacent floodplain alluvium, increased discharge at the time of the arroyo cutting was necessary to transport the coarse debris. (This explanation is possible, but others are also. For example the very act of incision would concentrate flow and increase stream competence.) Secondly, several documentary records refer to particular floods as being, for example, 'greater than ever before', 'unprecedented', etc. at times when arroyos were developing.[38] This evidence is not proof of significant hydrological changes, however, because the experience of observers was limited to a timespan too short to indicate whether large floods reflected rarer events in constant magnitude-frequency relations or whether flow probabilities had actually changed. And there is in any case a tencency for the most recent disaster to be perceived as the most serious, especially if damage to people and property is greater than before. Thirdly, there is no doubt that major floods and droughts did occur, and continue to occur, in all the basins under consider-ation.

Although the question of changed discharge remains unanswered, these observations call for the examination of assumptions and hypotheses relating to climatic and vegetational change in southern Arizona during the last hundred years. The possibilities of climatic change are considered first, and these are followed by a review of vegetational change and an evaluation of the various changes in terms of valley-floor discharge.

The Precipitation Record

(a) Review A fundamental cause of hydrological change in a drainage basin may be a change of climate, and it is possible that certain climatic variations could have led to valley-floor entrenchment. In this section some possibilities of secular and short-term climatic change are examined in the light of daily precipitation records from various stations in southern Arizona.

The initial argument for adopting climatic change as a partial explanation of entrenchment in the late nineteenth century arose from archaeological and geological evidence of erosion and sedimentation episodes at times in the past when human influence on the environment was unlikely to have been significant. The stratigraphic record in southern Arizona during and since the Wisconsin period certainly appears to include several periods of arroyo formation (e.g. Antevs, 1952; Haynes, 1968). But there has been considerable controversy over the nature of the climatic changes responsible for phases of erosion and deposition. Some, notably Antevs and Bryan, associated arroyo cutting with drought and poor vegetation, and arroyo filling with higher precipitation and improved vegetation. Others, such as Huntington (1914), argued that a tendency towards a drier climate would promote deposition, whereas humid conditions would favour gullying. More soundly based on the analysis of climatic and palaeobotanical evidence is the view that arroyo initiation is related to seasonal changes in the frequency of rainfalls of different intensities (Leopold, 1951a; Martin, 1964; Schoenwetter, 1962). Most of these hypotheses involve a secular change of climate, and most emphasize precipitation, rather than other climatic variables such as temperature. The possibilities must remain that short-term climatic variations, and contemporaneous changes of several climatic variables, could also produce conditions favouring entrenchment.

The main body of data for studying climatic change in the American South-West is the daily precipitation record. Several studies have been made of this record and the results pertinent to southern Arizona are briefly reviewed here.

In a well-known New Mexican study, Leopold (1951a) posed and answered the significant question: is there any evidence of important climatic variations in the past century that might have some bearing on the cause or timing of the epicycle of erosion? Leopold argued that not only total precipitation, but also frequency of rains of various daily intensities may vary from year to year or season to season, and that such variations could have a significant influence on vegetation, runoff, and erosion. Erosion, he suggested, is caused mainly by large rains (i.e. those equal to or exceeding one inch per day), whereas smaller rains (e.g. those between 0·01 and 0·49 inches per day) provide moisture to sustain shrubs and grasses that tend to protect the surface. Thus an increased frequency of heavy rains or a decreased frequency of light rains, or a combination of both, could be associated with a phase of erosion.

From a study of daily precipitation records from four stations since about 1850, Leopold concluded (1951a, p.351):

it seems clear that during the early portion of the past hundred years, New Mexico experienced a relatively low frequency of small rains both in summer and winter. At least in some areas, the early period of record shows a relatively high frequency of large rains. Such a circumstance must have been conducive to a weak vegetal cover and relatively great incidence of erosion. That the modern epicycle of erosion began in the Southwest about 1885 is well established ... We see, then, that not only was grazing tending to promote erosion at that time, but meteorological conditions were more conducive to erosion than during the period of the present generation. Thus there is established concrete evidence of a climatic factor operating at the time of initiation of southwestern erosion which no doubt helped to promote the initiation of that erosion.

Later in this section an attempt will be made to establish if Leopold's hypothesis can be substantiated in southern Arizona.

Previous work on historical climatic data in southern Arizona has been mainly by Hastings and Turner (1965), McDonald (1956), and Sellers (1960).

Hastings and Turner (1965, p.279) commented: 'An analysis of the rainfall records since 1895 for five stations in southeastern Arizona shows some affinities to the curves presented by Leopold. Whether there is general agreement before 1895 is a question on which judgment must be deferred.' Unfortunately these authors do not elaborate on their analysis of post-1895 data; data before 1895 are analysed below in order to answer their unresolved question. Clearly, as most arroyos were initiated before 1895, such an analysis is of crucial importance. Hastings and Turner also studied temperature changes since 1898 for three stations in Arizona (Phoenix, Yuma, Tucson) and demonstrated that there has been a slight increase in mean annual temperature which resembles changes elsewhere in the world. The implication of this increase is that, if rainfall has declined or remained the same, there could have been a secular trend towards aridity during the period.

That such a trend is a possibility is demonstrated in Figure II.13, in which 10-year running means for mean seasonal temperatures at 18 stations in Arizona and New Mexico can be compared with similar running means for precipitation (the latter data come from Sellers, 1960). It is clear that since the turn of the century there has been a slight decrease in summer precipitation and a greater decrease in winter precipitation, together with general, slight increases of temperature. These trends point towards greater aridity since 1898, reflected perhaps in greater evaporation and less soil moisture. Such secular changes could have greatly modified vegetation, but because they are so slight and protracted, it seems rather unlikely — even if they reflect a trend begun as early as 1860 — that they would have led to entrenchment at the critical period. And, of course, it is not yet clear that the trends since 1898 apply to the 1860—1898 period. It should also be

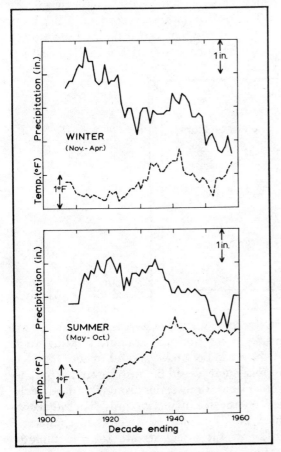

Figure II.13 Ten-year running means comparing mean seasonal precipitation at 18 Arizona and western New Mexico stations (after Sellers, 1960) with mean annual temperatures at 18 Arizona stations (after Hastings and Turner, 1965)

noted that Sellers identified a downward trend in total precipitation averaging an inch per 30 years, as well as the seasonal declines since 1905. And none of the trends is statistically significant. (McDonald, 1956, also noted a secular decline in precipitation since the 1920s.)

Most other precipitation studies of southern Arizona are more casual. Olmstead (1919) compared the characteristics of two 12-year 'rainfall cycles' for Fort Apache. Huntington (1914) pointed to the great annual and seasonal variability of rainfall at Tucson, a theme also pursued by McDonald (1956). And Peterson (1950) showed that between 1881 and 1884, when some arroyos may have been initiated in the South-West, annual rainfall was above average at several stations in southern Arizona.

(b) The daily precipitation record Long records of daily rainfall are scarce

in southern Arizona. In this study data were compiled for stations that are assumed to be reasonably representative of the major entrenched basins (Figure II.14 and Table II.1). The Fort Bowie-San Simon records were used to represent the San Simon Valley; Fort Grant is located between the Aravaipa and Whitewater basins; Tombstone (whose record only begins in 1897), was taken to be representative of the San Pedro Basin; Fort Lowell and Tucson data were combined to produce a record for the Santa Cruz Valley.

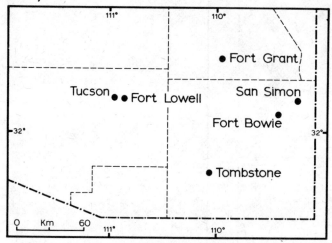

Figure II.14 Stations used for the analysis of daily precipitation

The data are not entirely satisfactory for several reasons. Firstly, no station record is complete. Omissions are normally minor, relating to a month or so in a year, and often they can be safely ignored. Where data for several months or whole years are missing it would be possible to interpolate the information to produce a continuous time series using standard techniques. This solution was rejected on the following grounds. The adjacent-station method (Paulhus and Kohler, 1952) is impracticable because adjacent stations are too few, too distant, and their records are too incomplete. Methods based on using data in years or months preceding or following the data gaps are rejected because of large data variability. In the following analysis, therefore, only original data are used to generate seasonal and annual values.

A second problem relates to the homogeneity of the data. In order to obtain sequences representative of the Santa Cruz and San Simon valleys, data from two stations at different locations in each area have been combined. In the case of Fort Lowell-Tucson, the locational differences are assumed to be climatically unimportant: indeed, data from the two stations have often been used as a single sequence before. The considerable differences in altitude and location of Fort Bowie and San Simon, in the San Simon Valley, are certainly significant (see also McDonald, 1956). In the analysis of these data, therefore, statistics have been calculated separately for

Table II.1

Station Data[+]

Station	Lat.	Long.	Alt. (ft.)	Period	Source* of Data	Years for which data is absent or incomplete	Remarks and History
1. *Fort Bowie* (a)	32°09'	109°26'	5000'	1867–83 / 1889–94	1 / 1	1884–8 / 1895–8	Post Surgeon and Signal Service data. One location higher, and SW. of San Simon
2. *San Simon* (a)	32°16'	109°14'	3609'	1897–1945	2	1897 / 1901–2 / 1912 / 1916–20	Gauge began at RR station; 4 small moves
(b)	32°19'	109°17'	3560'	1945–9	2		Downstream from (a) 5 miles
(c)	32°16'	109°15'	3608'	1949–66	2		Station moved back into town
3. *Fort Grant* (a)	32°37'	109°57'	4851'	1873–1900 / 1900–66	1 / 2	1879 / 1882–9 / 1905–19 / 1922–7 / 1929–31, 1937, / 1939, 1944–5 / 1947–8 / 1951–4	Post Surgeon and Signal Service data until 1905. Earlier data are available, but are for Camp Grant in San Pedro Valley
4. *Tombstone* (a)	31°42'	110°04'	4675'	1897–1966	2	1952	At seven different locations in Tombstone City with one brief excursion outside
5. *Fort Lowell* (a)	32°13'	110°58'	2387'	1867–73	1	1867	At Military Plaza, Tucson, 6 miles NE. of Tucson
(b)	32°16'	110°53'	2450'	1873–83	1	1875, 1879 / 1880, 1881, 1882, / 1883	
6. *Tucson* (a)	32°13'	110°58'	2400'	1883–91	1	1884, 1886	Southern Pacific Agent. One month at Fort Lowell in 1891. University of Arizona (5 locations)
(b)	32°14'	110°57'	2423'	1891–1966	2		

+ Source: U.S. Weather Bureau, 1956.
* 1 = National Archives, Washington.
2 = NOAA, National Climatic Center, Asheville.

each station. A related problem is that rain-gauge position has changed from time to time at most stations, and these moves may have influenced the data. Station histories (Table II.1) suggest that the moves were not normally into significantly different environments, and their possible effects have been ignored.

Thirdly, it is necessary to assume that the data are accurate. That this assumption could be unjustified can be emphasized by pointing out that military forts were not primarily scientific research centres but isolated defences, often in hostile Indian territory. On the other hand, the records appear to be extremely precise. The early records of the Post Surgeon and Signal Service, for example, are often embellished with informative and detailed notes, and are in some ways more valuable than the later U.S. Weather Bureau data. It might seem likely that early records would under-record precipitation, especially that from small rainfalls, but there appears to be no evidence of this. For instance, rainfall of 0·01 inches was being recorded at Fort Lowell in 1869.

Finally, it is unlikely that a single data sequence can fully reflect rainfall conditions in a large drainage basin of southern Arizona because the spatial variability of rainfall totals, frequencies, intensities, and durations is extremely great.

Despite these qualifications, the daily precipitation records undoubtedly provide the most detailed and precise means of testing notions of climatic change in southern Arizona during the last hundred years. Because the data are not entirely satisfactory, only the most conservative conclusions are drawn from them. Emphasis is placed on the Fort Lowell-Tucson data which provides the longest and most complete record (Figures II.15, II.16, and II.17).

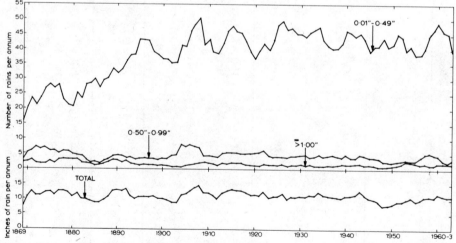

Figure II.15 Fort Lowell-Tucson: 5-year running means of total annual precipitation, and annual frequency of rainfalls in different categories

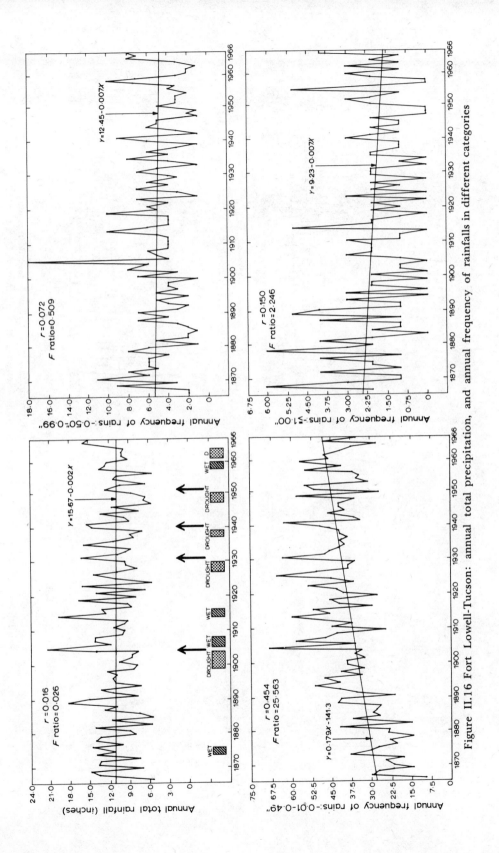

Figure II.16 Fort Lowell-Tucson: annual total precipitation, and annual frequency of rainfalls in different categories

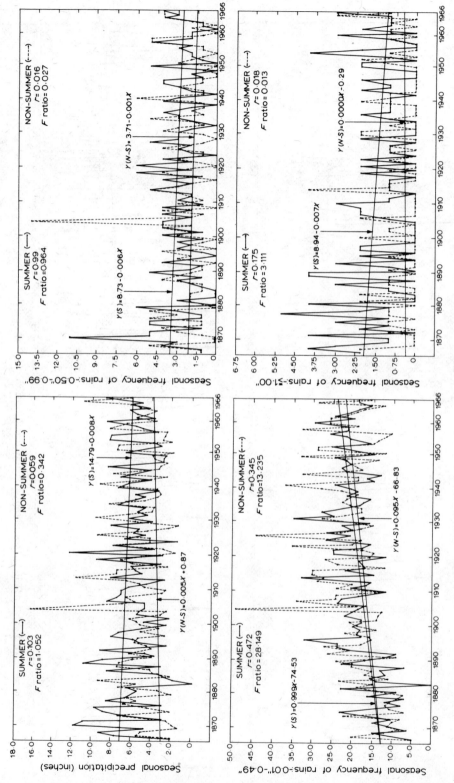

Figure II.17 Fort Lowell-Tucson: seasonal precipitation totals, and seasonal frequency of rainfalls in different categories (summer: June–September; non-summer: October–May)

Table II.2   *Fort Lowell-Tucson Annual Precipitation Data*
Tests of Significance of Difference Between Sample Means

	Period 1 (N = 51) (1866–1916)	Period 2 (N = 50) (1917–1966)

1. Light intensity
rainfalls (0·01″ − 0·49″
per day)

$\overline{X}$	33·70	42·76
σ	13·21	9·03

$t = 4\cdot026$. Significant at the 0·001 level

2. Medium intensity
rainfalls (0·50″ − 0·99″
per day)

$\overline{X}$	4·84	4·40
σ	3·02	2·45

$t = 0\cdot81$. Not significant

3. High intensity
rainfalls (1·0″ or over
per day)

$\overline{X}$	2·00	1·52
σ	1·56	1·18

$t = 1\cdot84$. Significant at the 0·1 level

4. Total annual
rainfall

$\overline{X}$	11·07	10·68
σ	3·79	3·09

$t = 0\cdot57$. Not significant

Statistical measures used in this analysis include means, running means, standard deviations, coefficients of variation, correlation and regression coefficients, and F-ratios. Because of the possibility of autocorrelation amongst regression residuals and the influence it might have on correlation coefficients and F-ratios, the Fort Lowell-Tucson data have been analysed using the Cochrane-Orcutt iterative technique for least squares regression and correlation (Cochrane and Orcutt, 1949). The regression coefficients on which Figure II.18 is based are derived from ordinary least-squares-regression analysis.

(c) Results

(i) Secular trends in annual and seasonal precipitation. Running means (Figure II.15), statistical comparison of the two equal halves of each record using the t-test (Table II.2), and correlation and regression analysis

Table II.3

Correlation and Regression Analysis: Fort Lowell-Tucson
(Period: 1867—1966 (100 years))

		Regression coefficient	Correlation coefficient	F-ratio
(A) *Precipitation Totals*				
Annual		−0·002	−0·016	0·026
Summer		0·008	0·103	1·052
Non-summer		0·005	0·059	0·342
(B) *Precipitation Frequency*				
(1) Annual	− light	0·180	0·455	25·563*
	− medium	−0·007	0·072	0·509
	− heavy	−0·007	0·150	2·246
(2) Summer	− light	0·099	0·472	28·149*
	− medium	−0·006	0·099	0·964
	− heavy	−0·007	0·175	3·111
(3) Non-summer	− light	0·095	0·345	13·235*
	− medium	−0·001	0·016	0·027
	− heavy	0·000	0·018	0·013

* Significant at the 0·001 level
Summer: June—September
Non-summer: October—May

(Table II.3, Figures II.16 and II.18) show that there have been no significant secular trends in annual precipitation totals in the last hundred years in southern Arizona. This conclusion accords with that of Leopold (1951a) in New Mexico. The same conclusion also applies to summer (June-September) and non-summer (October-May) precipitation (e.g. Table II.3, Figures II.17 and II.18).

(ii) Short-term changes: drought and wet periods. Despite the lack of secular trends in annual, summer, and non-summer precipitation totals, there is clearly considerable variation in precipitation from year to year (e.g. Figures II.16 and II.17). This variability can be described usefully for data sequences in terms of means, standard deviations, and coefficients of variation (standard deviations divided by the means), and these statistics are shown for annual precipitation totals in Table II.4. As McDonald (1956) has shown, coefficients of variation from Arizonan stations are higher than for most other stations in the United States.

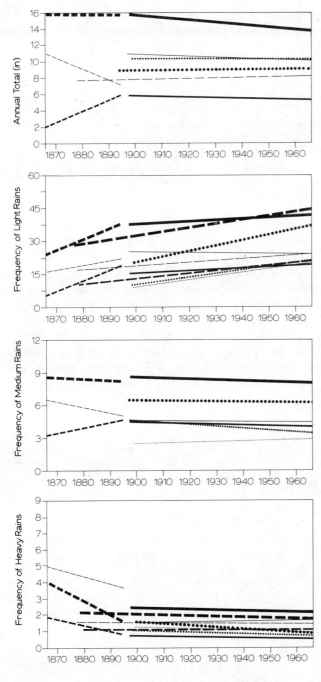

Annual Total (in)

Frequency of Light Rains

Frequency of Medium Rains

Frequency of Heavy Rains

	Annual Total	Non-Summer	Summer
TOMBSTONE			
FORT GRANT			
FORT BOWIE			
SAN SIMON			

Figure II.18 Secular trends in southern Arizona, represented by regression lines showing precipitation totals and annual and seasonal frequencies of rainfalls in different categories

Table II.4   *Variability of Annual Precipitation*

	Mean annual precipitation (in.)	Standard deviation	Coefficient of variation	Years of Record
Fort Lowell-Tucson	10·991	3·291	0·299	100
Tombstone	13·378	4·445	0·332	70
Fort Grant	12·724	3·847	0·302	45
Fort Bowie	13·639	3·356	0·246	22
San Simon	8·886	3·162	0·355	60

Relatively dry and wet periods can be defined in a variety of ways. For example, if such periods are arbitrarily defined as being composed of at least three successive years in which *annual* precipitation is above or below the mean, then several interesting features emerge (Table II.5, Figure II.16).

Firstly, spells of relatively wet or dry years are fairly common (Table II.5). Secondly, the spells are not always coincident in each valley. For example, the run of dry years at Tucson from 1899 to 1904 is matched by a longer spell, from 1897 to 1904 at Tombstone; and according to Lantow and Flory (1940) this drought extended from 1891 to 1904 at Willcox. And the relatively wet period in the San Pedro Valley between 1925 and 1933 (recorded at Tombstone) is absent from the Tucson record, and

Table II.5   *Drought and Wet Periods: Annual Data*

	Drought	Wet Periods	Period of Record
Fort Lowell-Tucson	1899–1904[+] 1927–30[+] 1937–40[+] 1947–50[+] 1960–3	1874–6 1905–8 1914–16 1957–9	1867–1966
Fort Grant	1902–4[*]	1893–5	1880–1966
Fort Bowie	1869–73[+]		1868–94
San Simon	1932–6 1945–8	1903–5 1926–8 1939–41 1957–61	1897–1966
Tombstone	1897–1904[+] 1940–8[+] 1950–3	1925–33 1957–9	1897–1966

* sequence terminated by lack of data
+ sequence terminated by wet year

there was actually a drought at Tucson between 1927 and 1930. A third point is that drought periods are often immediately succeeded by one or more relatively very wet years (Table II.5, Figure II.16). The possible significance of this is considered below but, briefly, it is that vegetation cover is depleted during the drought and takes more than a year to recover, so that in the wet year following a drought, heavy rains may fall on surfaces particularly conducive to runoff and erosion, and valley-floor floods may occur (as they did at Tucson in 1905).

Table II.6 *Drought and Wet Periods:*
Cumulative Precipitation Deficiency or Excess
between June and September at Fort Lowell-Tucson

Droughts	Cumulative Deficiency (inches below mean)	*Wet Periods*	Cumulative Excess (inches above mean)
+1884–6*	8·834	1866–9	5·72
1891–2	3·016	1871–2	11·47
1894–5*	3·606	1874–6	8·31
1899–1906*	10·794	1878–80	4·26
1912–13	3·866	1889–90	8·62
1915–16	0·966	1896–98	3·26
1932–4*	2·41	1907–11	7·83
1937–9*	3·45	1935–6	2·52
1944–5	1·90	1940–1	2·29
1947–9	8·44	1954–5	4·92
1951–3*	5·08		
1956–7	3·22		
1960–1	2·18		

+ Preceded by incomplete data
* Drought terminated by two or more relatively wet summers

The depletion of vegetation during droughts, and its possible effect on runoff, could be very important, so that a more detailed analysis of the precipitation data is instructive. Several range studies, such as those by Culley (1943), and Reynolds (1954) at the Santa Rita Experiment Station, indicate that over 90 per cent of perennial grass growth occurs in summer (June-September) and forage production is positively correlated with summer rainfall. Table II.6 shows the drought and wet periods at Fort Lowell-Tucson based on cumulative deficiencies or excesses of *summer* precipitation. Two very serious droughts and at least three very wet periods are evident in the period from 1867 to 1906. The possible significance of these periods is considered further below.

(iii) Rainfall frequency. Figures II.16 and II.17 summarize for Fort Lowell-Tucson the correlation and regression analysis of daily rainfall frequency, per year and per summer and non-summer period, of light (0·01″—0·49″ per day), medium (0·50″—0·99″ per day), and heavy (1 inch or more per day) rainfalls. Figure II.18 shows the regression lines for these variables for the other stations studied in southern Arizona.

The most important feature of the analysis is the increase in the frequency of light rains. This secular trend is apparent, to a greater or lesser extent, at all stations. The Fort Lowell-Tucson and Fort Bowie data (e.g. Figures II.16, II.17, and II.18) show clearly that most of the increase occurred during the late nineteenth century.

A second trend, possibly complementary to the first, is a decline in the frequency of heavy rainfalls, especially during the summer season. This trend is not pronounced or statistically significant, but it is apparent at Fort Lowell-Tucson, Fort Bowie (in the nineteenth century), and, to a lesser extent, at San Simon, Fort Grant, and Tombstone.

These two trends are similar to those identified by Leopold (1951a) in New Mexico.

(iv) Conclusions. 1. There have been no statistically significant secular changes in annual, annual summer, or annual non-summer precipitation totals during the last hundred years at the stations studied in southern Arizona.

2. Drought and wet periods are a feature of the precipitation pattern. Droughts are at times terminated by extremely wet years, and in these circumstances runoff and erosion might be expected to be particularly pronounced. But such circumstances are not confined to the period of arroyo initiation — they have certainly occurred since, and there is no evidence that they did not occur before.

Cumulative summer precipitation deficiencies during droughts — a useful climatic index that is closely related to forage production and hence to vegetation cover and, perhaps, to runoff and erosion — were particularly high at Fort Lowell-Tucson during the droughts of 1884—6 and 1899—1906. There have also been significant wet summer periods, such as those in 1871—2, 1874—6, and 1889—90.

3. Several stations show significant increases in the frequency of light rains, and these trends appear to be most pronounced towards the end of the nineteenth century. The results substantiate for southern Arizona the observation of Leopold (1951a) in New Mexico that during the early portion of the last hundred years the frequency of light rains, annually and seasonally, was relatively low.

It could be that, as a result of this secular change, the water available for grasses may have been reduced in summer, the critical period of growth in this region, and thus protective vegetation cover may have been weakened at the time of arroyo initiation.

4. There was a reduction at most places in the frequency of high-intensity rains. Such rains are those responsible for runoff. It could be, as Leopold (1951a) found in New Mexico, that there was a slightly greater frequency of runoff-producing rains in southern Arizona towards the end of the nineteenth century than there has been since. This change coincided with a relatively low frequency of light, grass-sustaining rains.

Vegetation Changes

Vegetation is a critical variable influencing the relations between rainfall on the one hand, and runoff and erosion on the other, mainly because vegetation utilizes a proportion of the available water and modifies the erodibility of the ground surface. In semi-arid lands it is also a variable that is particularly susceptible to alteration as the result of climatic change or the activities of man. Study of the nature and effects of vegetation changes in southern Arizona, however, raises numerous problems of which only a few can at present be conclusively resolved. In this discussion attention is directed towards answering two fundamental questions: (a) what is the broad pattern of vegetation changes in southern Arizona during the last hundred years? and (b) to what extent can such changes be attributed to changes of climate, to the effects of livestock, or to works of man?

(a) The pattern of vegetation change Reconstruction of the vegetation patterns encountered by the first white explorers in the South-West and their modification, has been attempted by several authors using a wide range of historical information, especially the diaries, field notes, memoirs, and

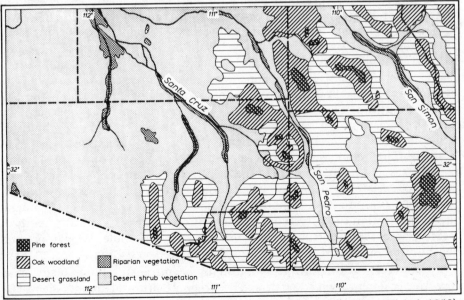

Figure II.19 Vegetation distribution in southern Arizona (modified from Nichol, 1952)

reminiscences of residents, explorers, and travellers, photographs, and the U.S. General Land Office survey notes. The advantages and drawbacks of these sources in examining vegetation history have been described by several authors (e.g. Buffington and Herbel, 1965; Hastings and Turner, 1965; Leopold, 1951b; Stoiber, 1973; Woodward, 1969; York and Dick-Peddie, 1969).

The major drainage basins of southern Arizona have a rich diversity of flora and they normally include sections of the principal 'life zones' in the region (Figure II.19). These zones, which are stratified altitudinally, include the desert, the desert grassland, the oak woodland, and, at the highest elevations, the pine and fir forests. Cutting across some of these zones, and important in the context of arroyos, are the swaths of riparian vegetation along valley floors. The most extensive zones in the area as a whole are those of desert shrub, desert grassland, and oak woodland.

(i) *The oak woodland* occurs mainly at altitudes between 4,000 and 7,000 feet (Rich, 1960). The woodland is dominated by *Quercus oblongifolia* Torr.,[39] *Quercus emoryi* Torr., and other oaks. Other trees include, at lower levels, Arizona rosewood (*Vauquelinia californica* Torr.), the one-seed Juniper (*Juniperus monosperma* Engelm.), and mesquite (*Prosopis juliflora* Swartz); at higher elevations woody plants are found such as manzanita (*Arctostaphylos* spp.), Arizona madrone (*Arbutus arizonica* Gray), and Mexican pinyon pine (*Pinus cembroides* Zucc.). This vegetation contains a high proportion of shrubby species at higher altitudes which are progressively replaced at lower elevations by grasses.

The most striking historical change in the oak woodland, as revealed in numerous photographs, has been the disappearance of oaks on the lower margins of the zone, and the complementary altitudinal extension of the desert grassland together with invasion by shrubs (or trees) such as mesquite, ocotillo (*Fouquieria splendens* Engelm.), and juniper (Hastings and Turner 1965). Hastings and Turner concluded that increased soil aridity was responsible for the upward contraction of oak woodland because the oak carcasses showed no signs of being tampered with by man, because the greatest decrease in oak numbers occurred at the hottest and driest limits of their range, and because at higher elevations the oak population appeared to be stable. They emphasize that because the vegetation in this zone depends on a biseasonal rainfall regime, the vegetation changes could have been related to a decrease in precipitation during either or both seasons. Equally, other changes could have promoted soil aridity, such as changes of temperature or infiltration capacity. Finally, some of the disappearance of trees must be attributed to felling by man, as in the Dragoon, Mule, Whetstone, and Huachuca mountains of the San Pedro Valley (Rodgers, 1965).

(ii) *The desert grassland* has undoubtedly been transformed in many areas since the coming of white settlers. The original nature of the grassland is a matter of heated debate, but it is clear that early in the nineteenth century the area was dominated by an exceedingly rich grass flora which included both perennial and annual grasses including the genera *Bouteloua, Hilaria,* and *Aristida* (Humphrey, 1958). The grasses were interspersed in places with low-growing trees and shrubs, notably including several varieties of mesquite (*Prosopis* sp.), creosote bush (*Larrea tridentata* (DC.) Colville), and species of *Acacia, Opuntia,* and *Yucca.*

The transformation of the desert grassland has been widely reported (e.g. Harris, 1966; Hastings and Turner, 1965; Humphrey, 1958). The grasses have suffered major reduction and have been extensively replaced by woody species, notably mesquite, acacias, creosote bush, and burroweed (*Haplopappus tenuisectus* Greene). Hastings and Turner recognized a total of 21 invading species. Evidence for these changes is extensive. A good illustration is found in Colonel H.C. Hooker's reply to a questionnaire from Griffiths (1901) in 1900.[40] Hooker, a perceptive and successful cattleman who owned Sierra Bonita Ranch near Fort Grant in the Sulphur Spring and Aravaipa valleys, estimated that grazing facilities in south-eastern Arizona had declined fully 50 per cent in 25 years and he attributed the decline principally to overstocking. Mesquite was the most aggressive invader and persistent competitor of grass. Originally it was largely confined to valley bottoms and drainage courses and to a sprinkling over the uplands. On a conservative estimate, perhaps half of the nine million acres of 'mesquite' land in Arizona has been colonized since about 1850 (Parker and Martin, 1952).

It would be wrong for several reasons to conclude that the changes occurred uniformly throughout southern Arizona. Firstly, the grassland vegetation was initially variable both in space and time (e.g. Hastings, 1958–9). There were areas of good and bad forage at any one time, and the quality of grasses varied from time to time at any one place. Woody plants were also initially present in some places. Secondly, good stands of grass are still to be found on certain soils, when weather is suitable. Parts of the Aravaipa, Altar, and San Pedro valleys provide examples. And some areas of initially poor grass still support poor grass. Thirdly, the changing pattern of perennial and annual grasses has probably varied from area to area. A fourth complication is that the spread of woody plants has not been uniform. The spread of mesquite, for instance, seems to have been particularly pronounced in the bottom lands of the San Pedro and Santa Cruz valleys. And finally, the prevalent notion of wholesale grassland deterioration appears to derive largely from the notoriously questionable testimony of old-timers and explorers; more recent analysis of the problem suggests that the idea of universal transformation is an exaggeration (e.g. Hastings and Turner, 1965; Leopold, 1951b). Possible causes of the transformation are considered briefly below.

(iii) *Desert shrub vegetation* occupies much of the lower land in southern Arizona and it is relatively more important in the south-west of the state.

The pattern of desert vegetation is complex, reflecting local variations of water availability, terrain, aspect, soil, and microclimate. The vegetation is luxuriant on the higher slopes where 40 per cent or more of the surface may be covered by the crowns of woody and succulent perennials, such as paloverde (*Cercidium* spp.), ironwood (*Olneya tesota* Gray), and the majestic saguaro cactus (*Carnegiea gigantea* Engelm.). In addition there are numerous other shrubs including cacti and bursage (*Franseria deltoidea* Torr.). Creosote and white bursage (*F. dumosa* Gray) dominate the plains.

There have been many changes to the desert vegetation in the past hundred years, but no simple pattern of change is evident (Hastings and Turner, 1965). It seems that semi-woody perennials like bursage have declined; the saguaro seems to be stable on rocky slopes but appears to have declined in level areas of homogeneous soil; paloverde species may have increased in the upper part of their ranges and declined in the lower part; and mesquite has migrated upwards (Hastings and Turner, 1965).

(iv) *Riparian vegetation* is a noticeable feature of most basin floors in southern Arizona (Figure II.19), being composed both of distinctive, riparian species and of denser and larger specimens of species common elsewhere (Campbell and Green, 1966; Shreve, 1951). There are several accounts of the riparian vegetation encountered by the first Anglo-Americans. According to Bryan (1928b), for example, the sacaton grass and swampy areas of bulrushes along the Santa Cruz Valley near Tucson have disappeared since 1880 and the original mesquite groves have been greatly extended. The picture is similar in the San Pedro Valley, where cottonwoods, willows, and grassy cienegas have withered but veritable forests of mesquite remain (Bryan, 1928b; Hooker in Griffiths, 1901). In addition, the alkali-tolerant phreatophyte, salt cedar (*Tamarix pentandra* Pall.), has spread with explosive speed through the valley floors of the South-West largely because of its ability to colonize bare surfaces of fresh alluvium created by sedimentation behind dams, its production of numerous wind-dispersed seeds during a long flowering season, and the clearing of riparian vegetation by man (Harris, 1966).

Some of these modifications of riparian vegetation — such as the disappearance of plants dependent on a high water-table and the establishment and extension of phreatophytes capable of tapping a relatively deep water-table — are clearly related in part to the decline of groundwater levels that has accompanied arroyo development and groundwater exploitation. In addition, it seems probable in many areas that riparian vegetation has been removed along roads, cattle tracks, and irrigation ditches etc., and has been replaced by different land uses where stock-rearing and irrigation have been practised.

(v) *Conclusion*. That vegetation in southern Arizona has changed significantly during the last hundred years is beyond doubt. All the major 'life zones' have been modified, especially at their margins. Hastings and Turner (1965, p.271) recognized an

upward displacement of the plant ranges along a xeric to mesic gradient . . . In some cases the humid upper margin of a species' range has expanded; in others the arid, lower boundary has contracted. In still others, changes have occurred in the mid-reaches of the range and these appear to be linked with microenvironmental characteristics, the decreases often occurring in drier parts and the increases on more humid patches of the environmental mosaic . . . Expressed in terms of what has happened to the habitat, then, the prevailing pattern has been a shift toward drier or hotter conditions, the plant species migrating upward to where the old, favorable conditions still prevail.

These conclusions are based on cautious and careful argument. They imply regional modification of vegetation; they point toward climatic change as the most likely cause. And yet other causes of vegetation change need to be examined before the effect of the changes on discharge are considered, because the changes diagnosed by Hastings and Turner are slow and protracted, and the explanatory need in terms of arroyo development is for profound and short-term changes towards the end of the nineteenth century.

(b) The causes of vegetation change In many ways the problem of explaining vegetation change is similar to that of explaining arroyos — the present patterns can be explained in a variety of ways and conflicting hypotheses have rarely been conclusively evaluated. Within this broad area of speculation and conjecture, by far the greatest attention has been given to the desert grassland. The arguments concern the invasion of woody plants and the decline of grass and, as described in several reviews (Harris, 1966; Hastings and Turner, 1965; Humphrey, 1958), they have become polarized around four possibilities: the activities of rodents, fire, overgrazing, and climatic change.

Rodents and other wild animals have been regarded as agents contributing to changes because some of them disseminate viable mesquite seeds and others facilitate mesquite colonization by eating grasses that hinder the growth of mesquite seedlings. The changes also improve the habitats of some rodents, thus promoting the growth of the rodent community and fostering still further the development of mesquite and the decline of grass. In addition, once a grassland has deteriorated, the activities of rodents might keep it in a poor condition. Although the ecological effects of rodents have been confirmed it is not clear why they should have flourished towards the end of the nineteenth century and it is improbable that they initiated range deterioration (Hastings and Turner, 1965). Humphrey (1958) concluded that rodents facilitated shrub invasion in some instances but were insufficiently effective to have been a major factor in an extensive shrub invasion.

The evidence of research workers such as Cable (1967) and many others lends support to the view that recurrent fires on the one hand severely restrict the establishment of certain shrubs, and on the other do not seriously prejudice the normal growth of grasses. Humphrey (1958) and Harris (1966) have both cited historical sources which indicate that range fires — of natural origin or ignited by man — were common in the past but declined in frequency with the coming of the white man. Thus, it is argued, fire has been a significant factor in maintaining grassland in the distant past and lack of fire in more recent times has permitted the invasion of shrubs. While the effectiveness of fire in controlling shrubs is not in doubt, it must be admitted that most historical evidence on fire frequency comes from tall-grass prairies; in southern Arizona such evidence is both limited and equivocal. Hastings and Turner (1965) concluded that fire probably did not occur frequently in the desert grassland (and, indeed, in adjacent vegetation zones) in the past and, therefore, that fire has been a relatively unimportant factor in grassland change in southern Arizona.

The third possible cause of range deterioration is overgrazing by domestic animals. The literature related to this theme is enormous and only a few comments are required here. Livestock are said to promote shrub invasion by disseminating viable seeds and scarifying seeds in their alimentary tracts, by opening up grasslands through grazing to facilitate shrub establishment, and finally, by reducing moisture content in the upper layers of the soil through grazing, thus favouring plants such as mesquite which can draw on deeper water supplies (Hastings and Turner, 1965). Overgrazing might also simply reduce grass cover. These processes are in some ways open to question (Hastings and Turner, 1965; Humphrey, 1958), but most authorities seem to agree that they made some contribution to change especially during the boom-and drought years between approximately 1880 and 1906. Nevertheless, there is an argument that appears to diminish the stature of the overgrazing hypothesis.

It is undoubtedly true that there was a great influx of livestock into southern Arizona after about 1880. But it is less well known that there was an earlier cattle period in the area between about 1790 and 1820, associated with Spanish-Mexican colonization[41] (Denevan, 1967; Haskett, 1935; Hastings and Turner, 1965). The precise numbers of livestock in this earlier period are impossible to determine and it is therefore unrealistic to compare numbers with the later cattle period. But it seems likely that cattle were important at this time. For example, Bartlett (quoted in Haskett, 1935), said in 1851 of the Babocomari Hacienda, which stretched some 25 miles along a tributary of the San Pedro River: 'This hacienda, as I afterwards learned was one of the largest cattle establishments in the state of Sonora (now Arizona). The cattle roamed the entire length of the valley; and at the time it was abandoned, there were not less than forty thousand[42] of them besides a large number of horses and mules.'

Cattle ranching was also important, it seems, in the Santa Cruz Valley. Haskett (1935, p.7) stated that the cattle overran the valleys and upland, and he quoted an interview with a centenarian of Tucson in the *Tucson Citizen* on 21 June 1873: 'As long as I can remember the country was covered with horses and cattle, and on many of the trails they were so plentiful that it was quite inconvenient to get through the immense herds ... This country then belonged to Spain.'[43]

The first and second cattle periods have another feature in common that may be of considerable significance: they both coincided with relatively dry periods.[44] Evidence for this coincidence comes from tree-ring analysis. In a tree-ring study of Douglas firs and Ponderosa pines in the mountains of southern Arizona, Schulman (1942) demonstrated a close correspondence between tree growth and winter precipitation. For instance, periods of 'minimum tree growth' were times of relatively low winter precipitation. By extension, it is conceivable that periods of minimum tree growth were also times of relatively poor grass growth (and cover) in summer. The second cattle boom coincided with the phase of 'minimum tree growth' between 1870 and 1905; the earlier cattle period coincided with the time between 1750 and 1825 when 'minimum tree growth' exceeded 'growth above normal'. A more recent study by Stockton and Fritts (1971) based on relating tree-ring and climatic data between 1899 and 1957 and using the results of this analysis to make probability statements about climate from tree-ring data from 1650 to 1899, points towards a similar conclusion: the periods 1773–92, 1804–23, and 1870–89, amongst others, were all times with an unusually high probability of below normal seasonal precipitation.

Thus, in seeking to explain vegetation change — indeed, in seeking to explain arroyos — one might legitimately ask why this first cattle period did not have effects similar to those attributed to the second cattle period, for there is certainly no evidence of grassland change or arroyo development in the earlier period. There could, of course, be good reasons for the difference, but because the point at which *over*grazing or *over*stocking occurs normally defies definition in a historical context — as it depends on many changing and unquantified variables such as range condition, management practices, livestock concentrations, and types of animals — good reasons are not easily elicited. One explanation could be that the coincidence of *severe* overstocking and overgrazing with *severe* summer drought (e.g. 1884–6 in the Santa Cruz Valley, Table II.6) *only* occurred towards the end of the nineteenth century. Such coincidences could have had exceptionally serious effects on forage cover and its subsequent recovery, as Nelson (1934) and others have suggested. However, it is equally possible that the overgrazing argument in the late nineteenth century is weakened by the fact that there may have been an earlier cattle boom in some of the major entrenched valleys which also coincided with a relatively dry period and yet apparently had no serious effects on the grassland and, even if it did, did not lead to arroyo formation.

The fourth factor controlling grassland changes, climate, has already been considered in some detail. It is sufficient here to stress two important points. Firstly, the most compelling argument for a climatic-change interpretation of vegetation change in southern Arizona rests on Hastings and Turner's observation that change has occurred, with much apparent consistency of trend, in all the major vegetation zones. Most other arguments, as the previous discussion indicates, refer principally to the grassland. A second point is that if a slow, long-period change of climate has progressively modified vegetation conditions, then clearly both sets of changes are relatively subtle, and they are unlikely to have made a rapid impact on discharge events in the short period of time when arroyos were initiated.

Thus within the ebb and flow of conflicting hypotheses no fully acceptable explanation of vegetation change emerges. It is clearly both possible and reasonable to maintain that the coincidence of several environmental changes — some related to natural factors, others caused deliberately or accidentally by man — led to regional modification of vegetation.

Climate, Vegetation, and Valley-Floor Discharge

The evidence for climatic change is fairly clear; the evidence for vegetation change is undeniable. If one accepts that such regional changes did occur towards the end of the nineteenth century, the important question remains — could they have so altered discharge along the major valley floors that arroyos were created as a result?

Answers to this question are often more or less explicitly cast in terms of two related hypotheses. The first acknowledges that under given vegetation conditions runoff variation is directly related to rainfall variation and therefore sees changes in rainfall as leading to changes in runoff. In terms of the second hypothesis, which assumes 'constant' climate, vegetational changes such as those described in the previous section, together with the trampling effects of livestock, are thought to have reduced infiltration capacity, decreased surface detention, reduced consumption of water, and therefore led to increased runoff. The increased runoff arising from either of these changes, or from both operating together, is then assumed, in addition to promoting surface erosion and sediment concentration, to have augmented total discharge or the 'peakedness' of discharge events along valley floors, thus increasing their erosiveness.

There is a body of contemporary evidence that goes some way towards substantiating in southern Arizona some of the principles upon which these hypotheses are based, but historical validation of these ideas is more difficult. [45]

One way in which runoff might have been increased is by the trampling of livestock, which reduces the infiltration capacity of the soil. This effect has been demonstrated in numerous studies, such as those by Lusby (1964 and 1970), Colman (1953), and Packer (1951). Unfortunately there have apparently been no precise studies of trampling effects on rangelands in southern Arizona, where soil responses to trampling could be different from those elsewhere, but Griffiths's (1901) qualitative observations suggest that trampling may have been significant. The effect of trampling, of course, is likely to be most pronounced where livestock are concentrated, such as along the margins of streams and around water-holes (Colman, 1953). Such localized activity may have had little effect on increasing runoff, although it may have helped to concentrate flow.

In southern Arizona, field plot studies by Osborn and Lane (1969), Schreiber and Kincaid (1967), and others at Walnut Gulch Experimental Watershed (Tombstone) have demonstrated that under approximately uniform vegetation conditions runoff volume is most significantly correlated with summer-storm characteristics and especially with amount of summer-storm precipitation. In one set of experiments, for example, precipitation quantity explained over 70 per cent of the runoff variance (see also McDonald, 1956).

A related result of these experiments is that runoff is normally only generated at the same experimental plots by rainfalls exceeding 0·26 inches (Osborn and Lane, 1969). To generate runoff in the floors of the major basins of southern Arizona, considerably higher precipitation is required. For instance, Dorroh (1960) estimated that 0·5 to 0·7 inches of rainfall is usually necessary before runoff occurs in valley floors. As rains of these magnitudes in southern Arizona are normally confined to summer months, floods are in the main a summer phenomenon. For example, 90 per cent of runoff at Walnut Gulch is in July and August.

Another empirical observation is that local runoff at test plots in southern Arizona is only a very small proportion of total precipitation — always less than 10 per cent, and often less than 3 per cent (Dorroh, 1960; Ogden and Hawkinson, 1970; Osborn and Hickok, 1968). This is important because it could be argued that, for a given rainfall, a small change of vegetation might produce a relatively large change in runoff.

But the role of vegetation and vegetation change in affecting runoff in southern Arizona is less clear than the role of precipitation. Field plot studies in Arizona, Utah, Idaho, Colorado, and elsewhere in the West have suggested that, in general, surface runoff is increased by *heavy* grazing or a similar depletion of vegetation cover (e.g. Colman, 1953). This conclusion is not entirely supported by plot studies in southern Arizona. For instance, plot studies at the Santa Rita Experimental Range (Santa Cruz Valley) by Ogden and Hawkinson (1970) showed that close-clipping treatments (comparable, perhaps, to heavy grazing without trampling), while reducing the basal cover of perennial grass, did not significantly influence runoff. At experimental sites in the Walnut Gulch research area, Kincaid and Williams (1966) were unable to find a significant relationship between runoff and three range treatments — clearing, pitting, and seeding to grass — although runoff was negatively correlated with vegetal crown cover. Similarly, Kincaid, Osborn, and Gardner (1966) concluded from unit-source watershed studies in the same area that runoff from predominantly shrub-covered and predominantly grass-covered watersheds was not significantly different. Perhaps the vegetation contrast here is comparable to a change in the past from grass to shrubs? [46]

It is, of course, unrealistic to argue that the contemporary patterns of runoff revealed by these experiments apply to changes through time on the grasslands of southern Arizona towards the end of the nineteenth century. But one is certainly justified in questioning the assumption that conversion of grassland to shrubs, or heavy grazing of grassland in the past, inevitably increased runoff. It could be that in much of southern Arizona the pre-grazing vegetation was seldom dense enough to exert much control over runoff in the first place, or that subsequent changes could have been inadequate to alter runoff significantly.

There are other obstacles involved in applying the results of plot studies to the hypotheses of increased valley-floor discharge. It must be remembered that plot studies are not designed to solve the arroyo problem — they are usually concerned with range management, grazing capacities, and soil erosion, rather than with valley-floor conditions. Thus it is necessary to relate site studies to the basin as a whole, which is a difficult task. For example, it cannot be assumed that increased plot runoff increases valley-floor discharge. This is because local ephemeral runoff may rapidly disappear by infiltration into the alluvial mantles it crosses. Such 'transmission losses' may be great. It has been estimated, for example, that within the San Simon watershed only about 20 per cent of the 'on-site' runoff reaches the vicinity of Solomonville (Dorroh, 1960). Add to this the important reservation that a specific vegetation change, from whatever cause, probably only affected parts of any drainage basin in the nineteenth century, and the hypotheses of increased valley-floor discharge look somewhat weaker.

There are two other ways in which runoff may have been significantly affected by climate and vegetation changes. The first relates to the secular changes in the frequency of light and heavy rainfalls especially in the late nineteenth century (Figures II.16, II.17, II.18). It seems reasonable to concede that these changes may have had the same effect in southern Arizona as that hypothesized by Leopold (1951a) for similar changes in New Mexico: in the early part of the last hundred years there may have been a relatively weakened grass cover and a relatively high incidence of runoff-producing rains.

Secondly, vegetation cover may be seriously depleted during droughts as a result of water shortage, overstocking, or both (Lantow and Flory, 1940; Nelson, 1934; Reynolds and Martin, 1968). Overstocking arises, at least in part, from the decline of forage (e.g. grasses and browse shrubs) availability during a drought. Reynolds (1954) plotted the relationship between cumulative summer rainfall deficiency and cumulative forage deficiency on foothill pasture relatively free of mesquite and dominated by black grama grass at the Santa Rita Experimental Range from 1923 to 1953. His curve is shown as a solid line on Figure II.20. If this line is projected, and the cumulative summer rainfall deficiencies during droughts in the last hundred years at nearby Fort Lowell-Tucson (Table II.6) are plotted on it, then it is clear that the two major droughts (1884–6 and 1899–1906) could have had a relatively enormous impact on forage production. This impact would have been even greater if overstocking existed at the same time. As Reynolds (1954) indicated, forage production does not increase immediately precipitation improves; and recovery may be delayed even longer if the range has been overused (Lantow and Flory, 1940; Nelson, 1934). Thus heavy rainfalls *during* droughts or the relatively heavy rains that often immediately *followed* them (or, indeed, the rains of the significant wet periods between droughts (Tables II.5 and II.6) could have fallen on surfaces depleted of vegetation and particularly conducive to runoff and erosion. One argument detracts from the merit of this persuasive case: droughts and their related heavy rainfalls are probably not phenomena peculiar to the last hundred years.

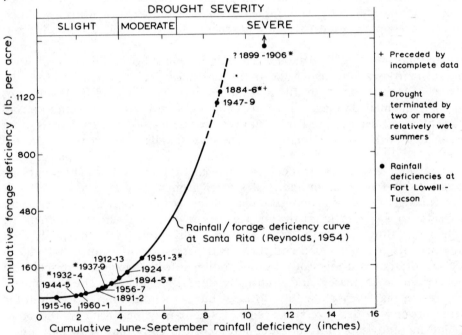

Figure II.20 Relations between cumulative forage deficiency and summer rainfall deficiency at Santa Rita (solid line, after Reynolds, 1954), with superimposed cumulative summer rainfall deficiencies at Fort Lowell-Tucson between 1867 and 1966

Thus, both secular and short-term climatic changes, and livestock activities, and their related vegetation changes, could have provided circumstances conducive to changed runoff and channel entrenchment at the time when arroyos are known to have been initiated in southern Arizona. But it must be emphasized that, although the logic of the hypotheses relating to increased valley-floor discharge and erosion is difficult to fault, it is also difficult to substantiate because the pertinent evidence is often far from clear.

HYPOTHESES OF VALLEY-FLOOR CHANGE

In this section two hypotheses relating to local changes of valley-floor conditions that would have altered flow velocities regardless of regional discharge changes are examined. The first concerns changes in the slope of longitudinal profiles due to differential deposition along them. The second involves drainage concentration and related changes on valley floors.

Slope Change and Arroyo Development

Most of the major morphological characteristics of the entrenched drainage basins in Arizona have been constant during the period of arroyo development. Drainage-basin area and relief, for instance, have probably been relatively unaffected by environmental changes in the last century, and their role in determining the nature of discharge along the valley floors has not changed.

One morphological variable that might change over fairly short time periods and might influence the timing and location of entrenchment is the slope of longitudinal profiles. Schumm and Hadley's (1957) study of gullying in small drainage basins in Wyoming, South Dakota, Nebraska, and New Mexico (discussed in Part I) showed convincingly that trenching is often associated with a steepening of the gradient in valley fills. It was suggested that alluviation along the valleys steepens their gradients in places until critical slope angles are reached, when trenching can occur. The trenching could result from one or more of several events, such as heavy rainfall or overgrazing. Localized deposition resulting in a steepening of gradient appears to be characteristic of valleys in semi-arid areas experiencing ephemeral flow. In these circumstances a discharge event normally first increases its sediment load and then, as it passes downstream, it is reduced by evaporation and especially by infiltration into the channel bed, sediment concentration increases, and eventually deposition occurs. The location of deposition may vary from flow to flow, but if accumulation proceeds in the same locality with successive events, gradient may be raised to the point where incision is permitted. Once initiated, the gully may grow and a new locus of deposition may be established.

Schumm and Hadley's hypothesis was specifically applied only to small drainage basins. But it is pertinent to consider for several reasons whether it could be applied, perhaps in modified form, to the much larger entrenched basins of southern Arizona. Firstly, the large Arizonan basins, like the small basins studied by Schumm and Hadley, are characterized by ephemeral flow. Secondly, the historical record reveals discontinuous entrenchment in some valleys, a feature similar but on a larger scale to that described by Schumm and Hadley. Thirdly, the reference in various documents to cienegas, marshy areas where water and sediments probably accumulated, suggests that there may be perceptible irregularities in the longitudinal profiles of the entrenched plains in Arizona.

An important consideration, of course, is the critical slope at which incision might occur. Schumm and Hadley (1957) found that in 0·05—0·5 sq.m. drainage basins, cutting into alluvium occurred on 2·5—5·4 per cent slopes; and in 0·6—19 sq.m. drainage basins, 1·5—2·5 per cent slopes were adequate. These data suggest that the critical slope may be inversely related to drainage area; if this is so, then the critical slopes in the large basins of Arizona would be very small. As Figure II.21 shows, the slopes of entrenched valley floors are indeed extremely gentle. A second important point, about which very little is known, is the time taken either for the progression of a complete deposition-incision sequence or for the slope threshold to be reached from given initial conditions.

In the following discussion an attempt is made to answer three questions that relate to the extension of Schumm and Hadley's hypothesis to the large drainage basins of southern Arizona. (1) Can steeper-sloping segments be recognized in the longitudinal profiles of the basin floors? (2) If so, are such segments entrenched? (3) Is there any evidence that arroyos have been initiated or rapidly developed at these locations?

The following procedure was adopted. For each basin the generalized contours of the valley-floor plains were constructed, thus eliminating the effect of any entrenchment on contour patterns and allowing reconstruction of pre-incision profiles. (A drawback of this method is that it makes no allowance for changes of gradient since incision in those parts of the profiles that have not been entrenched.) Tangent values of slope were then determined for each pair of contours by relating contour interval and the spacing of contours on the longitudinal profiles. In order to display the data as accurately as possible, contour spacings for constant contour intervals were plotted against distance downvalley from an arbitrary origin, and a scale of tangents (correct to four places of decimals) was added later. A steeper-sloping segment, representing an increase of slope downstream, was defined by two or more successive decreases in contour spacing downstream. These decreases are marked by heavy arrows on Figure II.21.

Given this procedure, the following conclusions are justified. With respect to question (1), steeper-sloping segments can be recognized in the longitudinal profiles and each entrenched valley has at least one such segment. Several features of these segments deserve comment. Firstly, they represent only very slight increases of slope; in all cases the increases are considerably less than 1 per cent. It could be that such changes are so small that they failed to affect significantly flow conditions in the basins by, for instance, increasing flow velocities. Secondly, most of the steeper segments appear to occur downstream of former cienegas. This is true in the San Simon (below Smith's 'alkali flat'), Whitewater, and (probably) Aravaipa valleys. In the San Pedro

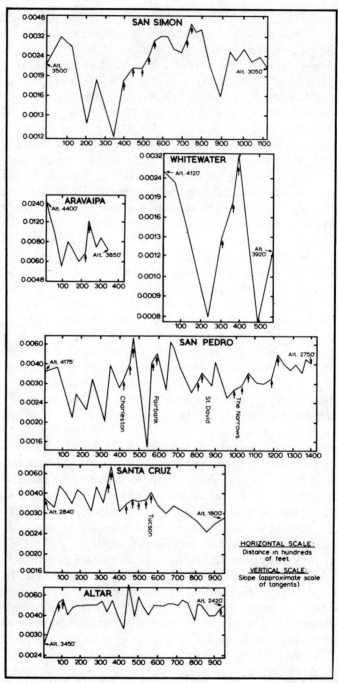

Figure II.21 Longitudinal profiles of valley floors in southern Arizona (for explanation, see text)

Valley, the steeper segments generally coincide with locations where 'base-ment' rocks appear at the surface and constrict the 'inner valley'; these segments also have former cienegas upstream (e.g. at Charleston, Fairbank, 'The Narrows'), although there are other cienega locations without down-stream steepening. In the Santa Cruz Valley, there is a steeper-sloping zone north of Martinez Hill and another in the vicinity of Tucson; the former is downstream of an old cienega (San Xavier), the latter approximately coincides with an old cienega. The very minor steepening near to the watershed of the Altar Valley is apparently unrelated to an old cienega. Clearly this preliminary survey links cienegas — which may be regarded as areas of water and sediment storage within the fluvial systems — with steeper-sloping segments in the longitudinal profiles of major valleys.

The answer to question (2) is clear: all the steeper-sloping segments are now entrenched. But question (3) is more difficult to answer because of the inadequacy of the historical record. The following comments summarize the available information. In the San Simon Valley, entrenchment was first recorded near Solomonville, but cutting *could* have occurred relatively early in the steeper-sloping segment along the line of the old road. In the Aravaipa Valley, incision probably began downstream of the steeper gradient and extended headward into it. Along Whitewater Draw the same is true, but *rapid* arroyo development is recorded in the steeper zone (e.g. in T.22 S.). In the San Pedro Valley it is possible that discontinuous entrenchment was initially associated with the steeper reaches and extended headwards into the adjacent alluvial basins, but the historical record is inconclusive in this respect. In the Santa Cruz Valley, entrenchment was initiated upstream of the Martinez Hill segment and within the second steeper-sloping segment, at Tucson. In both cases the cause of entrenchment is clear, as described previously, and it is probable that the coincidence of a steeper-sloping segment and initial incision at Tucson was fortuitous. But both zones experienced rapid arroyo development. In the Altar Valley, the steeper-sloping segment coincides with the locality where the arroyo most closely follows the line of the old wagon road; it is possible, but rather unlikely, that the arroyo was initiated in this remote, headwater area, although rapid arroyo development along the old road is probable.

Although there are steeper-sloping sections in the valley floors of southern Arizona, trenching was definitely initiated in only one of them, and there the coincidence was probably fortuitous. Equally, there is good evidence that the initiation of many arroyos was not in such localities. On balance, it seems unlikely that changes of slope in the longitudinal profiles of the original basin floors significantly influenced arroyo initiation — at least during the last hundred years — but the steeper-sloping segments may have been associated with rapid arroyo development.

In Part I, two other hypotheses relating slope change and entrenchment were reviewed, but neither of them appears to be relevant to the major arroyos in southern Arizona. Lateral shifts in channel position leading to entrenchment of tributaries did not affect the major valley floors, except in so far as migration of the Gila River could have promoted limited entrenchment along the Santa Cruz and San Pedro rivers where these tributaries join the main river (e.g. p. 47). Melton's (1965) hypothesis of drainage concentration due to steepening of *transverse* valley-floor slopes, while it may apply in the relatively confined situations he described, does not appear to apply to the broad floors of the major valleys, where marginal deposition would scarcely affect the geometry of the large floodplains.

Drainage Concentration, Related Valley-Floor Changes, and Arroyo Initiation

The hypothesis that arroyos were initiated as the result of drainage concentration and related changes along the major floors requires examination. In the discussion of evidence from the major valleys a recurrent theme was the coincidence between the location of drainage-concentration features and arroyos. This coincidence is summarized on Table II.7.

Table II.7

VALLEY	Drainage concentration feature associated with entrenchment	Date of origin of feature	Date of initial entrenchment
San Simon	a. Irrigation ditch at Solomonville	1883	1883
	b. San Simon wagon road	by 1875	after 1885
	c. Railroad embankment	1884	after 1885
Aravaipa	a. Fort Grant wagon road	by 1875	after 1886
Whitewater	a. Levees	—	after 1884
	b. Cattle trails	—	after 1884
San Pedro	a. Canals, roads	locally before 1851	before 1851 in places
	b. Railroad embankment	—	—
Santa Cruz	a. Greene's Canal	1910	1914
	b. Sam Hughes' Canal	after 1862	1883 or 1890
	c. San Xavier	by 1851/1883	by 1871/ c. 1883
Altar/Avra	a. Altar wagon road	by 1886	after 1886
	b. Flood control channel	c. 1950	by 1970
	c. Charcos	by 1886	after 1886
	d. Piped water	—	—
Papago Reservation	a. Flow concentration for flood farming	—	—

Given this considerable degree of coincidence between drainage-concentration features and arroyos, several questions require examination. Firstly, what were the hydraulic consequences of creating these features? Secondly, were the hydraulic changes alone adequate to permit entrenchment? And finally, if so, how can arroyos in areas without such features be explained?

The hydraulic implications of the drainage-concentration hypothesis are numerous. The first, and perhaps the most important effect of drainage concentration is to increase flow depth and hence flow velocity and flow erosiveness. Unfortunately it is impossible to estimate precisely how far erosiveness of flows was increased at particular sites, mainly because both the characteristics of the confined flow and the constraints upon them are usually unknown. But it is possible to make some reasonable guesses. The effects of flow concentration will, of course, vary with the type of feature — for example, the influence of an infiltration gallery in a large floodplain would be quite different from that of a railroad embankment marginal to a relatively narrow floodplain. Take as an example the case of a railroad embankment that effectively reduces the width of a 3,000-feet-wide floodplain by 50 per cent, and a discharge down that valley of 25,000 c.f.s. This example, assuming a slope of 0·01 and a roughness coefficient of 0·06, could very approximately correspond to an actual situation in the San Simon Valley (Figure II.12 shows that the predicted 100-year peak discharge at Solomonville is 26,339 c.f.s.). Figure I.3 shows that in these circumstances an approximate increase of *mean* flow velocity from 4·1 c.f.s. to 5·4 c.f.s. could be expected.

One needs to know if such changes in flow velocity would be adequate to initiate erosion. The answer to this problem must depend in part on other changes that accompanied drainage concentration.

One of these changes undoubtedly relates to vegetation. Riparian vegetation changes associated with entrenchment have been described in a previous section, but it is the vegetation changes preceding entrenchment that are important in this context. Of these, by far the most important is the removal of vegetation — the removal of forage on the floodplains and the localized destruction of vegetation along roads, ditches, etc. There are three major effects of such removal. Firstly, the interception and consumption of water by riparian vegetation is reduced so that relatively more water is available in the valley floors. Studies in the semi-arid western United States, including some in the Gila Valley, have shown that removal of riparian vegetation may significantly increase water yield (e.g. Colman, 1953; U.S. Geological Survey, *Professional Paper, 655*). Secondly, surface roughness is reduced so that flow velocities are increased. The precise changes are again difficult to determine, but Melton (1965) indicated that the retardance coefficient for dense cienega grass may be as much as 5—10 times higher than the approximate average n values of 0·02—0·05 for arroyos. The removal of riparian shrubs probably caused similar or even greater reductions of flow resistance.

A third effect of vegetation removal is that the alluvial deposits became directly exposed to erosion by flowing water. It is therefore important to know how erodible the newly exposed material is. A rough-and-ready study of the erodibility of arroyo-bank sediments from the San Pedro arroyo demonstrated that, despite superficial similarities of the predominantly silt-clay samples, the erodibility of the material by water is very variable but generally quite high. In the study 50-gramme samples were agitated in a water bath for one minute. The agitation was produced by a rotation machine which raised and lowered the sample by 2 cm at a rate of 26 cycles per minute. The percentage weight loss for each of the ten samples was as follows: 0·0, 1·8, 4·8, 5·2, 7·6, 9·0, 23·0, 34·0, 37·2, 90·4. Clearly the velocity of flow required to erode the material will vary according to the type of sediment, but it is likely to be much less than the permissible velocity of 6 f.p.s., reasonably estimated by Melton (1965) for *grass-covered* cienega deposits in southern Arizona.

The effect of trampling by livestock is another change related in some cases to drainage concentration. There can be little doubt that livestock trampling was most pronounced along valley floors, where water was most commonly available (e.g. Leopold, 1921). Thus compaction and reduction of infiltration capacity by trampling, and a corresponding increase of runoff, are likely to have been most marked along the drainage courses. Traffic on wagon roads probably had a similar effect. Both livestock and traffic would also have scuffed surface material, preparing it for easy removal by flowing water. Finally, livestock may have promoted drainage concentration by creating trails that focused on the valley floors.

The next problem is to determine if the hydrological changes that accompanied drainage concentration were alone adequate to permit entrenchment. That is to say, were they adequate to raise flow velocities above the erosion threshold? The short answer to this question is that the threshold could easily have been exceeded given changes, even relatively small changes, of depth of flow, surface roughness, and exposure of erodible material. Melton's (1965) calculation of changed mean velocity illustrates this assertion (p. 20). If the increase of hydraulic radius from 0·5 to 1·5 feet involved in his calculations in raising flow velocity to over 13 f.p.s. was achieved by a drainage-concentration feature — which is easily possible — then clearly the new velocity would exceed that permissible in grass-covered cienegas. And if the grass (or other vegetation) cover was depleted, the effect of the new flow velocity would be profound. Many calculations similar to Melton's are possible if the initial assumptions are varied, but as all assumed changes of valley-floor variables tend towards increasing flow velocity, the chances of exceeding the erosion threshold are high. (This theoretical discussion is extended in the Californian context on pp. 179–184.)

Drainage concentration and related changes were therefore almost certainly adequate by themselves to permit erosion. It remains an open question whether such features and changes were alone responsible for the initiation of arroyos or whether they merely provided the loci for erosion in a changing regional environment. One argument tending to favour the first possibility is that the chronological relations between the valley-floor changes and entrenchment are, where they are known, fairly close. For example, there was no arroyo on the Santa Cruz Plains before Greene's Canal was cut in 1910 despite the very large floods (e.g. 1905) and the overgrazing and climatic change in preceding years. Again, there was no arroyo at San Xavier until the infiltration galleries were cut; and yet the arroyo here was initiated before the major floods and overstocking of the late nineteenth century. In these localities, and probably in others as well, it seems possible that arroyos would not have been formed without the valley-floor changes, despite changes of discharge. Naturally, any regional changes of discharge, arising from climatic or vegetational changes, would have eased the task of erosion.

There remains the major problem that the drainage-concentration hypothesis has not been satisfactorily applied to all arroyos, notably those in the Whitewater and San Pedro valleys. As explained previously, evidence relating to the cause of Whitewater Draw is scarce and circumstantial, although the concentration of settlement and cattle along the original wash is certain. In the San Pedro Valley, there is clear evidence of entrenchment before Anglo-American settlement, but no evidence of its cause. Perhaps the Indian and Spanish-American activity along the valley-floor may have played a role. Or perhaps early entrenchment was related to irregularities of slope in the longitudinal profile of the valley floor. New entrenchment, and development of established arroyos since about 1870 could be related to drainage-concentration features on the valley floor, to extensive vegetation changes in the basin, or to a combination of both.

CONCLUSIONS

Many, but not all of the principal valley floors in southern Arizona are now at least partly entrenched. This study of varied evidence relating to the major arroyos has illustrated the difficulties of identifying causes of arroyo initiation and development and of disentangling the complex webs of cause and effect spun in Part I. It is probable that the arroyos arose from several interrelated environmental changes. Unfortunately the precise orchestration of the changes is uncertain from the scrappily preserved scores, but the available record strongly points to certain of them being much more important than others.

The evidence suggests that entrenchment was originally intermittent along many valley floors and subsequent changes have led to the coalescence of the initial trenches. There is strong evidence to indicate that specific valley-floor changes — such as the cutting of ditches and canals, the creation of roads, and the building of embankments — provided the loci for the initiation of many arroyos. It can be argued that such changes were adequate by themselves to permit entrenchment and that recourse to other environmental changes is unnecessary in most areas. Nevertheless, other changes occurred and they may have promoted arroyo initiation and development.

In so far as climatic data have been analysed, the argument for climatic change since about 1865 rests at present on two observations. Firstly, the frequency of light rains increased and the frequency of heavy rains declined slightly in the last hundred years, as the Fort Lowell-Tucson record reveals. This might mean that in the earlier part of the record, grass and other shallow-rooted plants largely sustained by light summer rains may have been depleted and surface cover correspondingly reduced, and increased runoff at that time may have resulted from the heavy rains. Secondly, droughts are often terminated by relatively wet years. This probably means that during droughts vegetation cover was depleted, vegetation had had insufficient time to recover in the wet year following a drought, and, as a result, runoff and erosion arising from heavy rains at that time were increased. This second phenomenon was certainly important in the *development* of arroyos, but there is no reason to believe that the pattern of dry-wet years was peculiar to the last hundred years.

Overgrazing — a fact noted in many historical records — may have increased valley-floor discharge and thus promoted arroyos, but the argument is weakened for two main reasons. Before the relatively dry period of the cattle boom and arroyo formation towards the end of the nineteenth century there was an earlier period of Spanish/Mexican livestock rearing that coincided with relatively dry conditions but during which arroyos were not apparently formed. And the effects of overgrazing — which was in any case always confined to only part of any drainage basin — on valley-floor discharge are uncertain.

The evidence for secular vegetation change is persuasive, but it seems probable that such changes were too slow, and perhaps even too late, to have produced significant increases in valley-floor discharge in the critical period of arroyo initiation.

Much emphasis has been placed in previous discussions on the coincidence between the time of arroyo formation and the period of overgrazing. This coincidence is not very precise. Some arroyos were formed before the 'Anglo-American' cattle arrived; others were initiated long after the cattle boom was over. The coincidence is better between arroyo formation and Anglo-American settlement, although even here it is not perfect. Valley-floor entrenchment coincides most frequently and most precisely with the creation of substantial drainage-concentration and related features.

Once initiated, arroyos have characteristically become deeper, wider, longer, and, in several cases, more sinuous. These developments are seen as reflecting a general tendency towards creating within the old floodplains new channel systems capable of accommodating discharge events of widely different magnitudes and frequencies. The main processes of enlargement appear to have been erosion by floodwaters, and arroyo-bank collapse at times of low flow — due mainly to piping. Arroyo enlargement has been marked in places by the creation of cut-and-fill terraces. Some arroyos or parts of arroyos have changed relatively little in recent years and they may have already attained a fairly stable condition.

It seems reasonable to conclude at present that the best hypothesis to explain arroyo formation along the major valley floors of southern Arizona acknowledges the possibility of increased valley-floor discharge due to climatic and/or vegetation changes but emphasizes the role of drainage-concentration features and related changes along valley floors.

PART III

Arroyos in Coastal California

INTRODUCTION

Whereas much of the early work on arroyos was in Arizona and several basic explanatory hypotheses were developed there, very little attention has been paid to entrenchment in California. During the first half of the twentieth century, the growing arroyo literature accumulated only one reference to channel erosion within the state, a brief assertion in a monograph on the geology of southern Utah that 'the streams of southern Nevada and southern California likewise are developing arroyos' (Gregory and Moore, 1931, p.143).

Naturally, the progression of modern erosion has not been entirely ignored by previous workers. The populous state of California now has numerous universities, governmental agencies, and private organizations that are concerned to some extent with erosion and associated environmental changes. A survey of published geological reports, water-supply papers, soil surveys, conservation brochures, regional studies, touring guides, and text-books yielded occasional photographs and brief descriptions of valley-bottom gullies in several, scattered locations. But none of these studies mention South-Western arroyos, or attempt to evaluate various explanatory hypotheses. Typically, causes are implied, asserted, or assumed. Most explanations involve either vaguely defined natural processes (English, 1915; Upson and Worts, 1951; Shelton, 1966) or bland assumptions of cultural causes (Kennan, 1917; Sauer, 1929; Russell, 1932). The first and only significant Californian study of arroyos is that by Bull (1964b), who documented nineteenth- and twentieth-century elongation and deepening of stream channels on alluvial fans along the west side of the San Joaquin Valley and examined the changes in the general context of arroyo development in the South-West.

Well-developed arroyos are not uncommon features in certain areas of California. But the facts concerning them — their distribution, dates of origin, environmental context, and circumstance of initiation — are almost entirely undiscussed. Sources of data relevant to these facts are perhaps richer in California than in any other part of the South-West, and yet they are largely unexploited.

The portion of California selected for detailed examination comprises a coastal zone approximately 70 miles wide and 350 miles long, extending from the Los Angeles Lowland to Monterey Bay (Figure III.1). This area, hereafter called coastal California, covers approximately 25,000 square miles of diverse terrain and includes numerous arroyos.

Environmental and Historical Context

Coastal California is a very varied environment. High, forested mountains contrast with adjacent, narrow, debris-filled basins and broad alluvial plains; moist, often foggy, and forested coastal zones contrast with parched deserts a few miles to the east.

The Coast Ranges, the mountains of the northern half of the region (Figure III.1), exhibit pronounced north-westerly structural and topographic trends that are mirrored in the trends of isohyets and isotherms, and strips of oak woodland, chaparral, grassland, and irrigated farmland. Alluviated valley floors also follow sympathetic trends, often in structural depressions, and commonly parallel to the strike of Tertiary deposits and structures in older crystalline rocks. In the south, the less continuous mountain and basin blocks of the Transverse Ranges trend from east to west. Poorly consolidated Tertiary sediments and volcanic rocks dominate the mountains in the west; east of the Santa Clara and San Fernando valleys, crystalline rocks compose the San Gabriel and San Bernardino ranges. Geologically the whole region is relatively recent and it is still frequently affected by seismic activity, which is associated especially with the San Andreas fault zone and its numerous related structures.

Climatic variation is largely the result of topographic effects. The storm systems that bring most marked weather change and almost all precipitation arrive from the west and north-west during the cool season. Although their frequency and severity decline southwards, these Pacific storms dominate winter weather throughout the region. Similarly, anticyclonic circulation associated with a persistent, well-developed high-pressure cell over the eastern Pacific dominates the entire region during summer and effectively limits precipitation and convectional activity. Terrain — and notably its altitude and barrier effects — imposes local variety on this pattern. For example, precipitation is greatest at high elevations with unencumbered exposure to the ocean, and declines rapidly on east-facing slopes and in protected lowlands. Temperature conditions are similarly closely related to elevation and to the limits of inland penetration of the shallow, damp, and extremely temperate layer of marine air along the coast.

Because of the long summer drought and sporadic nature of winter precipitation, most flow in drainage systems is characteristically ephemeral or intermittent, with very high discharges during storms or for short periods during winter, only trickles over some reaches for the remainder of the cool season, and dry channels throughout the summer. Only the largest systems, with high mountain tributaries, alluvial reservoirs, and favourable geological conditions, manage discharges along favoured reaches during the summer. Evidence exists that formerly the flows of many more streams were perennial, but pumping from ground-water reservoirs and diversion of surface flow for irrigation have eliminated summer flows from many valleys.

Patterns of vegetation are complex. The enormous variety of elevation,

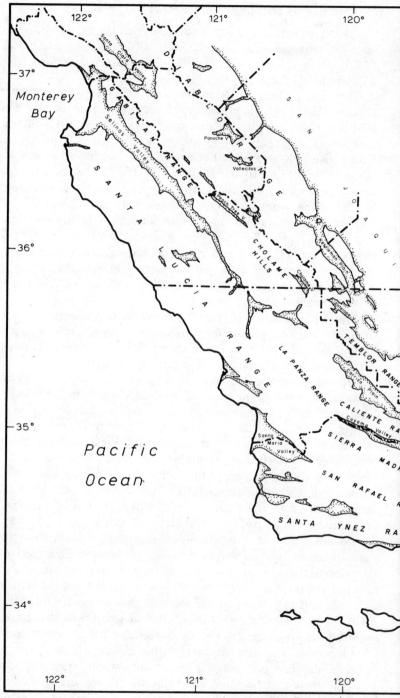

Figure III.1 Major mountain range

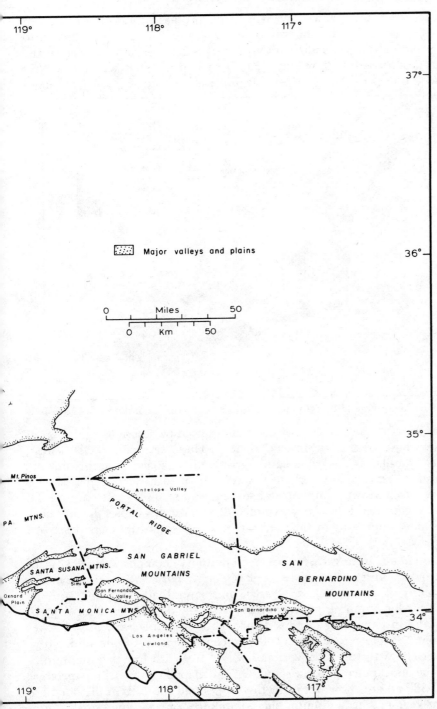

Major valleys and plains

al valleys in coastal California

slope, exposure, substrata, and available moisture has produced a mosaic of habitats populated by combinations of plants difficult to classify into distinct groups and equally difficult to map. Jensen's vegetation map of the state, as modified by Burcham (1957), is small in scale and highly generalized, but provides a reasonable introduction to the most common

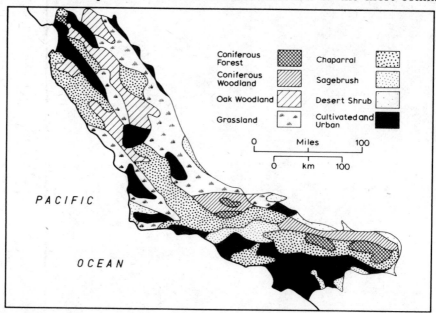

Figure III.2 Major vegetation types of coastal California (based on Burcham, 1957)

groups of plants (Figure III.2). All seven types used to describe vegetation of the entire state occur within the region. These are coniferous forest, coniferous woodland, oak woodland, grassland, chaparral, sagebrush, and desert shrub. Areas where agricultural and urban uses have replaced vegetation are also shown; in most instances these were once grass-covered. Of the seven vegetation types, oak woodland, grassland, chaparral, and sagebrush are most important in the context of arroyos, and they are described briefly below.

Oak woodland is a rather varied community composed basically of evergreen oaks and grass. Coast live oak (*Quercus agrifolia*), interior live oak (*Q. wislizenii*), blue oak (*Q. douglasii*), and several others, along with an admixture of digger pine (*Pinus sabiniana*) and the deciduous valley oak (*Q. lobata*), stand in clumps or dispersed through a cover of grass. Crown cover ranges from negligible to almost 100 per cent. Density of the understory varies inversely with crown cover, and where trees are few the community takes on the appearance of a grassland. On the map (Figure III.2), large areas of this woodland are shown only in the ranges and foothills in the northern half of the region. Further south, the community once formed small stands in hilly areas and narrow margins around grass-covered valley floors. Within mapped units there are numerous patches of chaparral on steeper slopes and in dry locations, as well as open stands of digger pine and shrubs at higher elevations in the southern Coast Ranges that have an appearance similar to coniferous woodland.

Grassland, or California Prairie, once covered most of the alluviated valley bottoms of the region and much of the rolling hilly terrain where it was underlain by poorly consolidated sedimentary rock that allowed rapid soil development. Significant stands remain along the dry western margin of the San Joaquin Valley and in coastal hills and valleys north and south of San Luis Obispo, but their character has altered. Numerous species of perennial bunchgrass dominated the prairies until well into the historical period, and these were accompanied by a large variety of spring-flowering forbs (Burcham, 1957). Contemporary stands along the edge of the San Joaquin Valley are essentially treeless and composed of short, rather widely spaced annuals. In more coastal locations stands are taller and denser and contain occasional oaks.

Chaparral dominates most of the rugged terrain of the region. Steep slopes, shallow stony soils, and the xeric conditions associated with them under prevailing mild-winter/dry-summer climates, have allowed this community of evergreen, broadleaf, drought-resistant shrubs to form dense thickets over large areas. Its impenetrability, vulnerability to fire, and ability to re-establish itself are renowned. Various plants, including chamise (*Adenostoma fasciculatum*), manzanita (*Arctostaphylos* spp.), ceanothus (*Ceanothus* spp.), and shrub oak (*Q. dumosa*), are the common dominants in some stands, but richness in constituent species is characteristic.

Sagebrush includes two somewhat distinct communities. Units mapped near the coast, the coastal sagebrush, are structurally similar to chaparral although they are usually less dense, shorter, more herbaceous, and contain more sub-shrubs. Major differences are floristic, with true sages dominant, but a number of species are shared with chaparral. The community extends along many rugged sections of the coast in stands too small to appear on the map. The unit near the south end of the San Joaquin Valley is a bastardized community appropriate to this isolated desert area. It is typified by a sparse ground cover of sub-shrubs and short grasses.

The earliest explorers found several economically similar aboriginal groups occuping coastal, lowland, and valley environments within the region who supported themselves by hunting, gathering, and, in some cases, fishing. The missions initiated a new way of life which superseded that of the natives within a few decades. Between 1770 and 1804, twelve missions, two military outposts, and an agricultural colony were established in the larger valleys and coastal plains of the region. Grain fields and irrigated gardens and orchards were developed around the new settlements, both to supply needs and to occupy hands, and the grass-covered valleys and hills were transformed into rangelands for introduced livestock. Numbers of cattle, sheep, horses, mules, and goats increased, and by the 1820s livestock had become the base of the economy throughout the region. Cattle were most important, with hides and tallow the most valuable items of export and beef a significant component of the local diet. Herds on the widespread mission ranches, and those of a slowly growing number of privately operated *ranchos*, roamed largely untended and vied for forage and water, especially in dry years, with numerous herds of feral cattle and horses, which were evidently plentiful in inland locations of the region and the Central Valley (Burcham, 1957).

The missions were secularized in the mid-1830s, but the regional emphasis on cattle continued, and even intensified, especially during the early and middle 1850s, with the creation of a market for beef by the 'goldrush' to the Sierra foothills.

Overspeculation, evaporation of northern markets, and the flood and droughts of the early 1860s brought an end to this era of cattle-ranching. The following two decades were times of diversification, experimentation, and consolidation. Most large holdings quickly disintegrated and parcels were bought or appropriated by disenchanted gold-seeking Anglos, migrating war veterans, or other 'foreigners'. Sheep-ranching and extensive cash-grain farming assumed widespread significance. Breeding improved livestock herds, but these were relegated to rougher and drier parts of the region. Most valley-bottom lands and much of the rolling hill country were ploughed for the first time and sown to winter wheat or, somewhat later, barley. Fodder crops became significant and there were some scattered attempts at dairying and orcharding.

Since about 1880, major land-use changes have generally followed the development of transportation networks. Dry farming and ranching have continued to retreat into more isolated and less desirable areas behind waves of specialized irrigation agriculture and urbanization. The lowlands on the southern margin of the region were connected to northern California and the East by the Southern Pacific route through the Central Valley in 1876, and within a decade two direct lines eastward were completed. Population boomed (especially in Los Angeles), agricultural colonies were established, irrigation networks were constructed, and specialized commercial agriculture, dominated by the orange, made rapid progress. The northern end of the region was connected by rail to San Francisco in the 1870s which facilitated marketing of grain, some fruits, dairy products, and later, with improvements in refrigerated freighting and development of irrigation, the concentration on leafy green vegetables.

Relative to the southern and northern margins, the rest of coastal California remained isolated until after completion of the Southern Pacific's coastal route in 1901. With access to exterior markets, intensification of agriculture began in coastal lowlands and valleys and contributed to growth of local centres such as Santa Maria, San Luis Obispo, and Paso Robles. But away from the chain of valleys followed by the railroad and later highways, isolation has generally persisted. Compared with the Los Angeles area, the central portion of the region is still sparsely populated and devoted largely to ranching, national forests, scattered oilfields, and military reservations.

The Pattern of Arroyos

Figure III.3 shows the distribution of arroyos in coastal California. The map is based on a reconnaissance field survey of all areas within the region containing recent alluvial deposits (as they are shown on the 1:250,000 geological maps compiled by the California State Division of Mines). Each arroyo on Figure III.3 was personally visited at at least one location and, where access was limited, large-scale topographic maps or stereoscopic pairs of aerial photographs were used to record the approximate limits of the features. At times it was difficult to determine whether or not a channel should be classified as an arroyo. Difficulties were greatest in urban areas where many semi-natural channels function as stormdrains, and many such channels have been ignored. Elsewhere, if there was a definitional difficulty, two criteria indicative of recent entrenchment were used: steeply sloping or vertical banks separating the channel bottom from a smooth alluvial terrace surface above, and strong field evidence that flood discharges do not now inundate the terraces. In general, the recognition of arroyos has been rather conservative.

The pattern of arroyos prompts several observations. The distribution is patently irregular. To a large extent this irregularity reflects the configuration of the region's terrain. As might be expected, arroyos are absent within the rugged mountain areas where alluvial accumulations are uncommon. In addition, the occurrence of discernible entrenchment decreases with distance from the mountains, and disappears along the lower courses of large streams crossing the flat coastal plains or broad valleys.

Most arroyos are found in sub-humid and semi-arid areas which were covered, at least initially, by grassland or grassy oak woodland. Within these areas, two types of sites commonly contain arroyos: the upper slopes of alluvial fans, and the alluviated floors of narrow valleys where they pass through hills comprising poorly consolidated rock or old basin fills.

Channel conditions may be very variable even within these 'arroyo environments'. In any one valley, there may be found discontinuous or continuous arroyos, shallow washes, unchannelled flats, and well-defined channels apparently adjusted to adjacent floodplains. The tributaries of the Salinas River illustrate this variety. Pine Valley (7b in Figure III.3) and several of its tributary valleys are cut by a network of trenches which were formed for the most part since 1859[47] and are still eroding. Similar drainage systems a few miles to the south and north possess quite different channel forms — Pancho Rico Valley contains a wide, sandy channel between what are probably premodern (but probably post-Pleistocene) terraces standing up

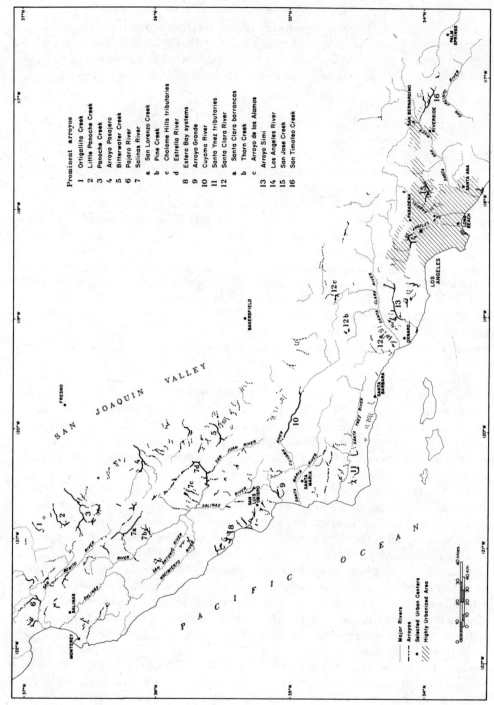

Prominent arroyos

1 Origalliita Creek
2 Little Panoche Creek
3 Panoche Creek
4 Arroyo Pasajero
5 Bitterwater Creek
6 Pajaro River
7 Salinas River
a San Lorenzo Creek
b Pine Creek
c Cholame Hills tributaries
d Estrella River
8 Estero Bay systems
9 Arroyo Grande
10 Cuyama River
11 Santa Ynez tributaries
12 Santa Clara River
a Santa Clara barrancas
b Thorn Creek
13 Arroyo de los Alamos
14 Arroyo Simi
15 Los Angeles River
16 San Jose Creek
17 San Timoteo Creek

Major Rivers
Arroyos
Selected Urban Centers
Highly Urbanized Area

Figure III.3 Distribution of arroyos in coastal California

to 70 feet above the channel bed. The gently sloping floor of Long Valley, on the other hand, is devoid of a channel except for shallow swales here and there that are occasionally erased by ploughing and harrowing along the farmed valley floor.

Sources of Data

Sources of information pertinent to arroyo formation in California are extensive. In the following discussion the most important of them have been quarried, in particular the U.S. General Land Office survey field notes and plats, old editions of Geological Survey topographic quadrangle maps, published and unpublished daily precipitation records, census materials, and a variety of historical accounts relevant to the study of the livestock industry and ecological change. A number of sources of considerable general potential, but which did not appear to be directly valuable to the specific case studies of arroyos presented below, have not been used. They include newspapers, photographic collections (e.g. the Fairbank and Shantz collections at the University of California, Los Angeles, and the University of Arizona, Tucson, respectively), railroad surveys and engineering reports, county property records, and the plethora of reminiscences, explorers' journals, and other accounts in local archives. In the following discussion of a group of arroyos, emphasis is placed not only on archival information but also on field measurements and interviews with local residents.

EVIDENCE FROM THE VALLEYS

Of the many arroyos in coastal California (Figure III.3), only eight have been studied in detail. The choice has been constrained by several practical considerations of scale, location, and availability of reliable historical data. Many arroyos are only very short, or are in urbanized or heavily cultivated areas where artificial drains and other structures obscure the erosional forms. Moreover, many arroyos in the coastal region are situated on lands owned privately before California was incorporated into the United States in 1848 and which were never surveyed systematically by the U.S. General Land Office. Within these areas of Spanish and Mexican land grants, accurate early descriptions of channels are rare and normally they only refer to the boundaries of the grants or to surveys of unofficial township boundaries projected through some of the grants. Copies of *diseños* (crude sketch maps filed with original grant applications to the Mexican government) are available for some land grants, but their details commonly allow little understanding of drainage or channel conditions, and at times it is difficult to recognize even gross terrain features.

The following accounts relate mainly to San Timoteo Creek (Figure III.3, 16), Arroyo de Los Alamos (12c), Thorn Creek (12b), Estrella-Cholame Creek (7d), Panoche Creek (3), Little Panoche Creek (2), Arroyo Pasajero (4), and Bitterwater Creek (5). All except Thorn Creek are described in field

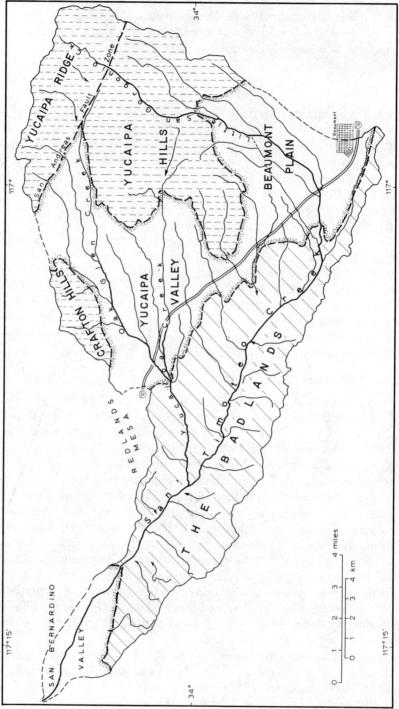

Figure III.4 The drainage basin of San Timoteo Creek

notes of General Land Office surveyors between 1850 and 1900 and all were initiated or extended during this period. A few other arroyos are briefly mentioned.

San Timoteo Creek

San Timoteo Creek originates on the high southern slopes of the San Bernardino Mountains and drains the western approach to San Gorgonio Pass. The intermittently flowing creek follows in its lower course a gently sloping ribbon-like valley about 15 miles long and seldom more than a half-mile wide developed in The Badlands (a chain of rugged hills in poorly consolidated Plio-Pleistocene sediments). Along the entire length of this valley, San Timoteo Canyon, the creek is deeply entrenched. Most, and possibly all, of this entrenchment occurred after 1871.

The drainage basin of San Timoteo Creek above its confluence with the Santa Ana River (Figure III.4) contains about 125 square miles of land, including crystalline blocks forming mountains and hills up to 8,800 feet high in the north-east of the basin, broad embayments of partially dissected alluvial slopes at the base of these uplands, and The Badlands. The mountains are covered by a patchwork of chaparral and pine forest, but the latter is rare below 7,000 feet except on steep, north-facing slopes and in valley bottoms. The alluvial surfaces immediately upslope from The Badlands lie between about 2,500 and 3,500 feet in elevation. They are in places deeply dissected with flat-bottomed valleys. They were covered by grassland, oak woodland, and chaparral at appropriate sites until the last few decades of the nineteenth century. Until at least 1899 a large cienega was situated on the south-west margin of Yucaipa Valley above the point where Yucaipa and Oak Glenn creeks enter The Badlands.[48] The Badlands occupy the lower south-western third of the basin and are characterized by an intricate pattern of ridges and ravines developed on north-east-dipping, poorly indurated clays, silts, sands, and gravels that comprise the Plio-Pleistocene San Timoteo Beds (Frick, 1921; Burnham and Dutcher, MS.). Except where they are entrenched, the floors of San Timoteo Canyon and other large valleys in The Badlands (and the floors of small tributary valleys for some distance above where they join the larger valleys as low-angle, channel-less alluvial fans) are alluviated and nearly flat. The steep slopes of The Badlands are commonly clothed with a cover of low chaparral. Prior to cultivation in the 1870s, the valley floors evidently supported stands of grass, woodland and various riparian vegetation communities.[49] Almost all of the valley floor is, or in recent years has been, devoted to agriculture, especially citrus orchards in the lower canyon, barley fields, and patches of irrigated alfalfa or pasture. The lowest reach of the creek enters the deeply alluviated basin of San Bernardino Valley, and joins the Santa Ana River in an area which was a large cienega during the nineteenth century (Burnham and Dutcher, MS.).

As throughout coastal California, the Quaternary geomorphological history of the drainage basin is extremely complex. Numerous abandoned erosional and depositional surfaces may be seen within the upland and alluvial zones (Russell, 1932) and there is good reason to suspect stream piracy in at least three different locations. Evidence for tectonic activity is widespread: fault dislocations may be traced through old alluvial deposits in several places on the Beaumont Plain and through Yucaipa Valley (Burnham and Dutcher, Ms.) and the active San Andreas Fault zone crosses the north-east corner of the basin. However, as far as The Badlands, San Timoteo Canyon, and the modern arroyo alone are concerned, there is little evidence in the form of old surfaces, terraces, unconformities, or deposits to confirm

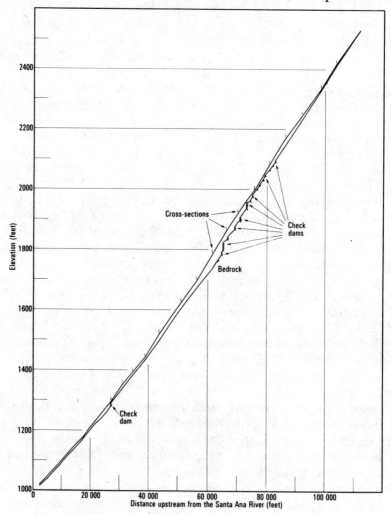

Figure III.5 The longitudinal profile of San Timoteo arroyo, 1966

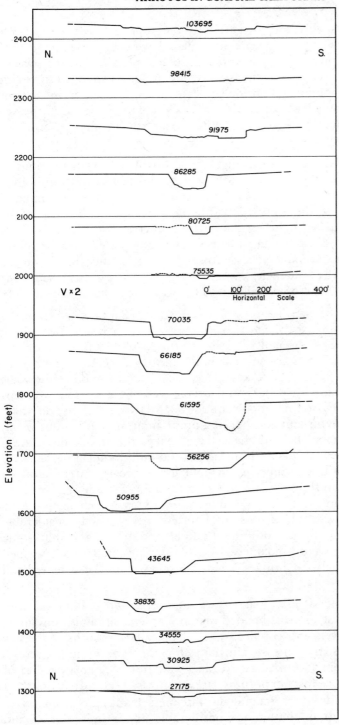

Figure III.6 Cross-sections of San Timoteo arroyo, 1966 (number in each cross-section refers to distance upstream, as shown on Figure III.5)

the truth of the eventful history suggested by the upper areas of the drainage basin. San Timoteo Canyon appears simply to have been eroded and then filled perhaps by as much as a few hundred feet of alluvium to the level of the present valley floor, prior to incision of the present arroyo. In surveying the entire length of the arroyo on foot no evidence was found in the alluvial sections of the arroyo walls that the creek has undergone the repeated episodes of filling and cutting so frequently described in other parts of the American South-West.

Figures III.5 and III.6 show the longitudinal profile and cross-sections of the San Timoteo arroyo in 1966. Depth, width, and details of morphology vary greatly from place to place. A maximum depth of 47 feet is attained in the central portion of the canyon. Width measured perpendicular to the flow-line exceeds 500 feet in a few places. There is a variety of forms within the arroyo: arrays of both cut and fill terraces (some paired) can be found along the channel in several reaches, although none is traceable for more than a mile along the channel. Some of the terraces reflect sediment accumulation behind structures designed to control arroyo enlargement.

From the mouth of San Timoteo Canyon to the Santa Ana River the channel is almost wholly artificial: San Bernardino County maintains dikes and occasionally dredges the bed to facilitate flows. Within the canyon the Southern Pacific Railroad Company has built, mostly since 1938, numerous concrete check dams in the arroyo and it has attempted to stabilize the walls in many reaches with rock rip rap and debris fences where erosion threatens to undermine sections of this important route. At two locations, one near the mouth of the canyon and another at a point about nine miles upstream, accumulation of sediment behind check dams makes the arroyo discontinuous. These dams, as well as dikes within the arroyo built by local farmers and ranchers to straighten the meandering channel and to prevent lateral erosion, have greatly influenced flow conditions and morphology in adjacent reaches. Despite these measures, the arroyo undergoes extensive changes during occasional major flows, such as those of February 1969 when considerable widening occurred in places, and the channel and terraces within some reaches of the arroyo were fundamentally altered. The 1969 floods washed out three of the four road bridges across the arroyo and also halted rail traffic through the canyon.

Materials comprising the floor and walls of the arroyo strikingly differ. The channel is lined with cross-bedded medium to coarse sands containing small amounts of gravels and cobbles, especially near the mouths of the few entrenched tributaries. In contrast, alluvial sediments exposed in the arroyo walls are highly variable from place to place but notable for a paucity of current-laid deposits. Most exposures are comprised almost wholly of silty-sand or sandy-silt layers ranging in thickness from several inches to about 10 feet and often containing considerable admixtures of clay and scattered small stones. When dry, these beds are extremely hard and frequently fissured along vertical planes oriented parallel and perpendicular to the arroyo wall. Bedding is discontinuous both along and normal to the canyon's axis. A few exposures in the middle reaches of the canyon contain thick sequences of fine-grained, almost varve-like, cienega deposits. The configuration of beds at the mouths of small tributary valleys and the often asymmetrical profile of the canyon floor suggest that most of the debris filling the valley was derived locally from small watersheds in The Badlands, and not carried into the canyon from the upstream parts of the creek's drainage basin. Valley fills at the upper end of the canyon are noticeably more friable and coarser than those within the canyon and the relative inability of these deposits to maintain steep walls and confine flows is largely responsible for the gradual widening, shallowing, and eventual disappearance of the arroyo here. According to one resident[50] this reach was entrenched during floods in 1927 to form an arroyo perhaps '12 to 15 feet deep and 30 to 40 feet wide'; it subsequently widened and filled until the spring of 1938, when incision reoccurred along a slightly different course; by 1966 the 'arroyo' in this reach had the appearance of a braided wash approximately 400 feet wide confined by sloping banks 3 to 6 feet high (Figure III.6, section 98415).

Little is known of the condition of the canyon bottom prior to 1850. An *asistencia* of the prosperous mission San Gabriel was established about a mile from the mouth of the canyon in 1819 and there are descriptions by the mid-1820s of fields and roving cattle in this locality (Beattie, 1939). Two sketchy *diseños* filed in 1841 suggest that no defined channel connected a creek bed in San Timoteo Canyon to the Santa Ana River, and that small cienegas existed in the upper canyon. These cienegas are also shown on Land Office township plats.

Land Office surveyors have worked in the canyon on several occasions since 1850, and their observations on the creek are noted in Figure III.7. At the canyon mouth in the 1850s and downstream for a few miles the channel appears to have been a broad, sandy wash ranging in width up to 500 feet and having banks which were pronounced at some locations and undistinguished at others. The name 'arroyo' or 'dry arroyo' was applied, but an inspection of numerous surveyors' notes of the time leaves little doubt that this term denoted only a stream bed (usually dry) or a wash, and had little or no connotation of shape, size, or setting. None of the earliest surveyors made either quantitative or qualitative reference to channel depth, and along one section line in 1857, two independent survey teams failed to mention any drainageway at all, although their field notes are filled with references to numerous small arroyos, brooks, draws, and ravines elsewhere. In the upper end of the canyon there was a wash about half the width of the present trench which disappeared within a mile downstream into the sandy valley bottom. The canyon floor evidently possessed a stream channel only below section 35 of T.2 S., R.2 W., where cienegas located in tributary valleys

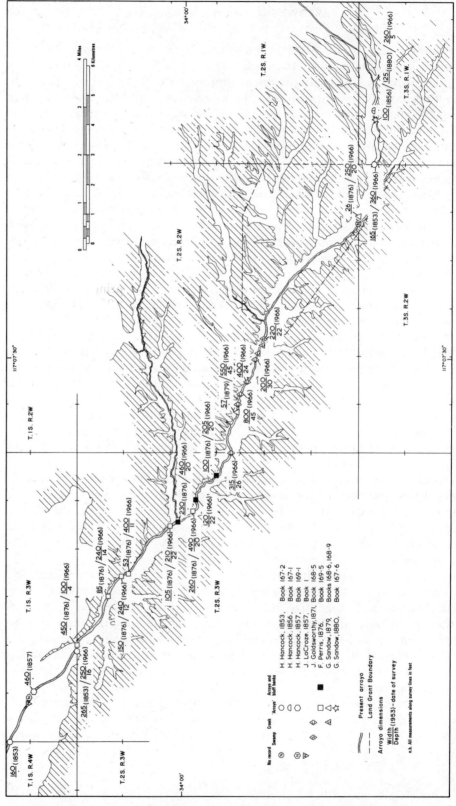

Figure III.7 San Timoteo arroyo: historical data

drained north-west along a course some distance north-east of the present trench.

Major channel changes within the central portion of the canyon seem to have occurred shortly after surveys in 1871, possibly following railroad construction in 1871–2. At the boundary between Ranges 2 and 3 W. of T.2 S. and along all section and quarter-section lines upstream from this boundary, descriptions of drainage in January of 1871 are consistent. A shallow creek from 4 to 5 feet wide flowed either through a 'willow swamp' or on an apparently flat valley floor. A resurvey of some of these same cross-sections in 1879 indicated that a trench had worked upstream past the boundary between sections 19 and 20 (T.2 S., R.2 W.) but that little change had occurred on the east side of section 20 or upstream from there. Observations along Yucaipa Creek where it flows through The Badlands also indicate that this creek was not entrenched until after 1871.

Section and quarter-section lines in most of the lower canyon were not surveyed until March 1876, and at that time the entire reach through T.2 S., R.3 W. possessed a channel with definite banks. Above the mouth of Yucaipa Creek the surveyor, John Perris,[51] referred to 'bluff banks' and 'steep bluff banks' on three of the nine lines he surveyed across San Timoteo Creek, phrases that do not occur elsewhere in his notebook. In this narrow two-mile strip of the canyon, Perris also described a stream 3 to 10 feet wide flowing between the bluffs and a small *zanja* (irrigation canal) on the valley flat, and he included the general note: 'Land level. Soil 1st and 2nd rate. Swamp.' Certainly this reach was then entrenched and, if the land was still swampy along the valley bottom, incision probably preceeded 1876 in this area by only a short period of time. Below the mouth of Yucaipa Creek the 'banks' were evidently lower, the channel was dry, and its width was considerably less than that of the present trench. Whether this reach was entrenched at the same time as the reach upstream, whether it was an older trench (perhaps cut during the catastrophic floods of 1862 or 1867 (Beattie, 1939)), or whether it was simply a shallow wash, is impossible to determine. Nevertheless, the distances between banks along all lines surveyed by Perris compared to measurements between contemporary trench walls along these same lines indicate considerable channel widening since 1876 of between 60 and 650 per cent.

According to Charles Singleton, who was born in the canyon and was its oldest living resident in 1966, the head of the arroyo lay in the vicinity of the school house (section 20, T.2 S., R.2 W.) by about 1890 and extended rapidly headwards sometime thereafter, possibly in the early years of this century. He also recalled that major changes occurred along the channel in 1927, and these produced a number of washouts of Southern Pacific track.

Several members of the Haskell family related stories of rapid extension of the trench near to their ranch headquarters during a summer storm in 1904. Although none was old enough at the time to remember details personally or to be absolutely sure of the date, they indicated this extension involved several miles of the arroyo, possibly up to the east end of the canyon (in T.3 S., R.1 W.)

From the preceding account, numerous other descriptions, and personal field observations (e.g. dates inscribed on check dams), development of the trench may be summarized as follows:

(a) Entrenchment in the middle portion of the canyon near to the mouth of Yucaipa Creek definitely predates 1876, and it is possible that the entire arroyo may have formed after 1871.

(b) Despite extremely wet years in the 1880s, some of the wettest on record in California, headward extension between 1876 and the first few years of this century was quite limited. The head may have been stabilized in the eastern half of section 20, T.2 S., R.2 W., throughout most of this period; headward migration between 1879 and the early 1890s was certainly less than one mile. Artificial control measures may have been used but there are no records to support this suggestion.

(c) A great extension of the arroyo occurred during the first few years of this century, possibly in 1904, and this may have lengthened the trench by as much as 7 or 8 miles to approximately its present upstream limit. Surprisingly, there were no major rainfalls recorded at nearby stations within several years of 1904, although some of the preceding years, 1897 to 1900, comprise one of the major drought periods recorded in southern California.

(d) Since the early 1900s the detailed topography of the arroyo has changed greatly, especially during major flows in 1927, 1938, 1941, 1966, 1969, and probably other times, but these changes have apparently involved trench width and depth without significantly affecting length, except possibly near the mouth of the canyon, where grading slopes for citrus orchards and channelization measures have narrowed the creek and forced entrenchment of a short reach.

Cañada de Los Alamos

Cañada de Los Alamos is located in the Transverse Ranges several miles south-east of Tejon Pass and the settlement of Gorman (Figure III.8). The lower 4 miles of the cañada, above its junction with the valley of Piru Creek at the head of Piru Gorge, are followed by U.S. Highway 99. The cañada contains the most spectacular historic arroyo in coastal California. Although the main branch of the trench is less than 4 miles long, it is up to 70 feet deep and is confined between precipitous walls seldom more than 300 feet apart.

The physical geography and underlying geology of the drainage basin tributary to Cañada de Los Alamos, which occupies about 60 square miles, are complex and not unlike those of the San Timoteo system. Elevation ranges from about 2,350 to 8,000 feet and together with terrain configuration accounts for significant variations in climate and vegetation. Alluviated

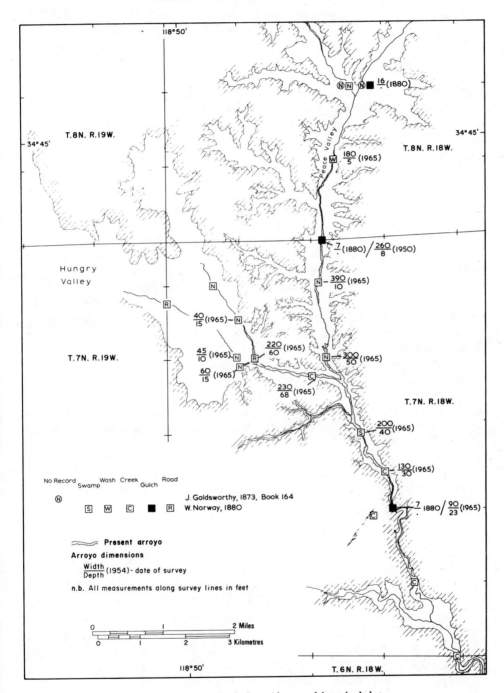

Figure III.8 Cañada de Los Alamos: historical data

valley bottoms in the cañada and its broad up-valley continuations, Hungry Valley and Peace Valley, probably receive little more than an average of 12 inches of precipitation per annum, and are covered by varied mixtures of grasses, evergreen oaks, Chrysothamnus, buckwheats, Russian thistle, sagebrush, mustard, and numerous other shrubs and broad-leaf annuals. The highest elevations on the slopes of Frazier Mountain receive about 25 inches of precipitation per year and are dominated by forests of Jeffrey Pine, but high mountains form only a very small portion of the drainage basin. Intermediate slopes and those of low ridges support grass with varying admixtures of chaparral and oak or pinyon-juniper woodland, depending on elevation, exposure, declivity, and substrate conditions. Most of the drainage basin is used for cattle-ranching, as it has been for well over 100 years, but the valley floors contain some grain fields, prominent rights of way for highways, pipelines and transmission lines, and a few small settlements.

The geology of the area has been described by Crowell (1950, 1952, 1954). Most of the basin is underlain by a wedge of generally north-west-tilted and moderately folded Pliocene continental sediments, the uppermost members of the Ridge Basin Group. Age and degree of consolidation of these sediments generally decrease upstream. Rugged slopes flanking narrow lower portions of Cañada de Los Alamos and Peace Valley are formed on Middle Pliocene sandstones, siltstones, and shales (Crowell, 1950) which California Department of Water Resources field maps suggest are susceptible to landsliding. A diverse assemblage of poorly consolidated conglomerates, sandstones, and siltstones, the Upper Miocene Hungry Valley Formation, underlies most of the rest of the basin and has been eroded into a network of broad valleys interfingering with low but intricately dissected and steeply sloping hills. Western and northern margins of the basin are rimmed by crystalline rocks, parts of which are massive granitic thrust plates separated from the sedimentary formations by the San Andreas fault zone, which traverses the northern margin of the basin. These rocks attain high elevations and exhibit steep rugged slopes except where they are covered by remnants of Pleistocene alluvial fans which continue downslope unconformably over the Hungry Valley Formation at some locations.

Crowell's observations (1950) leave no reason to doubt that orientation of the area's drainage southwards had been established during accumulation of the Hungry Valley Formation and thus predates numerous deformations and the mid-Pleistocene uplift of the region. The broad outline of the present network of valleys was formed by the upper Pleistocene. A few terrace deposits probably conformable with deposits in the upper portions of Hungry and Peace valleys were mapped by the Department of Water Resources on terraces in the cañada less than 100 feet above the channel of Los Alamos Creek. Valley widths throughout most of the basin seem well adjusted to lithological differences; for example, the expanses of Hungry Valley and its tributary valleys give way downstream to narrow canyons at the contact between the Hungry Valley Formation and Peace Valley Beds, and Cañada de Los Alamos is quite narrow for about 1·5 miles above its mouth where it consistently cuts across the strike of the Peace Valley Beds.

Unconsolidated alluvial deposits up to 90 feet deep line the bottoms of major valleys from about 1·5 miles upstream of the mouth of the Los Alamos Creek almost up to the basin's watershed in some locations. Where exposed in arroyo walls the textures, coloration, and stratigraphic characteristics of these materials are indistinguishable from those in San Timoteo Canyon. Thin-bedded cienega deposits are prominent in some locations. Logs of numerous exploratory wells drilled through valley fills of the lower cañada by the California Department of Water Resources show interbedded sandy silt and silty sand with frequent inclusions of organic sandy clay or clayey sand which generally give way to gravels and cobbles near the base of the fill. Landslide debris is present near the valley side in at least one location. Well logs also provide some information on the geometry of the valley beneath the fill. The transverse profile is only slightly more concave than the almost flat fill surface. The longitudinal profile of the bedrock surface slopes at a gradient considerably less than that of either the fill surface or the flow line of the trench (0·0136 compared with 0·0214 and 0·0167 respectively), reflecting substantial deepening of the fill upstream, at least below the junction of Hungry and Peace valleys. The fills appear to be significantly sandier and at least as thick as those near this junction for several miles upstream along the axes of both Peace and Hungry valleys.

Figure III.9 illustrates morphological variations along the arroyo. Data for longitudinal profiles along Gorman Creek (Peace Valley) and Los Alamos Creek below its confluence with Gorman Creek were taken from maps obtained from the California State Division of Highways (Project VIII-LA-4J, sheets 13–16, scale 1″:200′, C.I.5′), and although they represent conditions in 1954, there seems to have been little change since except for construction of two small dams in the trench and alluviation along two short reaches. Other longitudinal profiles and all cross-sections were surveyed in 1966.

Between Piru Creek and about point 10,000[52] there is little evidence that the canyon bottom contained deep fills for a long time. The cañada is quite narrow in this reach, and construction of U.S. Highway 99 involved extensive artificial cuts and fills and several relocations of Los Alamos Creek that may have removed fill remnants. But the projection through this reach of the valley-floor longitudinal profile suggests that the modern fill surface did not extend down the cañada to Piru Creek. A few debris deposits, coarse in comparison to fills upstream and possessing moderately sloping surfaces that show soil development, represent either Pleistocene terrace remnants or remains of a more recent fill that was entrenched long before the period of historical record. Between points 10,000 and 12,200 Los Alamos Creek is flanked by alternating terrace remnants which project to heights between 7

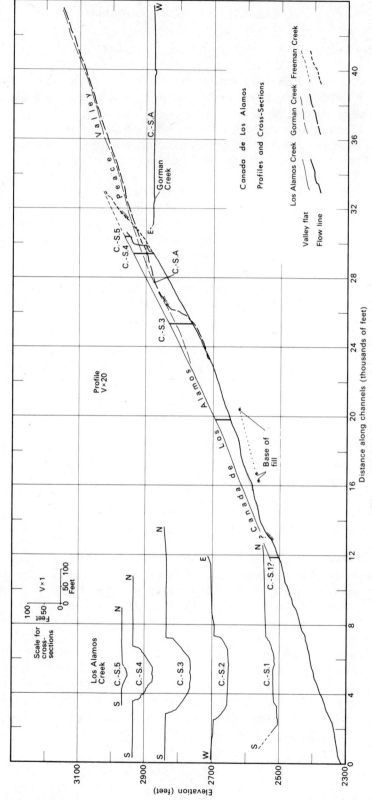

Figure III.9 Cañada de Los Alamos: profiles

and 30 feet above the present level of the creek (Figure III.9, cross-section 1). In this short reach there appear to be at least two terrace levels, the lowest being underlain by sandy alluvium at most locations.

Upstream between 12,200 and 15,500 there is only one terrace level, the valley floor, but the arroyo walls through this reach are not particularly steep. Highway construction displaced the channel westward by about 200 feet through part of this reach and may be indirectly responsible for exposing bedrock (shale and sandstone) along the channel between 12,200 and 13,500. The channel profile steepens noticeably over this material which, although soft and friable, evidently functions as the local baselevel for the trench upstream.

Near 15,500 the trench assumes a characteristic arroyo-like form that is maintained upstream to an artificially stabilized head near 30,000 and up four tributary trenches, which enter this reach from Apple, Coyote, and Freeman canyons and Peace Valley. Effects of the joining of drainage from Peace Valley and the cañada on valley-floor and arroyo morphology are especially difficult to decipher. The trench deepens gradually from about 25 feet near 15,500 to about 65 feet at the confluence of Los Alamos and Gorman creeks. From there upstream to the head, the gradient of Los Alamos Creek steepens to parallel that of the valley floor above, and the arroyo maintains nearly constant depth. This steepening may be related to reduced discharge above the confluence, but control by the dense cover of willow, cottonwood, cattail, sedge and other hydrophytes which clog the bottom of the arroyo upstream from point 22,000 may be of major importance. The profile of Gorman Creek also appears to be slightly steeper than that downstream, but the trench in Peace Valley shallows appreciably in the half-mile above the confluence. This shallowing is due in part to the indirect course of Gorman Creek relative to the axis of the valley floor, but there is also a very real difference between the gradients of valley flats in Cañada de Los Alamos near and upstream from the confluence (0·025) and the flatter Peace Valley (0·019), despite the latter's smaller drainage area.

Trenches in the cañada, Freeman Canyon, and Peace Valley possess steep headwall slopes containing springs nourishing perennial swamps or small brooks downstream within the arroyo. The head of the main trench (point 30,000) is partially stabilized by a concrete flume and check dam built on a once-buried bedrock spur, combined with dikes which direct flow to the side of the valley floor where bedrock is near the surface and thence through the flume. Despite these efforts, a narrow arroyo up to 20 feet deep has formed above the flume and extends for 0·75 miles upstream. A similar attempt has evidently been made to force flow from Freeman Canyon over bedrock, but although the poorly consolidated coarse sandstone members of the Hungry Valley Formation have narrowed the trench to a slit 20 feet deep and less than 3 feet wide in some locations (between 31,000 and 32,000), erosion has reached and formed a wide arroyo in sandy valley fills upstream. The complex head of the deep trench in Peace Valley (26,000) seems to have been stabilized effectively in the same manner, with a criss-cross of abandoned channels attesting to past efforts. For 0·25 miles above this head the valley flat is smooth and grassy and the main channel is reduced in places to a swale less than a foot deep and 10 feet wide. For about 8 miles further upstream, as far as Gorman, the appearance of the channel alternates between that of an arroyo-like form with well-defined walls 3 to 12 feet high and containing clumps of willows, and that of a sandy wash with poorly defined banks.

At least one 'cycle' of entrenchment and refilling has previously occurred in the cañada. Terrace remnants near the downstream limit of the valley flat are suggestive of such an event, but an exposure at point 19,950 provides unequivocal evidence (Figure III.9, cross-section 2). Here a small terrace lies 4 to 5 feet below the general level of the valley flat and continues along both sides of the trench for about 100 yards. Along the west wall of the trench the slope behind this terrace is continuous with an unconformity in the fill underlain by a dark grey layer presumably stained by organic remains up to a foot thick. The gently sloping unconformity is apparent for a distance of less than 30 yards, but the roughly horizontal bedding both above and below it is clear.

The history of this reach, at its simplest, involved (a) excavation of the valley, (b) accumulation of fill to a depth of about 90 feet, (c) excavation in the valley floor of a channel which eventually reached dimensions of the order of 15 feet deep and up to 300 feet wide, (d) filling of this trench to within 5 feet of the previous valley floor, and (e) incision of the modern arroyo to a depth up to 70 feet. Other incisions and refillings may have occurred, but evidence for them was not observed.

Surveyors' notes make it quite clear that neither Cañada de Los Alamos nor Peace Valley contained arroyos of significant size in 1880. The valley bottom was described as containing bunch grass, oak, willow, cottonwood, sycamore, barley fields, and a few dwellings. There may have been a perennial stream in the cañada downstream from about point 30,000; field notes dated between 25 May and 1 June describe a creek between 7 and 13 feet wide and one 'swamp' 120 feet wide where section lines cross the valley bottom. [53] The only indication of a deep channel in this reach is a reference to a 'gulch' 7 feet wide near the present position of Los Alamos Creek where it enters the narrow section of the cañada (point 12,000). Traverses along section lines in Peace Valley encountered narrow washes, gulches, or no channel at all. There is some suggestion that portions of the trench lie where the road to Fort Tejon was recorded in 1880 (points 14,500 and 33,800) but survey lines are only approximately located on topographic maps and it was impossible to locate section corners in the field.

Mr. Morrow, Foreman of the Circle K (Kinsey) Ranch, reported that the channel cut back past a ranch house, located near to the junction of the cañada and Peace Valley in 1911, and that the house was moved several miles north in 1912. Whether the entire trench upstream from point 12,000 was formed at the same time or not is unknown. Morphological evidence suggests that the reach below point 15,500 may be somewhat older.

Thorn Meadows

Like Cañada de Los Alamos, Thorn Meadows is situated along a tributary to Piru Creek and was initiated in the early years of this century, but the size and some environmental aspects of Thorn Meadows differ sharply from those of most California arroyos. The term meadow conjures up an appropriate image, that of a small, high-elevation, marshy, grass- and sedge-covered flat surrounded by forested mountains, although some of these conditions were modified by incision of an arroyo-like trench to depths exceeding 25 feet. Thorn Meadows now contains a complex array of terrace remnants which provides some indication of how entrenchment progressed.

The small drainage basin containing the meadows occupies an area of only 1·24 square miles and ranges in elevation between 4,850 and 6,450 feet. Except for the alluviated surface of the meadows, the basin is divided into steep slopes developed on very friable and occasionally cobbly, south-west-erly-dipping sandstones. These slopes support a varied cover of trees and shrubs, ranging from stands of forest and open woodland dominated by Jeffrey Pine, to a sparse cover of brush on steep south-facing slopes. Lower slopes surrounding the meadows are frequently typified by widely scattered fire-scarred trees rising above rock almost devoid of soil. Fills outline the maximum dimensions of the meadows and extend upstream about 1·5 miles from a point near the narrow mouth of the basin and obtain a maximum width of about 800 feet. Sedge and grass with some sagebrush dominate the downstream third of the valley floor but pine and a brush form of willow become increasingly significant upstream and on terraces within the arroyo. Mean annual precipitation over the entire basin probably approaches about 20 inches with a substantial portion of this total falling as snow.

The valley fills clearly reflect the lithology of the drainage basin and characteristics of the depositional environment. Sand predominates every-where, but upward through sections exposed in trench walls, downstream along the trench, and toward the axis of the valley there are general tendencies for (a) reduced numbers of clasts of sizes larger than sand, (b) increased amounts of organic debris, (c) better segregation of materials into discrete beds, and (d) a tendency for these beds to become thinner. Typical exposures near the axis of the valley exhibit beds of unconsolidated sand up to 8 inches thick frequently alternating with layers of white to black sandy clay as much as an inch thick. Sands are mottled with orange stains which also line root casts in the clay, but presumably this is a result of post-entrenchment oxidization. The almost varve-like alternation of sands and clays suggests that occasional flows of large magnitude swept large amounts of sand on to portions of the meadow surface, but intervening periods probably of several years in length were characterized by re-establishment, growth, and decay of meadow vegetation on top of each successive sand deposit. Some exposures show substantial amounts of peaty material mixed with sand, and well-preserved trunks and branches of sizeable trees protrude from trench walls at a few locations. These fills are extremely soft. When moist it is easy to dig into trench walls by hand or to cause sections of walls to collapse. When dry, the sandy clays are fairly hard, but interbedded sands remain very friable. It is quite apparent that the ability of the fills to maintain steep slopes is related to their content of cohesive fine material and organic debris, and further, that trench widening is certainly as much a result of wetting of fills as runoff activity in Thorn Creek.

The earliest topographic map of the area (Mt. Pinos, 30' sheet) was based on a 1901 survey and uses the symbol for freshwater marsh to designate roughly all of the area now possessing fills. Mr. Tifft, a resident of nearby Cuddy Valley who used to run a large cattle operation in the area and who retired from the Forest Service in 1965, claimed that Thorn Meadows was 'cut' about 1916 or 1918 or possibly as early as the channel in the Cañada de Los Alamos (1911). Although he lived only seven miles north of Thorn Meadows in Lockwood Valley since 1911 and ranged cattle in the meadows, he could be no more specific.

A detailed examination of the valley flat reveals a generally convex longitudinal profile containing numerous undulations and carved into several terraces. Although incision of the trench in the 1,500 feet upstream from the mouth of Thorn Creek might conceivably be related to slight incision or lateral shifting of the South Fork of Piru Creek, it is clear that most and probably all modern entrenchment of Thorn Meadows resulted from conditions or changes acting within the drainage basin of Thorn Creek; the trench is discontinuous and the channel above point 1,500 is separated from downstream reaches by a waterfall formed where the channel encounters resistant rock at the side of the meadows.

Figures III.10 and III.11 present, respectively, longitudinal profiles of the present flow-line of Thorn Creek and associated surfaces, and nine cross-sections surveyed across the meadows. The letter and number combinations T1 to T5 denote interpretation of the morphologic sequence of events, with T1 representing a high terrace, T2 probably the valley flat at the turn of the century, and T5 the present stream bed. Numerous additional sedge-covered terraces which lie less than 5 feet above the creek bed are not illustrated, but these are discontinuous and often relatable to obstacles along the channel.

In sequence, geomorphic events in the development of Thorn Meadows may be summarized as follows:

(a) Erosion of a valley across the strike of bedrock.

(b) Accumulation of fills in a meadow environment to a level (T1)

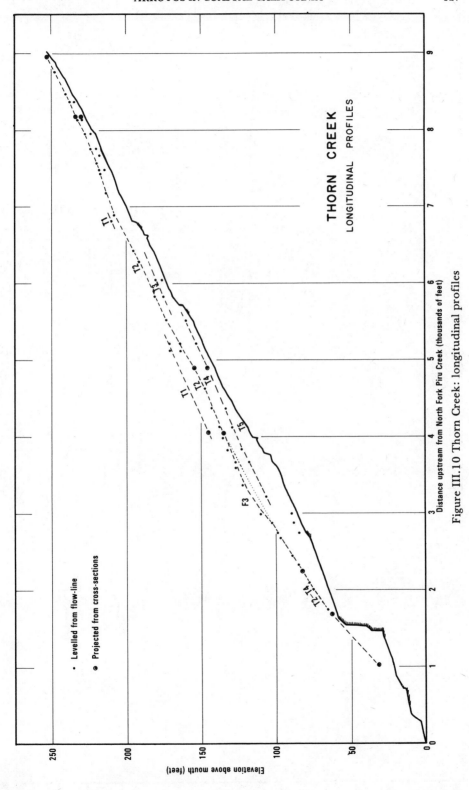

Figure III.10 Thorn Creek: longitudinal profiles

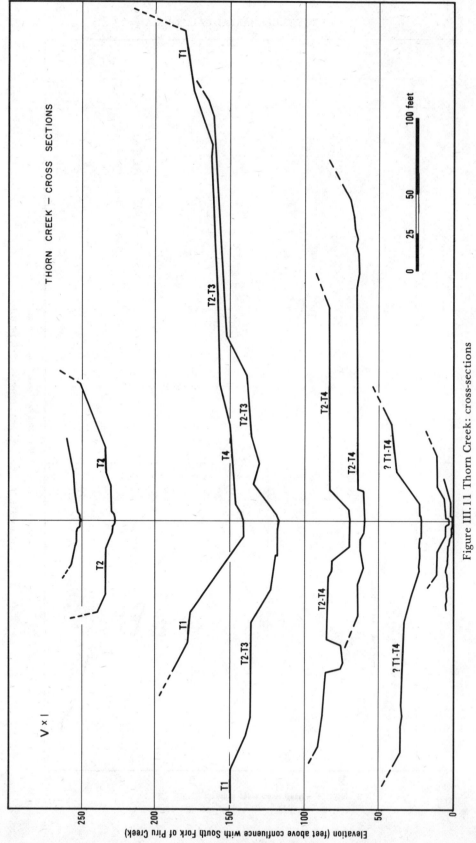

Figure III.11 Thorn Creek: cross-sections

represented by well-preserved terrace remnants which now support some large pines with basal trunk diameters exceeding 2 feet. The shape of this surface below point 4,000 is not apparent but was probably quite similar to that of subsequent fills.

(c) Entrenchment and probable removal of nearly all fills along the valley axis.

(d) Aggradation, also in a meadow, to the extensive T2 surface which, by inference from the Mt. Pinos Quadrangle (30', 1903), remained intact at the turn of the century. The final event in this filling may have been debris accumulation (conceivably as a result of fire in headwaters of the basin), which created the relatively convex longitudinal profile upstream from point 5,000.

(e) Modern entrenchment, which probably involved the following in close association: (i) entrenchment upstream from about point 5,000 and deposition of much debris removed from this trench to form a convexity (F3) on the meadows downstream. Together these formed a surface (labelled T3) which is well preserved at only a few locations along the creek; (ii) incision in the vicinity of this convexity and headward extension of a subsequent trench, remnants of which are easily reconstructed into the bench labelled T4; (iii) further incision, probably initiated near point 2,000, responsible for the present channel profile (T5). The downstream limit of this is marked by a decrease of channel depth to about one foot where the channel is superimposed on a resistant bedrock spur.

Incision further downstream through the narrow valley between point 1,500 and the mouth of the creek may have succeeded all of these events or, on the other hand, may predate erosion of the T2 surface. In any case, development of the trench upstream from about point 1,500 appears not to have been a consequence of erosion near to the mouth of the creek.

Two other small basins in the upper reaches of the Piru Creek basin are worthy of note. Upper Mutau Creek, which abuts Thorn Creek's watershed on the south, possesses an arroyo-like trench for a distance of about a mile, although there appear to be no older terraces or conformable benches associated with it. According to Mr. Tifft, incision was approximately contemporaneous with that of Thorn Meadows. About 2 miles north of Thorn Meadows a broad valley about 1·5 miles long and 0·25 miles wide appears to be filled quite deeply with alluvium. Most of the valley bottom is completely channel-less and at the mouth of the valley there is a 'dry' meadow. At the lower margin of this area where the valley narrows between steep ridges, the valley floor steepens appreciably and the surface is scarred by a number of small, sub-parallel discontinuous gullies. The situation appears ripe for the creation of an arroyo.

Estrella River and Cholame Creek

In the headwaters of the Salinas River, long reaches of the Estrella River and

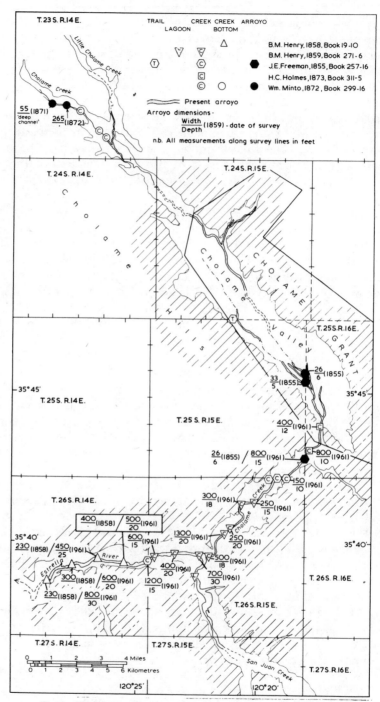

Figure III.12 Estrella River-Cholame Creek: historical data

its tributary, Cholame Creek, form a discontinuous arroyo with an over-all length of approximately 35 miles (Figure III.12). Where best formed in its lower course, the arroyo is up to 30 feet deep and frequently exceeds 600 feet in width; its floor is in many places filled with cottonwood trees and other riparian vegetation. Much of the middle and upper reaches of Cholame Creek courses along a series of alluviated valleys marking the location of the San Andreas fault; through these valleys the channel of the creek is in places entrenched with a typical arroyo, and in others it is a broad wash, a shallow channel with sloping floodplain, or a gentle swale. San Juan Creek, the major tributary to Estrella River, is entrenched for only a short distance above its confluence with Cholame Creek.

Drainage tributary to the arroyo comes from an area of several hundred square miles covered largely by grassland and oak woodland although coniferous woodland and some chaparral can be found in headwater areas which reach in places to elevations over 4,000 feet. Most of the area is devoted to cattle-ranching, as it has been for well over 100 years, and fields of irrigated forage crops supporting this activity can be found in various valley-bottom locations.

Survey records provide some information on arroyo development. Downstream from section 21, T.26 S., R.14 E., the steep walls of the arroyo gradually give way to less abrupt terrace scarps in Pleistocene alluvium. For about 3 miles upstream of this area the river was apparently incised to some degree before 1858: the surveyor, Brice Henry,[54] made specific reference to entering and leaving the 'creek bottom' on either side of what was then called San Juan Creek, although no note was made of its morphology. For the next 7 miles upstream, Henry referred only to a creek about 30 feet wide — often with pools of brackish water and adjacent willows — and a lagoon and slough on San Juan Creek above its junction with Cholame Creek. A few years earlier in 1855, another surveyor[55] failed to note banks or escarpments in this same reach, reporting only a dry creek bed 35 feet wide and flanked by willows. Entrenchment through most of this reach must have taken place subsequently to the surveys. Further upstream there are few observations (noted in Figure III.12), but those available show that short entrenched segments existed at very early dates. In all probability a discontinuous arroyo was present then as now.

Panoche Creek

Descriptions by Bull (1964b) of arroyos in western Fresno County fit reaches of numerous intermittent and ephemeral streams that issue from hilly and mountainous areas along the north-eastern margin of the Coast Ranges (Figure III.3). All of these streams terminate on semi-arid or arid piedmont areas, usually in low-angle alluvial fans composed of fine material which merge imperceptibly into alluvial plains and embayments that slope towards the axis of the San Joaquin Valley. In most cases, trenches are best

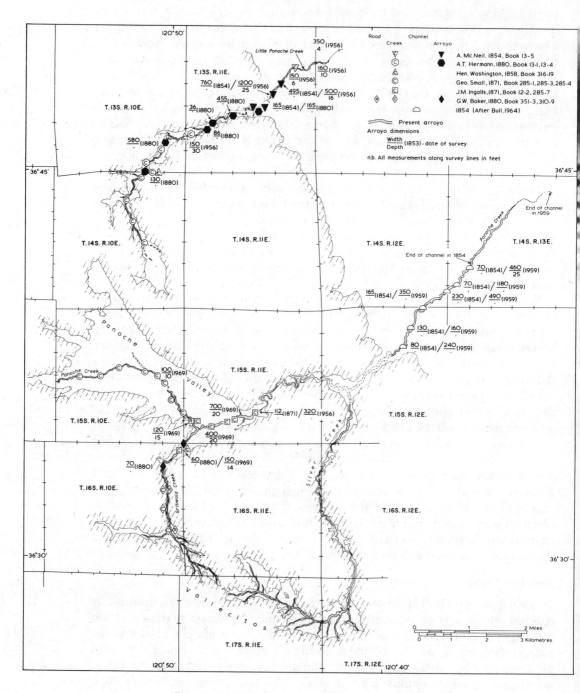

Figure III.13 Panoche and Little Panoche creeks

developed near fan apexes and gradually shallow to meet adjacent surfaces some distance downslope. Their development upstream is limited, except along relatively large intermittent streams that possess narrow alluviated valley floors for some distance back into the hills or pass through isolated alluvial basins in upstream reaches.

Some of these trenches certainly existed, at least in part, before settlement. As Bull (1964b, p.252) emphasized, they are '. . . natural features of alluvial fans, and terraces and abandoned gullies can be found on several fans'. However, he was able through use of survey records and accounts of settlers to date entrenchment or very substantial enlargement of all the channels he described to the period between 1875 and 1885. Bull was also able to correlate prominent terraces along channels and he attributed them to renewed incision after 1935.

Arroyo Ciervo and Arroyo Hondo, both described by Bull (1964b), are typical examples of the majority of arroyos in this area. These are morphologically simple, short, confined to upper fan slopes, and associated with drainage basins of intermediate size (about 5 to 50 square miles). On steep fan slopes at mouths of small canyons, channels deepen over short distances into narrow barranca-like forms, commonly over 25 feet deep, then gradually shallow, and disappear in low sandy delta-like deposits on fans or at edges of cropland areas. Their length is seldom more than a few miles.

The drainage system of Panoche Creek (Figure III.13) is one of the largest in this area and contains a complex network of discontinuous arroyos. The drainage basin above the fan apex includes about 300 square miles and the associated fan occupies a similar area. The headwaters lie in the Diablo Range where a few peaks exceed 4,000 feet in elevation. Annual precipitation reaches about 20 inches and slopes are covered with coniferous or oak woodland and chaparral. The dominant portion of the basin contains rolling hills composed of poorly consolidated sandstones, mudstones, and shales and broad valleys filled with Pleistocene basin deposits and unconsolidated alluvium. Precipitation probably ranges between 8 and 15 inches, and a sparse cover of short grass predominates except on occasional steep slopes or on cultivated patches in the valley bottoms. The fan surface is extremely smooth in most locations and composed of friable, extremely fine, deposits, some of which are subject to considerable loss of structure and subsidence when wetted (Bull, 1964a).

Bull (1964b) documented extension and widening of Panoche Creek across its fan subsequent to Land Office surveys in 1854 (Figure III.13). Two large alluviated basins situated upstream, Panoche Valley and Vallecitos, also contain extensive arroyo networks. Upstream from the head of the fan, the creek flows through a valley about half a mile wide which contains paired terraces formed in recent alluvium, but these show considerable evidence of erosion and probably predate the historical period. Between this valley and Panoche Valley the main stream winds for about 4 miles through a narrow canyon cut in resistant Cretaceous sediments. Silver Creek, the principal tributary, follows a similar but longer canyon from the eastern edge of Vallecitos. The almost flat floor of Panoche Valley possesses an arroyo-like trench which is perhaps 600 feet wide and 25 feet deep. The arroyo gradually narrows, shallows, and acquires continuous unbroken walls along a meandering course upstream for about 10 miles across the valley. The mouth of the valley, with its pinching out of alluvial fills, eroded trench walls, at least one old scarp in recent alluvium, and perennial flow (which rises and maintains stands of riparian vegetation along the trench bottom a few miles upstream), presents a situation analogous to that of Cañada de Los Alamos. The same may be said of Vallecitos, of which one half is drained by Griswold Creek through a narrow canyon to Panoche Valley and the other half by Silver Creek. At both exits there are deep arroyos, and upstream these subdivide into networks of trenches which cross the floor of the valley and merge with gullies on the soft sediments surrounding it.

The history of entrenchment in Panoche Valley and Vallecitos is difficult to interpret from early land-surveyors' notes (Figure III.13). No channel depths were reported, banks were described in only one location, and in most places arroyos follow the course of 'creeks' described in 1857, 1871, or 1880. Existing arroyos are considerably wider than creek widths recorded then. But surveys across both Panoche Creek (between sections 30 and 31, T.15 S., R.11 E.) and Griswold Creek between section 1, T.16 S., R.10 E. and section 6, T.16 S., R.11 E.) immediately above their confluence definitely place entrenchment in this vicinity between 1871 and 1880: present arroyos lie at some distance from creek positions recorded in 1871[56] and a resurvey across Griswold Creek in 1880[57] notes the correct position and reports 'deep bluff banks'. It is possible that none of the headwater channels of Panoche Creek was entrenched before 1871; but it is equally possible that arroyos already existed along some reaches at that date, and that they were still shallow enough to be ignored by surveyors. It should be noted that by 1871 there were numerous roads and grain fields in Panoche Valley, and one surveyor complained of the destruction of earlier survey markers '. . . by the droves of cattle and sheep that are continually grazing in and about this vicinity'.[58]

Little Panoche Creek

Little Panoche Creek (Figure III.13) drains a hilly area about a quarter the size of Panoche Creek's drainage basin and it is generally lower in elevation, drier, and typified by a sparse grass cover. Through much of the basin, Little Panoche Creek is incised into the alluviated floor of a narrow valley that averages less than one quarter-mile in width. The arroyo extends out on to an alluvial fan for only a few miles and here recent aqueduct and highway engineering work has now obliterated the former channel.

Again, survey records allow only a partial reconstruction of arroyo development. Near the fan apex and in the lower part of the valley the creek appears to have been entrenched by 1854,[59] but it terminated only a short distance down the fan and had not reached as far upstream as the boundary between ranges 10 and 11 E. by 1858.[60] In this reach the arroyo lacks the well-defined vertical walls common further upstream. By 1880 most of the valley possessed a creek with 'steep' banks or bounded by 'bluffs' at least as far as the boundary between townships 12 and 13 S.[61] No arroyo existed at this site in 1871, and at several locations upstream there was only a 'dry brook' ranging in width from 7 to 10 feet.[62]

The simplest interpretation of these observations is that the arroyo existed near the mouth of Little Panoche Valley in the 1850s and perhaps had been entrenched to some degree at the fan apex for much of its geomorphological history; headward erosion from this location may already have been underway in the 1850s. Most, if not all, of the current length of the arroyo had been established by January 1880, and at least some and perhaps most of this extension occurred after May 1871. The morphology of the arroyo has changed considerably since 1880.

Arroyo Pasajero

Arroyo Pasajero is the name applied to the lower course of Los Gatos Creek where it is deeply entrenched into the almost flat floor of a broad alluvial embayment, Pleasant Valley, and the gently sloping alluvial fan downslope of this embayment (Figure III.14). The tributary drainage basin occupies about 400 square miles and is similar in geology, terrain, elevation, climate, and vegetation cover to that of Panoche Creek.

Land surveys in the vicinity of the arroyo were completed in 1853 and 1854, and from these it is apparent that an arroyo 30 to 35 feet deep with 'bank perpendicular' existed near the boundary between ranges 16 and 17 E. at that time.[63] There is no record of depths or bank conditions at any other location along the channel, but there are descriptions of a wide creek, either dry or flowing, filled with 'underbrush' and cottonwoods and some mentions of a 'slough'.

The 1912 edition of Coalinga 30' topographic quadrangle indicates the existence of an arroyo (or even an intermittent stream) only downstream from the north end of the Guijarral Hills. By 1933 the arroyo was 25 to 35 feet deep with near vertical walls at the north edge of these hills and had also extended east downstream through T.20 S., R.17 E. At the same time, the trench had increased greatly in width and filled to a depth of only 12 to 15 feet in the eastern portion of T.20 S., R.16 E. (Polvadero Gap 15' Quadrangle, 1940). In 1933 the head of the arroyo lay near the town of Coalinga (Coalinga 15' Quadrangle, 1935) in approximately its present location. Upstream from the town, Los Gatos Creek and its major tributary, Warthan Creek, are broad washes, often with indistinct banks, although both channels have been artificially controlled to some extent. The lower reaches

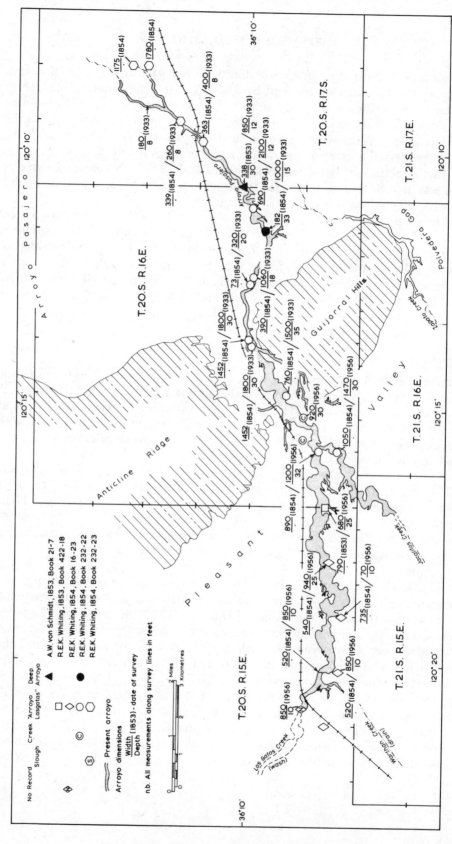

Figure III.14 Arroyo Pasajero

of the arroyo (in T.20 S., R.17 E.) have been filled and greatly altered by cotton farmers on adjacent lands during the past 30 years and now have the appearance of a shallow, overgrown drainage canal.

Bitterwater Creek

Bitterwater Creek (Figure III.15) drains a rugged foothill area of about 50 square miles on the edge of the San Joaquin Valley. The Temblor Range which occupies most of the drainage basin is composed of soft mudstones, shales, and sandstones and in this area reaches elevations above 3,000 feet; the climate of the entire drainage basin is semi-arid and sparse stands of short grasses and xerophytic shrubs dominate the hills and valley floors. The entire area is devoted to cattle-ranching. Headwaters of the creek flow for short distances through valleys marking the San Andreas fault zone, but fills in these valleys are not noticeably entrenched. The floor of Bitterwater Valley is relatively flat and contains an arroyo commonly 200 to 400 feet wide that has a maximum depth of 25 feet. The arroyo would form a continuous trench about 9 miles in length were it not for the construction of a small livestock tank (reservoir) midway along the valley.

The history of the arroyo is sketchy. Only three lines were surveyed across the creek in the 1850s, and one of these yielded reference to a 'gulch' 6 feet deep at the upper end of the valley.[64] Numerous survey field notes made in 1893 and 1895 describe what appears to be a discontinuous arroyo, with a deeply entrenched segment at least 2 miles long in the upstream end of the valley and a network of deep narrow gullies near the mouth of the valley separated by a reach through which the channel had definite banks but a depth unworthy of note. Since the 1890s there have been a number of changes: the creek has incised the middle segment of the valley and extended the arroyo beyond the mouth of the valley, depth has increased in some places, and width has increased quite notably in most locations, even uniting three adjacent gullies into a single arroyo at one place (the boundary between ranges 18 and 19 E.).

HYPOTHESES OF REGIONAL CHANGE

Introduction

Hypotheses attributing arroyo incision to regional changes have been introduced in Part I and discussed in the Arizonan context in Part II. Ultimate responsibility for entrenchment in these hypotheses is assigned either to various types of climatic change, or to extensive landscape changes associated with human activities, notably the rapid expansion of an economy based on domesticated livestock. All such changes supposedly acted through increasing amounts or rates of runoff from slopes within watersheds which produced erosive valley-bottom discharges of a size or frequency unknown or extremely rare in the past. In most hypotheses of regional change,

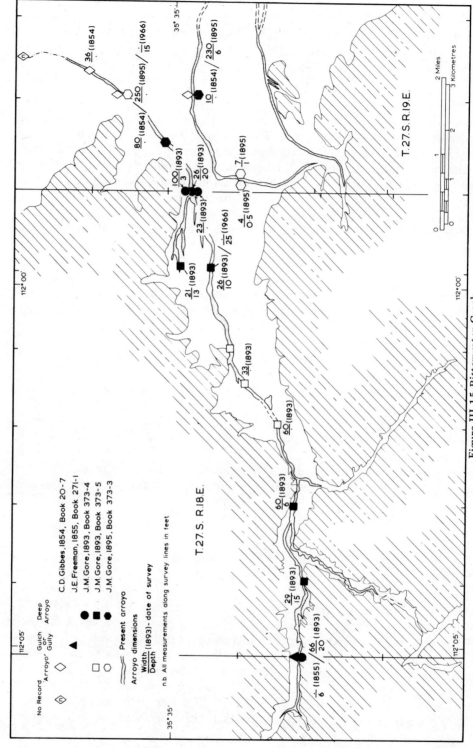

Figure III.15 Bitterwater Creek

vegetation depletion provides the fundamental link between climate or human activities and increased runoff.

As in Arizona, direct consideration of slope runoff and stream discharge in nineteenth-century California is obviated by a complete absence of reliable historical data. It is true that major floods and droughts have occurred and have been described ever since literate settlers arrived in California in 1769 (Lynch, 1931), but there is no way of objectively comparing the descriptions of these localized events with one another or of applying the information to other areas. In addition, evaluation of more recent instrumental streamflow records is obscured by gross uncertainties about the effects on runoff of long-continued and often ambitious stream-regulation programmes.

Yet there is sufficient pertinent historical information on California's climate, livestock populations, and vegetation to permit direct examination of their changes through time, and this information can be used to speculate on the nature and impact of runoff changes. In quantity, length of record, and, perhaps, reliability, California's archive evidently surpasses that for any other area in the South-West. Continuous precipitation records for three stations began by 1850. Quantitative data on livestock numbers date from the first colonial settlement at San Diego in 1769, and have been recorded at ten-year intervals with reasonable consistency and for fairly stable geographical units since the seventh U.S. census of 1850. Information on the condition and evolution of nineteenth-century vegetation is less uniform and more difficult to evaluate, but there are some valuable observations on the nature and causes of vegetation change.

Precipitation Trends

For several reasons, the form of analysis of precipitation data for California differs from that used for southern Arizona. Although there is considerable uncertainty concerning the dates of arroyo initiation in coastal California, entrenchment may have extended from before the 1850s to the present: certainly some arroyos existed at least in part by 1850, active incision is known to have occurred in valleys from about 1875 to as recently as 1911, and there has been some significant entrenchment as recently as the 1940s (Bull, 1964b). Thus the period of interest is longer than in southern Arizona. The climatic records are more complete in coastal California, so that regression analysis is less necessary for projecting trends across data gaps: other techniques suitable for detecting climatic fluctuations can be safely used. In addition, coastal California's abundance and geographical spread of climatic observations, together with the fact that precipitation within the region is largely controlled by the same large-scale cyclonic events, allow aggregation of data into a regional composite record that is desirable for purposes of display, generalization, and evaluation. Finally, the dry-summer, wet-winter precipitation regime of California requires different temporal units of observation and different parameters for the study of seasonality.

Nevertheless, the fundamental question is the same as that posed for southern Arizona: has precipitation, or any specific attribute of it, changed in historical times in any ways that might have led to increased runoff and thus promoted entrenchment? The underlying assumption is also the same as it was in Part II: if significant precipitation changes have occurred they are discernible in existing instrumental records and demonstrable in terms of statistical significance.

(a) The precipitation record Coastal California, and especially the Los Angeles region, currently contains a very high density of officially maintained rain-gauges, but the limited length of record precludes their use in our analysis. Examination of records reveals the names of some twenty-five stations that exist today and were also operational when published data began to appear in 1897. But because of grossly inconsistent and discontinuous records for many of these stations, only seven are acceptable for analysis. To these, five other stations have been added: two Central Valley stations (Fresno and Bakersfield) in order to allow some estimate of precipitation patterns and trends on the eastern flanks of the region, for which there is no representative long-record station; and three stations near the region's periphery that have exceptionally long, continuous records (San Francisco, Sacramento, and San Diego). General information pertinent to these twelve stations is listed in Table III.1, and station location is shown in Figure III.16.

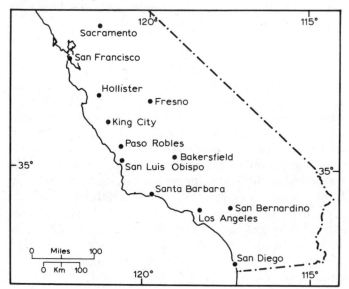

Figure III.16   Location of climatic stations

All of the twelve stations have been relocated, some of them many times, and most used non-standard rain-gauges during the early years of record. In addition, little is known about gauge exposures and height of gauges above

Table III.1   Stations Used for Analysis of Precipitation Trends

| Station | County | Location | | Ground Elevation | Gauge Relocations | Record from |
		Longitude	Latitude			
Bakersfield[2]	Kern	35° 25'N.	119° 03'W.	475'	1	1889
Fresno[1]	Fresno	36° 46'N.	119° 43'W.	331'	4	1878
Hollister[2]	San Benito	36° 51'N.	121° 24'W.	284'	3	1874
King City[2]	Monterey	36° 12'N.	121° 08'W.	320'	1	1887
Los Angeles[1]	Los Angeles	34° 03'N.	118° 14'W.	270'	5	1877
Paso Robles[2]	San Luis Obispo	34° 38'N.	120° 41'W.	700'	6	1887
Sacramento[1]	Sacramento	121° 30'N.	121° 30'W.	19'	10*	1849
San Bernardino[2]	San Bernardino	34° 08'N.	117° 16'W.	1125'	4	1870
San Diego[1]	San Diego	32° 44'N.	117° 10'W.	13'	7*	1850
San Francisco[1]	San Francisco	37° 47'N.	122° 25'W.	52'	13	1849
San Luis Obispo[2]	San Luis Obispo	35° 18'N.	120° 40'W.	300'	6	1869
Santa Barbara[2]	Santa Barbara	34° 25'N.	119° 43'W.	120'	4	1867

* Number of relocations before 1871 is not known.
Sources: [1] U.S. Weather Bureau (1952–); [2] U.S. Weather Bureau (1958).

ground level, two factors significantly affecting rainfall measurements, during early years. The effects of these changes of location and equipment are unknown for most stations, and caution is necessary in drawing conclusions about long-term trends, especially from the record of a single station. Most shifts in gauge location probably produced only minor deviations in measurement, but some may have resulted in significant changes caused by differences in exposure, elevation of gauge above ground, or actual differences in received rainfall.

The record for San Francisco is instructive in this context. A note in the California section of *Climate and Crops* for July 1902 documents definite changes in the catch of the official Weather Bureau gauge relative to other gauges in the city following movement of the station to the top of the Mills Building (154 feet above the ground) in 1892. The note concluded that (p.4) 'The catch of the gauge on the Mills Building is probably 33 per cent below the true catch, and all amounts recorded in the period 1892–1902 are probably in error that amount . . . ' Decreases in recorded rainfall were attributed to greater wind velocities on top of high buildings, resulting in both a functional reduction of gauge cross-section for raindrops having strong horizontal components of motion, and increased eddying and up-drafts around the mouth of the gauge. Piper (1959) applied double-mass analysis to data for San Francisco, Oakland and San Jose for their 83-year period of common record, and concluded that in order to achieve con-sistency between the three stations, recorded annual precipitation for San Francisco would have to be increased by about 30 per cent from 1892 to 1906, and should be adjusted from plus 1 to minus 5 per cent during the other 68 years of common record. But gauges in the two other cities were also moving to higher levels and thus the common datum may be misleading.

Gauges at many other urban stations, notably in Los Angeles, Sacramento, and San Diego, have also been moved upwards as they have been placed on the roofs of higher and higher buildings. An artificial trend towards reduction of rainfall and other false trends arising from urban gauge data might suggest that such stations should be excluded. But it is useful to include them because they have the longest records, give the only quanti-tative indication of rainfall conditions prior to the period of large-scale entrenchment, and the 'tall-building' effect was probably not important until the last years of the nineteenth century.

Precipitation data were taken from a number of U.S. Weather Bureau publications and unpublished records. Published sources, together with the years for which data were used, are shown in Table III.2. Daily rainfall values for years preceding 1897 were obtained from station record books stored at the National Climatic Center, National Oceanic and Atmospheric Adminis-tration, Asheville, N.C.

(b) Analytical procedures Steps in the analysis of precipitation data involve (i) selection of simple measures to represent attributes of precipitation

Table III.2

Sources of Climatic Data

U.S. Weather Bureau Publication	Annual Precip.	Monthly Precip.	Daily Precip.	24-hr. Max. Precip.
Monthly Climate and Crop Report (U.S.W.B., 1897–1906)			1897–1906	1887–1906
Climatological Service Bulletin (U.S.W.B., 1906–9)			1906–9	1906–9
Climatological Data (U.S.W.B., 1914–)	1930–68	1930–68	1914–68	1914–50
Monthly Weather Review (U.S.W.B., 1872–)			1909–13	1909–13
U.S.W.B., 1903 U.S.W.B., 1934	1849–1930	1849–1930		1871–96
National Summary (U.S.W.B., 1950–)				1950–68

thought to be critical in determining runoff; (ii) aggregation of annual values for each of these measures from the twelve stations to establish a composite picture representing the region as a whole; (iii) graphical portrayal of the composite record so that possible fluctuations and trends can be seen; and (iv) application of simple statistical tests to such variations.

(i) *Selection of measures.* Four aspects of precipitation – amount, seasonal distribution, frequency, and intensity – are analysed for change. To avoid dividing the rainy season at its peak by using the calendar year as the time unit, the twelve-month period extending from 1 July to 30 June has been used as the time period for all annual measures; there is a precedent for the use of this unit in California (U.S. Weather Bureau, 1934). Precipitation totals within these twelve-month periods, referred to below as 'annual precipitation', provide the measure for changes in annual amount of precipitation – i.e. trends towards more or less precipitation, and the occurrence of droughts and wet periods.

Seasonal distribution is represented by two measures: an index of relative concentration based on the proportion of annual precipitation falling in the early months of the rainy season, and by a simple sum of October, November, and December precipitation in each year. Precipitation frequency is measured by the number of daily precipitation observations in each of three size classes during the July-June period, and the values adopted to define the classes are selected to suit California's precipitation ($0.01''-0.24''$; $0.25''-0.99''$; and $1.00''+$). Three measures are used to examine fluctuations in precipitation intensity: mean daily intensity (annual precipitation divided by the number of rainy days during the year); maximum daily intensity (the greatest observation-day precipitation reported each year); and, for first- and second-order Weather Bureau stations only (i.e. San Francisco, Sacramento, San Diego, Los Angeles, and Fresno), the greatest annual 24-hour precipitation.

(ii) *The composite record.* Composite records, which are based on various methods of combining and weighting of data from several stations to produce a single representative statement, have occasionally been used in regional analyses of precipitation and temperature trends (Kincer, 1941; Burcham, 1957; Sellers, 1960). The Weather Bureau for many years published composite precipitation and temperature values for entire states each month in *Climatological Data.* Composite records have three main advantages. In an area having a high degree of meteorological uniformity, as in the region studied here, composite records tend to be conservative – to reduce the significance of localized meteorological 'accidents', measurement errors, and the effects of gauge relocations. They can also result in usable sequences dating back as far as that of the earliest established stations employed in their construction, although confidence in the records decreases and variations usually increase as fewer stations are used. There is also a real advantage in efficiencies of discussion and display where large bodies of data from numerous stations are to be considered simultaneously.

Although some reference is made below to the records of individual stations, a twelve-station composite record is the basis for most of the subsequent analysis. This record is derived by applying the following set of procedures for each variable: tabulating annual values for each station; computing mean values for each station over its period of record; calculating annual deviations from these means; algebraically summing deviations for all twelve stations by year; and averaging these annual sums. For plotting purposes, average annual deviations are added to or subtracted from a composite average of the twelve-station record means to achieve values with dimensions comparable to values actually recorded in the region.

Such composite values for each year should be regarded as index numbers, numbers that are helpful in understanding rainfall conditions for periods of years and in evaluating trends but which are possibly misleading in considering individual years. Neither distributional nor temporal weighting is attempted, and the effects of the region's varied terrain are ignored. Values might be considered representative of a location on the lower slopes of a fairly broad valley somewhere near to the centre of the region. Most of the stations comprising the record have this type of setting; the composite record means are strikingly similar to those for the station in the city of Paso Robles.

(iii) Graphical presentation of data. None of the several types of graphs that have been used to portray climatic time series is completely satisfactory. For instance, simple line plots of precipitation values by year and families of such plots representing several stations are commonly used in analysis of rainfall trends, but the interpretation of trends from them is often difficult and extremely subjective. Great year-to-year fluctuations may obscure long-term trends or periodic oscillations present in the data. Yet attempts to diminish the effects of annual fluctuations by using smoothing techniques may produce misleading impressions.

Moving averages (running means), or variations based on them, have long been a favourite mechanism for eliminating erratic and short-term movements in time series (e.g. Kincer, 1933, 1941; Hoyt *et al.*, 1936; McDonald, 1956; Burcham, 1957; Thomas, 1962; Hoel, 1966). Thomas (1962, p.22) summarized some of the advantages and disadvantages of moving averages as follows:

... they depict not only long-term cyclic fluctuations, but also any long-term trends that persist throughout the period of record; and they permit direct comparison of stations having great differences in length of record. However, there are the disadvantages that cyclic fluctuations may be obscured or amplified depending upon the method and time interval chosen for "smoothing"; and a single year of outstandingly excessive or deficient precipitation creates a plateau or trough whose significance is to be discounted.

Most of the weaknesses of moving averages are based on two characteristics that should be remembered when graphs of moving averages are interpreted (Hoel, 1966). Firstly, averaging distorts reality, and the extent of distortion or abstraction increases with length of the averaging period employed. A value plotted for a given year is not necessarily indicative of conditions during that year as the value is always dependent in part on conditions during previous and subsequent years, and plots of moving averages tend to anticipate and to prolong variations in actual values. Secondly, averaging techniques have a tendency to introduce spurious cycles, as Lewis (1960) dramatically showed.

Despite these cautions, moving averages seem to be best suited for displaying long-term precipitation tendencies, and they are superimposed on the plots of annual values in the graphs which follow to restrict the tendency to attribute undue significance to them. For ease of computation and application of significance tests, weighting is avoided and a ten-year base period is used. Calculation is based on the formula:

$$y = \frac{1}{10} \sum_{i=1}^{10} x_i$$

(III.1)

where x represents each of the successive annual values and y the ten-year mean. For example, in constructing graphs of ten-year moving averages the sum of values for the first to the tenth year of record is divided by 10 and the quotient plotted in a position half-way between the fifth and the sixth year. The mean of the second to the eleventh years is plotted between the sixth and seventh year.

Much of the interpretation of graphs is visual and qualitative. Objective conclusions are precluded by numerous arbitrary decisions on, for instance, the period of change required to initiate a trend and the amount of fluctuation required to distinguish a cycle. Interpretation is aided, however, by applying statistical tests to moving averages and unaveraged data.

(iv) Tests of significance. Two simple significance tests are used to aid the identification of precipitation trends or cycles. One, the so-called 'runs test', is applied to the composite record and the records of individual stations. The other test employs mathematical filters and is only used on the composite record.

The *runs test* is based on the argument that most sets of time-dependent data will contain fewer sequences of consecutive values above or below the median of these data than a set which is randomly distributed in time (Siegel, 1956; Hoel, 1966). With the existence of cycles and/or trends there would be a tendency towards longer runs of values above the median and of values below the median, and thus a tendency for the total observed numbers of runs, U, to be fewer than the number expected if the series were entirely random. For random sequences of values, the large-sample estimate of number of runs, μ_u, and standard deviation about this number for numerous samples, σ_u, are:

$$\mu_u = \frac{2n_1 n_2}{n_1 + n_2} + 1 \tag{III.2}$$

and

$$\sigma_u = \sqrt{\frac{2n_1 n_2 (2n_1 n_2 - n_1 - n_2)}{(n_1 + n_2)^2 (n_1 + n_2 - 1)}} \tag{III.3}$$

where n_1 is the number of values lying above the median and n_2 the number of values below. To test whether U is less than μ_u by an amount sufficient to rule out random fluctuation in the data, the difference between the two is transformed into z values by the relationship

$$z = \frac{U - \mu_{\hat{u}}}{\sigma_u} \tag{III.4}$$

and randomness is rejected, i.e. time dependence is assumed, according to a 5 per cent one-sided test if $z < -1.64$.

Thus the test is not able to differentiate cyclic and secular tendencies; this is normally left to visual interpretation. The value of the runs test lies in its ability to limit quickly subjective speculation about a set of data and to indicate whether or not effort should be made with more sophisticated and time-consuming searches for trends.

A second test, which tests for fluctuations suggested by plots of moving averages, consists of applying two independent mathematical filters to the same time series, one that passes high-frequency, year-to-year variations, and the other, a simple ten-year moving average that tends to preserve only low-frequency variations (Craddock, 1957). The artificial series generated by these filters are then used to obtain two independent estimates of the variance, and the ratio of these estimates is compared by means of Snedecor's F-test. If the estimates are similar, there is no reason to believe that the original series is not random. But if the estimate of variance derived from ten-year moving averages is considerably greater than the estimate based on the 'random element', the original series is considered to contain significant fluctuation. Further, if warranted, confidence limits may be derived from high-frequency variance estimates, superimposed on plots of ten-year moving averages and used to differentiate cyclic from secular trends.

Procedures followed in evaluating each series of precipitation data were: (1) to filter the series twice, once with the equation

$$y = -x_{i-1} + 2x_i - x_{i+1} \tag{III.5}$$

and once with the moving average given by equation (III.1); (2) to calculate the variance of the resulting high-frequency series (σ_s^2) and the variance of the averaged series (σ_{10}^2); (3) to find 60 $\sigma_{10}^2 / \sigma_s^2$, the ratio of the two estimates of the original series variance; and (4) to check this ratio for the number of terms in the original series against a plot of critical values at the 5 per cent significance level (Craddock, 1957).

(c) Results Data on amount, seasonal distribution, frequency, and intensity of precipitation in coastal California were analysed using the techniques described above. The record relevant to a consideration of amount and seasonal distribution begins in the winter of 1849—50; for frequency and intensity studies, the starting-point is 1871—2, the years in which manned U.S. Weather Bureau stations were established at four locations and reliable observations of light rainfalls began. Results of the analysis are discussed below.

(i) Variation in amount of precipitation. Previous studies of precipitation fluctuations and trends in California rely almost exclusively on annual totals and have arrived at remarkably different conclusions. An analysis of instrumental data and descriptive accounts of annual precipitation records in Los Angeles since 1770 led Lynch (1931, 1948) to conclude that there has been a general downward trend in the amount of rainfall in southern California during the last 200 years. Gray (1934), using regression analysis on records from 100 stations distributed throughout California, discerned a reduction of about 8 inches in annual precipitation for the state between 1850 and 1920! In contrast, Burcham (1956, 1957), working with data from twenty 'rangeland' stations situated mainly on the east side of the Central Valley, found no pronounced trend in annual precipitation since 1850. Similarly, Hoel (1966) used the annual precipitation record for Los Angeles as a textbook example of a trendless time series. Bull (1964b) emphasized the existence of periods of abundant rainfall, but did not specify any long-term tendencies.

The graph depicting annual precipitation values for the twelve-station composite record (Figure III.17) illustrates several points about variations in amount of precipitation in coastal California through time. Firstly, the record shows extreme variability in both amounts and sequence: annual values (represented by dots) show that wet years may experience many times more precipitation than dry years and the difference is commonly great between precipitation received in consecutive years. Secondly, neither annual values nor moving averages of these values (solid line) indicate a single continuous trend in precipitation amount over the entire period of record; indeed, the mean of the first 59 years of record differs from that of the last 59 years by only $0.43''$, a difference less than one would be likely to obtain if the two samples were drawn from the same population. Thirdly, if trends exist in annual precipitation the record is either too short to illustrate them, or they are short and cyclic.

The plot of moving averages does suggest cyclic tendencies, at least for the

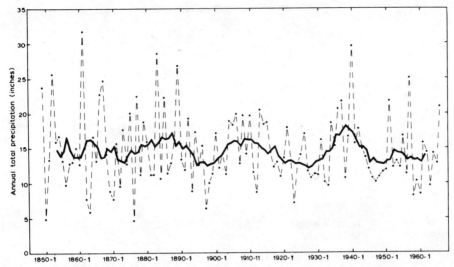

Figure III.17 The 12-station composite record: annual precipitation

central 90 years or so of record, with cycles having an amplitude of 4 to 6 inches and a periodicity of between 25 and 35 years. A number of predominantly wet years dominates the periods 1883—90, 1904—16, and 1936—44, although each of these periods contains years of normal or sub-normal precipitation. Intervening periods contain more than a usual number of dry years. Whether or not these apparent cycles define trends that are meaningful in terms of either atmospheric controls or general effects on watershed conditions and runoff is unknown, but statistical tests offer an objective and practical yardstick for evaluation.

The runs test failed to detect statistically significant variations (Table III.3). The composite data possess approximately the same number of runs as would be expected in a completely random series of comparable length. Application of the test to annual precipitation data for each of the twelve stations yielded only one significantly deviant case, Paso Robles, and this seems to reflect a rather significant gauge relocation. Filter analysis, which considers not only sequence but also magnitudes of observations, gives a variance ratio less than 1·0, i.e. the variance of the ten-year moving averages is somewhat less than an estimate of variance based on the year-to-year fluctuations contained in the annual precipitation data, whereas the presence of significant trends or cycles demands that variance of the averaged series should be considerably greater than that derived from short-term fluctuations (Table III.4).

Annual precipitation data may also be used as an index of drought and wet periods. In the analysis of precipitation records in southern Arizona, the termination of long-continued droughts by spells of unusually high rainfall was discussed. Table III.5 lists the principal wet and dry periods in California

Table III.3
Results of Runs Tests

Aspect of Precipitation	Station												
	Sacramento	Fresno	Bakersfield	San Francisco	Hollister	King City[1]	Paso Robles	San Luis Obispo	Santa Barbara	Los Angeles	San Bernardino	San Diego	Composite Record[2]
Annual Precipitation													
years of record	118	89	78	118	93	80	80	98	100	90	97	117	118
obs. no. of runs	55	42	37	67	54	38	33	54	51	51	48	54	57
est. no. of runs	59	45	40	60	47	41	41	50	51	46	49	59	57·5
probability	0·227	0·260	0·247	0·902	0·929	0·250	0·036*	0·792	0·500	0·855	0·419	0·172	0·462
Seasonal Distribution Index													
years of record	118	89	78	118	93	80	80	98	100	90	97	117	118
obs. no. of runs	62	44	41	50	45	44	34	44	57	45	47	49	59
est. no. of runs	60	43	39	60	46·5	41	39·5	50	50	44	47·5	57	58·3
probability	0·644	0·585	0·679	0·032*	0·376	0·750	0·104	0·111	0·922	0·587	0·458	0·063	0·552
Early Season Rainfall													
years of record	118	89	78	118	93	80	80	98	100	90	97	117	118
obs. no. of runs	59	48	41	63	49	42	44	52	61	43	46	55	57
est. no. of runs	60	44	40	60	47	41	41	50	51	46	48·5	59	57·5
probability	0·427	0·740	0·590	0·710	0·663	0·589	0·750	0·658	0·978	0·261	0·303	0·228	0·462
Precipitation Frequency													
years of record	90	79	70	96	70		70	73	70	90	70	95	96
0·01–0·24 inches per day													
obs. no. of runs	36	41	22	45	28		22	26	28	40	36	45	41
est. no. of runs	42	38	32·4	46	33·5		34	33·5	33·5	43	32·4	45·5	42·5
probability	0·092	0·756	0·004*	0·416	0·085		0·001*	0·032*	0·085	0·254	0·821	0·456	0·373

0·25—0·99 inches per day												
obs. no. of runs	51	53	30	38	40	35	28	32	47	30	31	45
est. no. of runs	46	42	31	42	36	32·5	34	33	46·5	32·4	34·5	46
probability	0·855	0·993	0·397	0·192	0·833	0·739	0·068	0·400	0·542	0·271	0·190	0·416
1·00″+ per day												
obs. no. of runs	39	25	28	36	28	32	24	20	37		28	29
est. no. of runs	43·8	28·6	29·5	38·7	31	31·9	28·5	22·6	42·8		28·7	37·9
probability	0·147	0·187	0·347	0·264	0·189	0·510	0·111	0·207	0·099		0·425	0·018*
Precipitation Intensity												
24-hour Maximum												
years of record	96	95		90					96		79	90
obs. no. of runs	41	48		40					51		43	48
est. no. of runs	46·4	47·5		46					49		39·5	46
probability	0·127	0·542		0·100					0·659		0·789	0·666
Maximum Day												
years of record	70		70		70		70	70		70		
obs. no. of runs	38		36		36		38	44		29		
est. no. of runs	34·8		36		36		36	36		34		
probability	0·785		0·500		0·500		0·685	0·973		0·108		
Daily Mean												
years of record	96	95	70	90	70	73	70	70	96	70	79	90
obs. no. of runs	53	54	42	50	42	40	24	38	51	29	48	37
est. no. of runs	46	47·5	36	46	36	37	35	36	49	36	40	46
probability	0·932	0·920	0·926	0·802	0·926	0·767	0·004*	0·685	0·659	0·046*	0·966	0·028*

1. Incomplete record of daily rainfalls. Used only in consideration of amounts and seasonal distribution.
2. Based on 12 stations in tests examining amount and seasonal distribution and 11 stations in tests of frequency and intensity.
* Significant at the 0·05 level.

Table III.4   F-Tests of Filtered Precipitation Series

Factor	Years of Record	Variance of High Frequency Series-V	Variance of Low Frequency Series-V_{10}	F-Ratio $60\dfrac{V_{10}}{V_s}$	Critical Region ($\alpha = 0.05$)
Annual Precipitation	118	176·90"	2·15"	0·73	$\geqslant 2\cdot00$
Seasonal Distribution Index	118	1131·37%	21·74%	1·15	$\geqslant 2\cdot00$
Early Season Precipitation	118	40·38"	0·51"	0·76	$\geqslant 2\cdot00$
24-hour Maximum Precipitation	96	1·2601"	0·0368"	1·75	$\geqslant 2\cdot10$
Maximum Daily Precipitation	70	2·4396"	0·0492"	1·21	$\geqslant 2\cdot50$
Mean Daily Intensity	96	0·02214" per rainy day	0·000379" per rainy day	1·03	$\geqslant 2\cdot10$
Falls of 0·01"—0·24"	96	135·046 days	1·495 days	0·66	$\geqslant 2\cdot10$
Falls of 0·25"—0·99"	96	117·177 days	1·276 days	0·65	$\geqslant 2\cdot10$
Falls of 1·00"+	96	17·849 days	0·460 days	1·55	$\geqslant 2\cdot10$

during the last 120 years. Both 'wet periods' and 'droughts' are complex concepts, depending largely on amount and frequency of precipitation and the time-periods between falls. In Table III.5, 'wet years' are those that received more than 5 inches above the long-term mean; 'wet periods' consist of two or more consecutive years in which precipitation exceeded the mean by 3 inches. 'Dry years' and 'dry periods' are defined by the same arbitrary amounts below the mean.

According to these standards, coastal California has experienced in the last 120 years 14 dry years and 8 dry periods which, when considered together, represent a total of 15 separate droughts. The number of separate wet periods is slightly greater. There does not appear to be any particular pattern of dry and wet periods in the time sequence.

Termination of droughts by wet years may have resulted in increased runoff and flooding, as argued in Part II. Droughts were followed immediately by wet years on three occasions since 1850 — during the winters of 1877–8, 1883–4, and 1913–14. The winter of 1883–4 was the third wettest in the composite record. It is conceivable that some instances of arroyo growth and possibly initiation were directly linked to these events, but there is no reason to suppose that they represent anything more than a temporal coincidence.

(ii) Seasonal distribution of precipitation. Year-to-year variations in the seasonal distribution of precipitation have significant effects on plant growth and vegetation cover in California (Bentley and Talbot, 1951; Burcham, 1957) and they may thus be important in controlling runoff. In the arroyo context, Bryan's (1925a) brief and apparently inaccurate reference to a statement by Visher provides the only direct assertion of this possibility, although several authors who discuss areas in the South-West, where atmospheric controls on summer and winter precipitation differ, have emphasized the role of summer precipitation (Martin, 1964; Leopold, Emmett, and Myrick, 1966).

Table III.5   *Wet Years and Periods,*
                     Drought Years and Periods

Wet Periods	Wet Years	Dry Years	Dry Periods
	1849–50		
		1850–1	
	1852–3		
	1861–2		
		1862–3	Summer 1862–
		1863–4	Fall 1864

Table III.5 continued

Fall 1866– Spring 1868	1866–7 1867–8		
		1869–70 1870–1	Summer 1869– Fall 1871
		1872–3	
	1875–6		
		1876–7	
	1877–8*		
	1883–4*		Summer 1881– Fall 1883
	1885–6		
	1889–90		
		1893–4	
		1897–8	Summer 1897– Fall 1900
Fall 1904– Spring 1907	1906–7		
	1908–9		
	1910–11		
Fall 1913– Spring 1916	1913–14*	1912–13	
		1923–4	
			Summer 1928– Fall 1931
			Summer 1932– Fall 1934
Fall 1936– Spring 1938	1936–7 1937–8		
	1940–1		
			Summer 1946– Fall 1950
	1951–2		
	1957–8		
		1958–9 1960–1	Summer 1958– Fall 1961
		1963–4	
	1966–7		

* Drought year or period terminated by a wet year. Horizontal lines indicate intervening years with approximately "normal" precipitation. For other definitions, see text.

In coastal California, where an overwhelming majority of precipitation received has a common source (the Pacific Ocean) and similar dynamics (disturbances associated with cyclonic activity), fluctuations in seasonal precipitation distribution might involve comparatively minor climatic shifts. For instance, a predominance of storms may occur either earlier or later in the rainy season than normal. On the basis of the hypothesis that precipitation occurring early in the rainy season (during the months of October, November, and December) would be less beneficial to plant cover and more apt to contribute to runoff once soils are saturated than precipitation later in the season, the proportion of rainfall for these three months relative to annual precipitation totals was investigated. Results are then presented in percentages. For example, a value of 53 per cent for Sacramento for the 1852–3 season indicates that 53 per cent of the total precipitation received during the period between 1 July 1852 and 30 June 1853 fell in the months of October, November, or December. No claim is made that a very high value for a given season definitely indicates high runoff during that year. The values are simply indices which might show, at most, climatically founded tendencies toward entrenchment or stability or, at least, the existence or insignificance of this aspect of rainfall as a variable worthy of consideration.

Greater faith may be placed in the long-term uniformity of these data than in that for any other aspect of precipitation analysed. Measurement error deriving from station relocation is essentially eliminated by working with proportions; movement of a gauge that might have affected efficiency or resulted in actual differences in amount of catch presumably would not influence relationships between amounts recorded in various months, except in the rare case of relocation during the rainy season which might invalidate the value computed for that year alone.

Plotted values of the seasonal distribution index (Figure III.18) exhibit considerable year-to-year variation, but the moving averages suggest some possible patterns. There appears to be a succession of irregular cycles between 20 and 35 years in length, with an amplitude averaging about 10 per cent, superimposed on a much longer cycle. One might conclude that channel activity could be in some way related to a general downward trend of this average (i.e. a slow shift in seasonal distribution towards later months of the rainy season) or to a tendency for high proportions of early-season precipitation during the nineteenth century.

Both the runs test (Table III.3) and the filter analysis (Table III.4) strongly suggest that to conjecture about cycles is fruitless. Seasonal distribution behaves in an essentially random manner, or at least has done so in coastal California since 1850. Considering data for individual stations, only one of the twelve, San Francisco, possesses an inordinately small number of runs.

Comparison of moving-average plots for annual precipitation (Figure III.17) and the index of seasonal distribution (Figure III.18) suggests that a

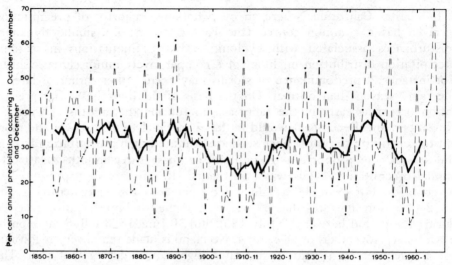

Figure III.18 The 12-station composite record: seasonal distribution index

second measure of seasonality should be examined. The two plots behave quite differently for the last 75 years, but before about 1895 (and especially during the 1880s) there is a reasonable correspondence between them. The correspondence in the 1880s of abundant rainfall with concentration of rainfall early in the season suggests that conditions then might have been more conducive to high runoff than in later years, although a year-by-year

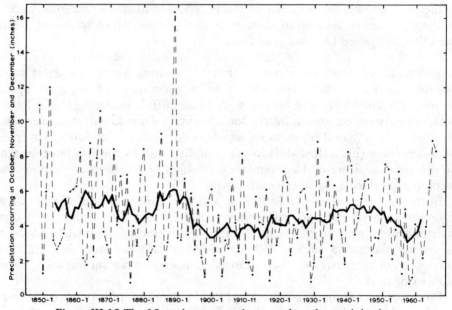

Figure III.19 The 12-station composite record: early precipitation

comparison of unaveraged values shows an excessive amount of rainfall in only two years (1885–6, 1889–90).

In an attempt to evaluate this phenomenon, it was decided to approach the relationship by examining the composite record for changes in amount of early-season precipitation. In a general way, this represents a combination of the seasonal distribution index with annual amounts, and should greatly accentuate differences between the 1880s and subsequent wet periods. Composite sums of October, November, and December precipitation are plotted by year in Figure III.19. As with previous plots, unaveraged values show great fluctuation, but there does seem to be a general tendency toward decreasing early-season precipitation through time. This trend is especially apparent for extreme high values; composite values exceeded 10 inches on four occasions, all before the turn of the century. The ten-year moving averages represent these tendencies well and indicate that a sharp decline in amount of early-season precipitation occurred in the 1890s, a drop amounting to approximately 1 inch per year if years of record before and after 1895 are compared.

Results of significance tests tend to minimize visual impressions derived from the graph; none of the tests, of either the composite or individual station records, indicated that suggested shifts in early-season precipitation are statistically significant. Because distribution of values is highly skewed, the runs test is probably much more valid than comparison of means. The sequence contains approximately the same number of runs as would be expected from a random selection of values, and the period before 1891 contains a proportionate number of years with values below the record median (50 per cent) and a proportionate number of runs. The variance ratio yielded by filter analysis is 0·76, far below the critical value of 2·00, implying that the shifts in amount of early-season precipitation in the 1890s is of doubtful importance in the light of the great year-to-year variation embraced by the series.

Whether or not apparent trends in early-season precipitation are significant to the problem of valley trenching or the more general question of modern climatic change is a matter of conjecture. It might be noted that the high arch of the moving-average graph is largely a result of one extremely wet month, December 1889, which was characterized by a very large number of not particularly intense falls. Throughout the 1880s and 1890s there were at least as many years with deficiencies in early season precipitation as there were years with surpluses.

(iii) *Rainfall frequency*. Results of Leopold's (1951a) analysis of rainfall in New Mexico and the analysis for southern Arizona make a consideration of possible variations in the frequency of light, moderate, and heavy rainfalls highly desirable in California. Some results already exist for California. Bull (1964b) visually examined data for Sacramento (1881–1958) and Mendota Dam (1901–58) using three-year moving averages of five-year moving aver-

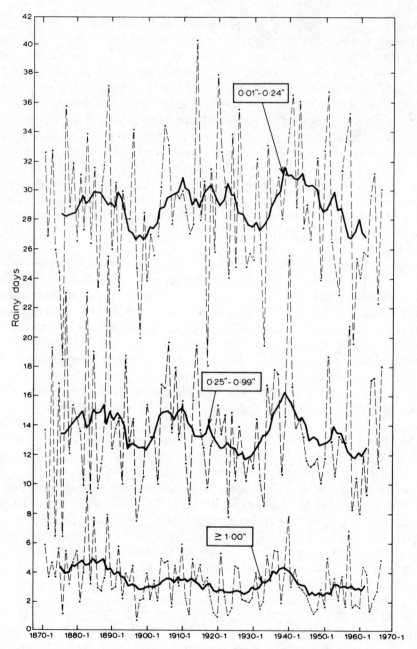

Figure III.20 The 11-station composite record: early daily precipitation frequency

ages for daily rainfalls in four different size classes. He found that (Bull, 1964b, p.258) 'The periods of most of the arroyo cutting (1875 to 1895, 1935 to 1945) also were periods of above normal daily and annual rainfall. A combination of high frequency of the large rainfalls and a low frequency of the small rainfalls coincided to produce above normal runoff, thus allowing the above normal runoff to erode the stream channels.'

In an unpublished study, Reeves examined daily precipitation since 1897 tabulated in six size classes for twelve stations and concluded that the data contained no significant cyclic or secular changes.

The number of daily rainfalls each year in three size classes $(0 \cdot 01 - 0 \cdot 24''$; $0 \cdot 25 - 0 \cdot 99''$; and $1 \cdot 00'' +)$ for an eleven-station composite record are plotted in Figure III.20. Only first- and second-order weather stations were used for the years 1871—96. King City was eliminated from the record because of gaps and discrepancies in reporting daily falls in 1917 and from 1920 to 1927.

Plots of annual values demonstrate considerable year-to-year variation, but 'smoothing' by the use of running means results in three lines with rather similar configurations. There appear to be cyclic fluctuations, much like those for annual precipitation, with peaks occurring about 1885, 1910, and 1940, and depressions at approximately 1900, 1930, and 1960. The curve representing large daily rainfalls $(\geq 1 \cdot 00'')$ seems to show a continuous downward trend amounting to perhaps one fall per year over the past 100 years.

Neither the runs test nor the filter analysis of the composite record indicates statistically significant deviations from randomness in any of the three series. But data for individual stations do suggest some time dependence in the light-rainfall category $(0 \cdot 01'' - 0 \cdot 24'')$: three stations possessed numbers of runs sufficiently low to be significant at the 5 per cent level. Whether or not frequencies of light or heavy falls may have differed by amounts sufficient to have affected stream channel morphology before 1870 is not established by this analysis. The analysis of data since that time shows no *regional* secular trends, but it is conceivable that specific light-rainfall trends at three stations could have affected local runoff conditions.

(iv) Precipitation intensity. Two aspects of precipitation intensity were examined for possible fluctuations — mean daily intensity and intensity of major storms.

Mean daily intensity is closely related to precipitation frequency and may be viewed in some respects as a summary statement of concurrent fluctuations in all three size classes. Mean daily intensity is calculated by dividing the precipitation received each year by the number of days on which measurable precipitation is recorded (Monkhouse and Wilkinson, 1963). The value thus obtained is scaled in inches per rainy day and is assumed to be indicative of the intensity of storms experienced during the year. Leopold, Emmett, and Myrick (1966) used the measure on data for Santa Fé (New

Mexico) to substantiate arguments for differences in erosional activity in the area before and after about 1880. It can be argued that changes in mean daily intensity might reflect runoff variations arising from either the influences of precipitation events on availability of water to plants and thus on the condition of vegetation, or through direct physical relationships between short-term intensities, soil infiltration capacities, and runoff production.

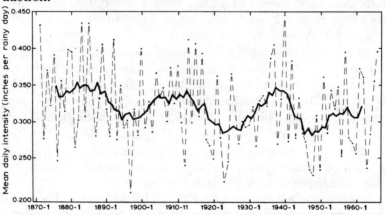

Figure III.21
The 11-station composite record: mean daily precipitation intensity

Data for coastal California are summarized by eleven-station composite values of mean daily intensity in Figure III.21. The plot of unaveraged values maintains considerable variability, but it assumes a cyclic appearance with high intensities common in the 1870s and 1880s, the first two decades of this century, the late 1930s and early 1940s and in the 1960s. Unusually low intensities mark the 1897–8 season and years surrounding 1920 and 1950. Moving averages greatly accentuate this pattern, describing three cycles with a length of about 30 years and an amplitude of about 0·06 inches per day which appears to decrease slightly with time. The first half of the record seems to possess a slight downward tendency. Statistical tests failed to identify any significant cyclic or long-term fluctuations for the region as a whole (Tables III.3 and III.4). On the basis of these tests, it appears that fluctuations of average annual intensity have, at least since 1870, behaved in a random manner.

It is possible that the initiation and extension of arroyos coincided with exceptionally heavy storms, storms that were perhaps heavier than those occurring in recent years. A measure of 'heavy storms' used here is annual maximum intensity. For official Weather Bureau stations – Sacramento, Fresno, San Francisco, Los Angeles, and San Diego – this consists of the greatest 24-hour rainfall in inches recorded each year. Absence of hourly data for co-operative stations – Hollister, King City, Paso Robles, Santa Barbara, and San Bernardino – led to substitution of maximum calendar-day intensities. San Luis Obispo and Bakersfield were omitted because of inconsistencies in the type of measurements reported.

As might be expected, correspondence between stations is not particularly close. On only rare occasions might a given storm be expected to set records at more than one station, even if stations are separated by only tens of miles, because areas of excessive precipitation, even in large-scale cyclonic disturbances, are localized and short-lived. The great storm on New Year's Day 1934 (31 Dec.–1 Jan.) in the Los Angeles area, which dropped up to 10 inches of rain at several lowland stations, was notable only at one other station analysed, San Bernardino. Variation from year to year at all stations appears erratic, although a few periods of years at some stations might be characterized by generally high or low maximum intensities as, for example, at Santa Barbara in the decade around 1910, and at Los Angeles in the 1880s and 1930s. Generalization about regional tendencies is difficult.

Five-station composite values for both maximum 24-hour and maximum daily intensities are shown in Figure III.22. Much of the complexity of individual station plots is reduced even by traces of unaveraged composite

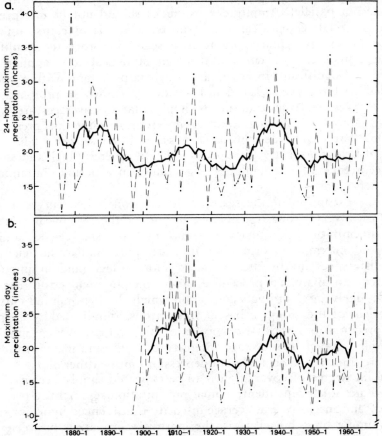

Figure III.22 The 5-station composite record: (a) maximum 24-hour and (b) maximum daily precipitation intensity

values. Ten-year moving averages of both 24-hour and daily intensities assume remarkably similar configurations, suggesting, once again, cyclic fluctuations with a periodicity of between 25 and 30 years. Intense storms were characteristic of the 1880s, the early 1910s, and the decade from about 1935 to 1945. Data from Weather Bureau stations tend to emphasize the latter period, and those from co-operative observers emphasize the period from about 1905 to 1915. This difference in stress could easily arise from imprecision of intensity estimates based on the calendar day, magnification of measurement error associated with gauge relocation by using the composite record of few stations, and/or sampling error. As with all other aspects of precipitation considered, tests failed to detect any significant fluctuation in either of these series (Tables III.3 and III.4).

(v) Relationships between aspects. Figure III.23 represents an attempt to summarize the tendencies of precipitation discussed up to this point. Ten-year moving averages representing each aspect of the composite record are plotted in parallel. Amplitudes of curves should not be interpreted to indicate the relative significance of aspects, which is of course unknown. Absolute values are replaced by relative scales in order to simplify and facilitate comparison of curves. Although statistical tests applied above indicated no significant trend in any single aspect, and with respect to controlled patterns even cast doubt on cycles shown so prominently by moving averages, it is not meant to imply that the averages are without meaning. Traces of moving averages *are* representative of precipitation conditions that were experienced. Depressions in curves genuinely indicate periods of below normal values; peaks indicate generally high values (or, at least, occurrence of outstandingly high values in a period containing few notable deficiencies).

With the exception of the seasonal distribution index, curves in Figure III.23 show a very strong resemblance to one another. Ten-year averages of annual precipitation, frequency of rains in three size classes, and both average and maximum storm intensities are quite similar, sufficiently for minor differences to be attributed to more-or-less random uncommon occurrences, to analytical procedures, or to measurement error. The last is especially likely in recording values upon which the light-rainfall curve, the most deviant of the group, is based. Wet periods, as indicated by the plot of annual precipitation, were also periods of higher than average number of rains of all sizes, greater average intensity of rains, and major storms. Dry periods are similarly associated with depressions in the other plots.

A certain degree of covariation is to be expected simply because aspects examined are not independent; annual precipitation represents a product of frequency and intensity and average intensity is influenced by major storms. What is interesting, however, is the positive correlation between storm frequency and intensity, a relationship that has existed certainly since 1870 and may be inferred well back into the nineteenth century. There is no

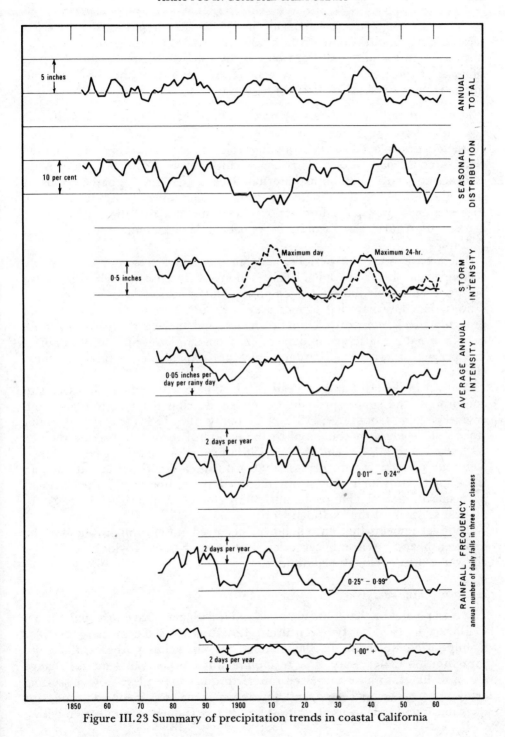

Figure III.23 Summary of precipitation trends in coastal California

evidence to support a mechanism similar to that hypothesized for New Mexico by Leopold. Comparison of these traces leads to the conclusion that in this region rainfall conditions during the wet 1880s, presumably the time of greatest erosional activity, were little different from those of the years immediately preceding the two world wars.

(d) Conclusions The analysis of precipitation records in coastal California gives no reason to believe that secular or cyclic changes in precipitation characteristics played a determining role in arroyo formation. Marked changes could have occurred in the decades before 1850, but there is no evidence to justify such an assumption. Secular trends are apparently absent since the middle of the nineteenth century. Quasi-regular fluctuations are suggested by some graphs, but statistical tests indicate that these are no more marked or regular than would be expected in a random series of observations.

There have been wet periods, and much channel erosion very probably accompanied them, as Bull (1964b) observed. Intense droughts have also occurred and contributed to temporary deterioration of watershed conditions that may have led to increases in runoff. But such wet periods and droughts hardly constitute climatic change, and there is no reason to think that their nature differed fundamentally from similar events before or after the period of arroyo initiation. They are expectable features of most climates.

At least in the last hundred years or so, climate within the region seems to conform to the simple probability models developed by hydrologists and engineers (e.g. Goodridge, 1969). Certainly the 1880s contained major storms, unusual when compared to the period of record, but so did the late 1930s and early 1940s, and the late 1960s seemed to be setting new records. Yet none of these storms necessarily constitutes a significant deviation from the climate of which they form recorded parts, nor would they present particularly unobtainable probabilities if predicted on the basis of any 20- to 30-year segment of the existing record.

The fact remains that entrenchment occurred in Californian valleys in the nineteenth and twentieth centuries. It seems advisable to look for causes elsewhere than in climatic conditions.

Livestock Numbers

There is no doubt that fundamental land-use changes have affected coastal California in the last two centuries: Los Angeles is the most spectacular manifestation of them. In the context of regional hypotheses of arroyo formation, it is necessary first to inquire which aspects of land-use change are most likely to have increased runoff through the valleys now possessing arroyos, when they occurred, and how much change was involved. Important questions relating land use to runoff are then examined in connection with a discussion of vegetation changes and vegetation-runoff relationships.

The extensive land-use changes most likely to have influenced runoff in coastal California during the late nineteenth and early twentieth century are cultivation, logging, burning, and grazing by domestic livestock. The first three of these can be quickly dismissed. Cultivation may be important in its hydraulic effects, but it probably had little to do with greatly increasing runoff upstream or upslope of arroyos because cultivation has affected few areas away from the valley floor itself, a small proportion of any drainage basin. Logging may have been important in some drainage basins, but most of those with arroyos have very small or poor and undesirable timber stands within their catchments. Burning could have been significant, but the available evidence suggests that burning practices were not particularly unusual at the time of arroyo formation. For instance, man-induced fires were less frequently used as a means of driving game from grass and shrubland in the nineteenth century than they were in the eighteenth century, and urban-fringe fires near Los Angeles were less frequent than they have been in the twentieth century.[66] Furthermore, many important components of the vegetation, especially in the chaparral, show sophisticated adaptations to repeated burning that evolved over a very long period of time.

The only widespread land-use change likely to have increased runoff in most watersheds containing arroyos was associated with the introduction of domesticated livestock. Livestock-ranching was a mainstay of the growing mission and secular economies by the end of the eighteenth century in coastal California (Cleland, 1941; Burcham, 1957). When the secularization of mission lands was completed in 1844, cattle-ranching was the focus of almost all economic activity in the region and it remained unchallenged until major droughts and declining markets in the 1860s resulted in a great reduction of the herds and a change to sheep ranching.

Quantitative data with which to describe precisely the changing livestock pressures on the land are rather poor before 1850. By 1780 there can have been no more than several thousand cattle, sheep, horses, and mules in the region, and between 1781 and 1848 it appears that natural increase alone sustained growth in numbers. Table III.6 lists several estimates of livestock numbers between 1769 and 1850, estimates that are certainly more thought-provoking than accurate. The figures exclude privately owned cattle and sheep, mission horses and mules, and feral animals. They do indicate, however, that before California was annexed there were already large numbers of livestock present. Cattle hide exports were estimated to be 200,000 annually in the years immediately preceding 1838, and another observer quoted a figure of 150,000 in 1841 (Burcham, 1957). Under sustained-yield conditions, these figures would require a cattle population of at least 500,000. Their distribution is not known, but in view of mission-land location, casual herding practices in the unfenced landscape, and feral livestock, it is clear that all of the subsequently entrenched drainage basins

Table III.6   Numbers of Cattle and Sheep Prior to 1850*

Source	Year	Cattle	Sheep	Remarks
Palóu, 1927	1769		94	Total for All Missions
Palóu, 1927	1773	205		Total for All Missions
Carmen et al., 1892	1790		1,700	Total for All Missions
Carmen et al., 1892	1797		6,000+	Total for All Missions
Dobie, 1941	1800	1,000,000+		California
Forbes, 1839	1831	142,901	153,455	Total for All Missions
Duflot de Mofras, 1844	1834	423,000	321,500**	Total for All Missions
Bolton, 1917	1834	396,000	321,000	Total for All Missions
Carmen et al., 1892	(1834)?		150,000	Maximum for All Missions
Engelhardt, 1920	(1834)?	186,000		Maximum for All Missions
Duflot de Mofras, 1844	1842	28,000	31,600**	Remaining at Missions

 * Source: Burcham, 1957.
**Including goats and hogs.

had been grazed by 1840, and some had been grazed as early as the 1770s.

Data from 1850 onwards are much more precise than early estimates, although they suffer from under-reporting. U.S. Census data for California livestock are shown in Table III.7. These totals do not reflect several important developments: expansion of the livestock industry away from the coastal zone, changes in stock-raising practices, progressive appropriation of the better land for crop agriculture, and a tendency for fewer and fewer livestock to be kept on rangelands.

Table III.7   *U.S. Census Tabulations of California Livestock*
1850—1950*
(in thousands)

Year	Cattle	Sheep	Horses and Mules	Goats
1850	263	18	23	
1860	1,180	1,088	170	
1870	611	2,768	229	
1880	664	4,152	266	
1890	1,367	2,475	454	
1900	1,445	2,563	508	109
1910	2,064	2,417	541	138
1920	2,008	2,400	468	116
1930	2,103	4,084	298	82
1940	2,056	1,707	189	58
1950	2,757	2,057	115	48

* Source: Burcham, 1957.

Burcham (1957) used data from numerous decennial census reports to refine information on livestock numbers. He considered sheep, traditionally extensive grazers in California, and 'beef cattle' as indices of range use. Burcham stressed that his figures, especially those for years before 1900, underestimate totals. For instance, independent estimates suggest the state data deficiencies for sheep in 1880 were 28 per cent, and for beef cattle, 21 per cent. Figures III.24 and III.25 show Burcham's county data assembled for units representative of most of the coastal region, and its northern, central, and southern sections.

Figure III.24 depicts the changes in range livestock numbers for the region and state from 1850 to 1950. To allow comparability between trends for different types of livestock, totals are presented in animal units, a measure representing grazing requirements of the average steer; the assumed relationship is that one steer = five sheep = one animal unit (Burcham, 1957).

The most noteworthy feature is the *lack* of substantial growth in numbers during the last half of the nineteenth century. Although relative numbers of sheep and cattle vary considerably, annual totals normally fall in the range

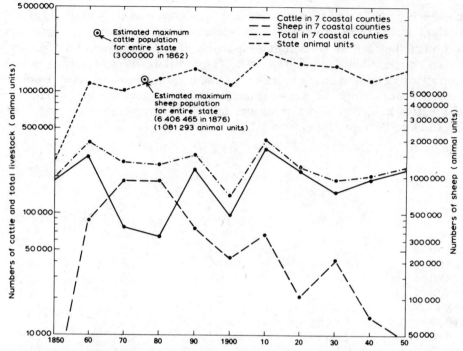

Figure III.24 Livestock numbers, 1850–1950 (based on Burcham, 1957)

200,000 — 400,000. If one accepts the 1834 estimates of Duflot de Mofras and Bolton (Table III.6) and allows the assumption that two-thirds of their estimate were in the coastal region, there is a real possibility that numbers did not increase significantly after 1830. There is corroborative evidence for this contention. Robinson (1947) estimated that in 1829 the San Gabriel Mission, in the southern part of the region, possessed 80,000 — 100,000 cattle, a number comparable to the highest figures reported for the entire southern third of the region since 1850. And in 1829 there were three other missions, several private land grants, and the Los Angeles pueblo within the same area. In short, much of coastal California may have attained or even exceeded its sustained yield livestock capacities before California joined the Union.

Two further arguments support this conclusion. Firstly, grazing practices before 1850, and to a certain extent until the 'Fence Laws' of the 1870s and 1880s, allowed livestock to roam the open range. Before fencing, it was of little advantage — indeed it was potentially dangerous — for a land owner to limit his herds and flocks: if his own livestock did not graze his land, his neighbours' livestock would. The short-term advantage went to the rancher who allowed his stock to grow to the maximum he could harvest. Also, wild cattle and horses, roaming on land largely free of natural predators, in general were able to multiply to the limits of available forage. If the range contained as few as 100,000 cattle in the mid-1830s, it is most unlikely that maximum sustained range capacities were not equalled or exceeded by the mid-1840s. Secondly, there is ample evidence (Burcham, 1957) that livestock numbers were flirting with the natural limits of the range in some areas as early as 1821 when, because of inadequate precipitation in the winter of 1820—1 and subsequent meagre forage, the colonial government initiated a programme to slaughter wild horses. The drought of 1828—30 prompted further killing and is said to have caused the starvation of 40,000 mission cattle (Burcham, 1957).

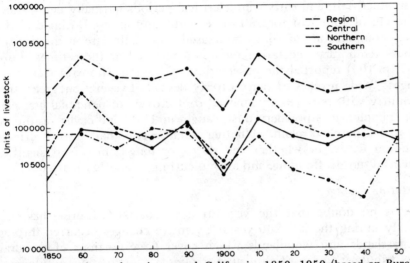

Figure III.25 Livestock numbers in coastal California, 1850—1950 (based on Burcham, 1957)

Figure III.25 shows that the decline of livestock numbers during dry years continued in the last half of the nineteenth century. The mid-1860s and late 1890s were especially disastrous, but there were other 'bad years'. Burcham (1957) reports estimates that the drought of 1856—7 killed 70,000 cattle in Los Angeles County alone. Wet years, together with a declining market for meat, in the late 1850s and early 1860s produced in 1862 what was probably the largest range-cattle herd ever in coastal California. But two consecutive years of drought that followed had effects that were reflected in cattle numbers for two decades: the state herd declined by between 200,000 and a million head; and half the cattle in Los Angeles County died (Burcham, 1957). Conversion of ranges to sheep production during the 1860s and 1870s resulted (Figure III.24), and this accounts in part for the maintenance of range use at high levels during these years.

The graphs for the three sections of the region show very similar trends to that for the region as a whole (Figure III.25), except that data for 1850 suggest initial expansion of livestock numbers on previously underused ranges may have been occurring in parts of the central and northern areas until the 1860s.

Intense pressures of livestock on the native vegetation of coastal California thus date back to the 1860s and in the more accessible and attractive locations such pressures were probably present some 20 to 40 years earlier. The only areas containing arroyos that escaped grazing by maintained herds of domesticated livestock before 1850 are the eastern slopes of the Coast Ranges, a few isolated areas within the ranges themselves, and the more rugged mountainous areas in the south.

It should be stressed that these pressures were not continuous. The normal rainfall regime dictated a marked annual fluctuation of pressures, with late-summer, fall, and early-winter critical periods normally being alleviated by growth of abundant forage in late winter and spring. During droughts, of course, competition for forage increased, especially late in the dry season. Serious, temporary vegetation depletion resulted at these times. Burcham (1957, p. 193) reported the observations of several who witnessed the 1864 drought: 'Wide reaches of range utterly devoid of vegetation; great stretches of country with only closely gnawed root crowns of perennial grasses; bare earth trampled to a powdery dust, caught up by "wind devils" as they raced across the parched plain.' Whether such events had *lasting* effects on vegetation cover, or whether the short- or long-term effects significantly influenced runoff, flooding, and arroyo cutting, is another matter.

Vegetation Change

There is no doubt that the vegetation of coastal California has changed radically during the last 200 years. Extensive changes occurred throughout the grasslands and woodlands which cover large portions of the drainage basins tributary to most Californian arroyos. Unfortunately, only one aspect of these changes is well documented — the floristic composition of the herbaceous cover. Those changes of vegetation presumed to be pertinent to the regulation of runoff are matters of speculation.

The success of exotic species invading the grass-covered areas of California is remarkable. Burcham (1957) noted that in some parts of the State '. . . it is possible to work on range surveys for several days at a time without recording a single native perennial herb' (p. 185), and 'few places on earth, if any, have had such a wholesale replacement of native plants by introduced species' (p. 198). Three plants probably preceded the Spanish missionaries into California and at least 15 more exotics were present by 1824 (Hendry, 1931; Hendry and Bellue, 1925). Robbins (1940) compiled a list of 526 exotic species growing wild within California and showed that 91 of these, including 20 grass species, were established by 1860. In the grasslands, most of the important introductions have been annuals, both grasses and forbs, and a large number of these are commonly considered to be weeds (Robbins, 1940; Clark, 1956; Burcham, 1957). With few exceptions, introductions were unintentional, unrecorded, and probably undetected for a number of years after their arrival.

Much of the responsibility for this invasion rests with the actions of immigrants, who both bridged natural barriers between potentially competitive plants, and introduced domestic livestock which placed heavy stresses on the palatable native species. But why the exotics were so successful is not clear. There was no similar success in the grasslands of southern Arizona (Hastings and Turner, 1965), New Mexico, Texas, or the Great Plains (Clark, 1956) despite some similarities of land-use history. Possible explanations may lie in the similarity between California's environment and those in which many invading species evolved, the rather unlikely possibility of relatively greater livestock pressures in California than elsewhere in the South-West, the distinctiveness of California's climates, soils, and aboriginal inhabitants, and the absence of significant pre-contact grazing pressures from indigenous faunas (Clark, 1956). Whatever the cause, complete transformation of the grasslands and the grassy understorey of woodlands followed closely behind settlement.

Three difficulties are involved in attempting to evaluate the relevance of these floristic changes to possible changes in runoff. First, the general character of the grassland prior to the establishment of exotics is not well known (Beetle, 1947; Clark, 1956) because most early descriptions postdate the establishment of the most common exotic species, such as wild oats (Avena fatua). Secondly, invasions of individual species are poorly documented and certainly occurred at different times and in different places, and their progress can only be recounted in terms of a few stages perceived to be of importance. Thirdly, estimates of the relative densities and seasonality of the original plant cover and its successors must be based on general information.

All descriptions of the dominant species and general appearance of the pre-Spanish grassland, oak woodland, and coniferous woodland of coastal California are necessarily historical reconstructions based on general descriptions, a few early botanical collections, and intuition. The consensus view is that the herbaceous cover was composed of perennial bunchgrass dominated mainly by various needlegrasses (Stipia lepida, S. pulchra, and S. coronata). Blue wild-rye (Elymus glaucus), pine bluegrass (Poa scabrella), deergrass (Muhlenbergia rigens), June grass (Koeleria cristata), California melic (Melica imperfecta), California brome (Bromus carinatus), and various three-awn grasses (Aristida spp.) were some of the important associated grasses. In certain situations perennial sod-forming grasses (e.g. beardless wild-rye, Elymus triticoides), or annuals (e.g. various fescues, Festuca spp.) must have been locally dominant, and some annuals were doubtless spread extensively through all associations. The cover also contained a variety of forbs, both annual and perennial.

Density and height of the cover varied greatly from place to place, season to season, and wet year to dry, but two factors bearing on runoff production should be kept in mind. Firstly, ' . . . native bunchgrasses, being disposed in clumps, did not wholly occupy the ground surface' (Burcham, 1957, p. 191), although the proportion of bare ground commonly exposed and changes in this proportion following introduction of foreign species are not matters of record. Secondly, whatever proportion of the surface covered by bunch-grasses, before the introduction of livestock their dried stalks and leaves remained largely intact through dry periods of the year, until replaced by new winter and spring growth, so that some of the surface area was permanently protected.

The cover of perennial bunchgrasses began to evolve with the introduction and spread of each new introduced plant. Changes were probably subtle during some years, but they were undoubtedly greatly accentuated by droughts, especially when they coincided with heavy grazing pressures. By using a few conspicuous species as indicators, Burcham (1957, p. 198) constructed a general sequence of grassland change for Californian range-lands.

There have been three major stages of succession in the annual plant cover;
... The first stage, characterized especially by wild oats and mustard, was most prominent between 1845 and 1855. The second stage, characterized by filaree, mouse barley, nitgrass and by native annuals like foxtail fescue, occurred from about 1855 to 1865 or 1870. The third stage, in which introduced barleys, red brome, silver hairgrass, and a number of forbs were dominant, began about 1870 to 1880 and is quite widespread today.
... This chronological sequence in dominance of the plant cover corresponds to the descending scale of annual plant succession on California ranges...

In coastal California and the San Joaquin Valley the first stage was apparent as early as 1833.

The possible effect of these changes on runoff are not readily apparent. Three aspects of the changing cover might be considered to increase runoff: decreased density, decreased height (a reflection of plant material present), and shortening of the growing season (Table III.8). It is possible that

Table III.8

	'Original' to Stage 1	Stage 1 to Stage 2	Stage 2 to Stage 3
Density	increase	decrease	decrease
Height	increase?	decrease	decrease
Growing season	decrease	decrease?	decrease
Possible effect on runoff	decrease?	increase	increase

replacement of native bunchgrass by wild oats, mustard, and associated exotics had, in itself, little effect on runoff. Indeed, a tendency towards decreased runoff may have accompanied this change (Table III.8), because 'Plants which replaced the pristine cover usually occupy the ground more completely than did the native perennials, densities of 50 to 70 per cent or higher being fairly common except on heavily used ranges' (Burcham, 1957, p.199). The wild-oat-dominated cover was probably also taller than the bunchgrasses, although the change to an annual habit may have had a compensating effect on runoff. Subsequent changes (stage 1 to 2; stage 2 to 3), if they had any general effects at all on runoff, probably only acted to increase runoff slightly. The probable ramifications for density, height, and seasonality are indicated by the character of existing stands of grass that appear, at least in species composition, to represent each of the three successional stages (Burcham, 1957). Average values for contemporary widely scattered samples of each stage show decreasing density of surface cover (from 40 per cent to 30 per cent to 25 per cent), and decreasing height, along with predominance of undesirable forbs under roughly equal grazing pressures. Seasonality of the cover is not specified by Burcham.

In terms of relative hydrological effects, however, the importance of these changes is uncertain. The vegetation transformation may have created general tendencies towards increases (or decreases) of runoff over at least the last 150 years. But short-term fluctuations of cover, especially those brought by drought, would probably have masked most of the secular tendencies and would probably have been much more important in directly influencing runoff.

Vegetation, Soil, and Runoff

The foundation of most regional hypotheses — that vegetation cover and soil conditions regulate the production of runoff from slopes during storms — is rather surprisingly one of the weakest links in the rainfall-erosion argument. Two observations emphasize this weakness. First, the overwhelming strength of rational argument that both decreased vegetation cover and disturbance of soil should act to increase runoff (Lull, 1964; Storey, Hobba, and Rosa, 1964) conflicts sharply with the results of some empirical field studies on the hydrological effects of removing vegetation from various watersheds in California. Secondly, if one assumes that rational arguments are correct (that runoff *is* controlled by vegetation and soils), it is difficult to arrive at estimates of how much additional runoff might have accompanied the various secular or short-term vegetation changes that are known to have occurred. It is quite possible, for example, that increases in discharge resulting from such changes in watershed conditions were insignificant relative to the hydraulic effects of localized modifications of valley floors.

(a) Results of empirical studies In California no empirical data are to hand on runoff from controlled experimental plots involving partial removal of herbaceous cover and slight compaction of soils (i.e. the kinds of changes that would presumably accompany increases in grazing pressures over *extensive* portions of watersheds). However, there are some studies that have attempted to evaluate the influence of complete removal of cover (largely

chaparral of varying densities) by burning on both amounts and rates of runoff. Unfortunately, these studies have used different procedures and neither their observations nor their general conclusions are conformable. Rowe (1944, p.85) summarizes some of the findings as follows:

The results of 15 years of rather extensive runoff- and erosion-plot and infiltration studies carried on by the California Station in woodland and chaparral types of the State show that burning of the vegetation has, almost without exception, resulted in decreased infiltration-capacities and increased surface runoff and erosion-rates. Infiltration-surveys made in connection with flood-control surveys by the United States Department of Agriculture in the Pajaro, Santa Maria, and Santa Yñez river drainages, and including more than 600 infiltration-capacity measurements, show that burning of the chaparral and forest cover in these watersheds results in reduced infiltration-capacities of all the soils tested. Findings closely parallel to these have also been reported by Dr. A.W. Sampson of the University of California as a result of his investigations in the chaparral and woodland types of northern California.

The magnitudes of increase in runoff that may be involved are suggested in an unpublished analysis by Rowe et al. of fire in small, rugged, chaparral-covered watersheds of southern California (reported in Storey, Hobba, and Rosa, 1964). Various generalized curves for 'fire-effect ratios' (peak discharge after burning ÷ peak discharge before burning) for a wide range of probable storm discharges and years since burning (vegetation recovery intervals) indicate that burning has great and lasting effects: for example, peak storm discharges of a magnitude expectable on an average of once a year are increased by about four times during the year immediately following burning, two and a half times during the second year, and about twice during the third; for the maximum storm with a recurrence interval of ten years, the increases are of the order of thirty times in the first year, six times in the second, and three times in the third!

The results of Veihmeyer (1950; 1951; 1953; Veihmeyer and Johnson, 1944) contrast with those of Rowe et al. Working with 17 paired plots monitored for as many as 18 years within chaparral areas in central and northern California, Veihmeyer found that runoff from burned plots was not significantly different from that of vegetated plots either in amount or frequency. He concluded that '. . . . removal of vegetation by burning has not impaired the infiltration capacity of the soil nor has the runoff of water been accelerated and erosion increased' (Veihmeyer, 1951, p.226).

It is difficult to accept that Veihmeyer's conclusions are generally applicable as they contradict most accepted beliefs and evidence from elsewhere (Lull, 1964). But they do illustrate a critical point: that broad generalizations about the effects of vegetation depletion on runoff, especially when they are subtle, may not apply to specific sites, or to extended periods of time at a wide range of sites.

(b) Estimates of possible increases in slope runoff The problem of estimating how much of an increase in runoff may have resulted from depletion of vegetation may be approached through several highly empirical engineering

techniques. Eight different techniques designed to predict runoff changes resulting from proposed 'land treatments' are summarized by Ogrosky and Mockus (1964) and by Storey, Hobba, and Rosa (1964). Some of these techniques are sophisticated and require extensive field measurement of watershed conditions, but four relatively simple methods seem suitable for an attempt to gain some crude estimates of how vegetation changes during the last hundred years might have increased runoff: the so-called 'Rational' method, the Cook method, the U.S. Soil Conservation method of runoff curves, and a multiple regression method developed for southern California by Anderson (1949).

Estimates based on such techniques are particularly sensitive to assumptions concerning the amount of vegetation change that occurred, the morphometry and geological conditions of any drainage basin examined, and the storm intensities and frequencies considered relevant for a given runoff occurrence. It is difficult to integrate all of these assumptions for entire watersheds tributary to arroyos; too many facts and factors are unknown or uncertain. For the sake of argument, an average reduction of vegetation cover over the entire watershed amounting to one half of the previously existing cover is assumed (e.g. from cover density of 50 to 25 per cent or from 'fair' to 'poor'). This is probably much more than can have occurred for any length of time in most drainages tributary to Californian arroyos.

By using a set of 'reasonable' assumptions about drainage basin and storm conditions,[67] the four different methods produced radically different estimates of peak or storm runoff that might obtain both before and after the vegetation changes assumed here. But changes determined by each method are at least in the same direction. The Rational method suggests that vegetation depletion might have produced an increase in peak runoff amounting to between 33 and 66 per cent of previous peak runoff; the Cook method, depending on how one interprets its descriptive terminology, suggests increases in peak runoff of between 50 and 200 per cent; the U.S. Soil Conservation Service method indicates increases in amounts of runoff ranging from 25 to 50 per cent for storm rainfalls greater than about 2 inches; and Anderson's regression equation yields an approximate doubling of peak discharge under a wide range of rainfall events.

Although all four approaches and the assumptions employed are open to criticism, it seems reasonable to conclude that probable increases in slope runoff during storm events which might have produced arroyos in most of coastal California were between the high and low estimates obtained in these calculations (i.e. between 25 and 200 per cent). A 'best estimate' might be that vegetation changes since the beginning of the nineteenth century could have *doubled* the sizes of major flows through the valley bottoms.

If this estimate indeed represents the reality of unrecorded events, then it is entirely possible that widespread grazing or the combination of grazing pressures and occasional droughts led to initiation of some arroyos in coastal

California. Resulting floods may bear the prime responsibility through their ability to increase erosiveness (velocity) of valley-bottom flows. But the magnitude of such increases must be viewed in relation to changes in erosiveness and erodibility that have accompanied local modifications of valley bottoms.

HYPOTHESES OF VALLEY-FLOOR CHANGE

Various valley-floor changes that may have affected erosiveness of flows independently of increases in discharge or that may have acted to increase the erodibility of valley-floor sediments have been described in Part I and analysed for southern Arizonan arroyos in Part II. It seems probable that three such changes could have occurred in coastal California: (a) local increases of slope; (b) concentration of flows; and (c) removal of valley-floor vegetation. In this section the evidence for each of these changes and their possible influences on entrenchment are examined, relative both to one another and to the increases of discharge that probably accompanied extensive alteration of watershed vegetation.

Increase of Slope

Once established, breaks of slope may greatly influence the development of channels in fine sediments. Such breaks, or headcuts, tend to maintain themselves and may even increase in height as they intermittently migrate upstream in association with surface erosion, piping, collapse, and sapping. Migration of headcuts associated with arroyo extension has been described in many parts of the South-West and it was certainly important in California. Indeed it may still be seen today during heavy storms, especially in small gullies tributary to large arroyos. But whether or not this mechanism bears prime responsibility for the arroyos that exist today is another matter.

Steepening of some tributary valley floors by rapid lateral or vertical erosion in principal valleys may have been involved in the creation of some Californian arroyos, including those in the Pine Creek system, some tributaries of the Santa Yñez River and San Timoteo Creek, and the lower reach of San Lorenzo Creek. But such local steepening of longitudinal profiles could not have been generally important, because most Californian arroyos either terminate downstream in alluvial fans or are separated from the base-level influences of principal streams by narrow bedrock canyons.

Schumm and Hadley's hypothesis (see above, pp. 90–94) is more difficult to evaluate. Irregularities certainly occur in the alluvial longitudinal profiles of valleys in coastal California and two aspects of them are worthy of comment: (a) their magnitude and (b) the correspondence between steeper gradients and the positions of early arroyos.

Figures III.5, III.9, and III.10 illustrate the irregularities in the longitudinal profiles of San Timoteo Canyon, Cañada de Los Alamos, and Thorn Meadows. Clearly the degree of irregularity, like the magnitude of slope, is closely related to drainage basin size. For instance, gradients of Thorn Meadows vary between 0·02 and 0·05 within a distance of only a few hundred feet (in a one-square-mile drainage area), whereas the longitudinal profile of San Timoteo Creek (in a drainage area of 125 square miles) varies between 0·012 and 0·016 over much greater distances. It is certainly possible that steeply sloping sections along the floor of Thorn Meadows might produce significantly higher flow velocities than those in other sections during major runoff events. The amount of acceleration there and along the floors of other small basins would have been strongly influenced by the shape of the valley floor, vegetation cover, and nature of discharge events, but it is conceivable that velocities in some steep reaches might have been twice as great as those in more gently sloping reaches. In the larger basins, such as that of San Timoteo, however, it is unlikely that minor variations of slope could alone have produced variations in velocities of more than 10 to 20 per cent for a given discharge: other hydraulic variables were probably more influential.

Arroyo depth and alluvial-surface slope are normally closely related: the deepest sections of most arroyos are usually found near the upstream margin of steeply sloping sections in the pre-entrenchment surface. But this correspondence probably reflects the hydraulic efficiency of the arroyo compared to that of the alluvial surface, and it says little about arroyo origin.

Historical evidence is not sufficiently detailed to reveal the loci of initial entrenchment of Californian arroyos, but examination of early channel descriptions in surveyors' field notes, modern field measurements, and data on topographic maps permit some comments on the relations between more steeply sloping sections and early arroyos. The association is not very strong. For example, many arroyos on the west side of the San Joaquin Valley were established by the early 1850s at canyon mouths where valley-floor and alluvial-fan slopes are steeper than those lower in the drainage systems. But slopes at and upstream of canyon mouths are normally regular over fairly long distances, and it is difficult to imagine points within them where slope might have significantly influenced flow velocity. Some early entrenchment in Cholame Creek coincided with slightly steeper slope segments in the valley floor, but relatively narrow floodplains and decreased flow width at these places may have been even more important in creating erosive flows. The arroyo of the 1870s and 1880s in San Timoteo Canyon and the small ravine reported in Cañada de Los Alamos apparently did not correspond with steeper sections in the valley floors.

Concentration of Flows

Reliable, direct evidence of flow concentration is scarce in coastal California. In a few places, such as Peace Valley, upper Panoche Creek, and Griswold Creek, arroyo development followed roads for short distances, and a drain reported along a tributary of San Lorenzo Creek is now an arroyo. Circumstantial evidence is more widespread. For example, the earliest reports of a deep arroyo in San Timoteo Canyon followed railroad construction by a few years, and the course of the arroyo is clearly determined in places by the railroad embankment. And many arroyos and other stream channels described in the nineteenth century follow routes that certainly could have coincided with pre-existing travel routes, irrigation ditches, or drains. Unfortunately, the areas where artificial drainage concentration would have been most probable are precisely those areas where land subdivision predates sytematic General Land Office surveys.

Flow concentration in terms of Melton's (1965; see above, p. 19) hypothesis may have occurred in southern California during the last 150 years. In San Timoteo Canyon the transverse slopes of the main valley floor may have been increased, and flow width correspondingly reduced, as small alluvial fans at tributary mouths impinged on the main valley floor; there certainly has been slope-sediment accumulation along the margins of the floodplain. For example, 0·5 miles of the county road along the side of the valley were buried by 2 feet of sediment during a storm in 1969; the foundations of a 40-year-old house on the valley-floor margin where there are no tributaries have been buried by 2 to 3 feet of debris on the up-slope side; and local residents recall a debris deluge that flowed from a small tributary basin following a fire in 1956, inundating the road, railroad, and a field in the valley bottom. The precise effects of such debris accumulations are difficult to determine, but they could have contributed towards flow concentration in the main valley floor.

Removal of Valley-Floor Vegetation

There is indisputable evidence that the vegetation cover on valley floors was radically altered during the nineteenth century. Cultivation of valley floors that are now entrenched was widespread by that time. Wheat fields, orchards, and other evidence of cultivation were mentioned in surveyors' notes at various locations in most of the valleys we have previously described. Furthermore, in accessible coastal valleys, where early private ownership meant that no Land Office surveys were undertaken, cultivated fields were certainly common, especially near to the missions.

The effects of farming are potentially great on both erosiveness of flows and erodibility of valley-bottom soils. The nature of valley-floor vegetation is not well recorded, but it was certainly quite variable, for the surveyors' notes refer to, for instance, densely vegetated cienegas, willow swamps, verdant groves of trees, and stands of shrubs and grasses. The influence of such communities on valley-floor discharge and on the protection of valley-floor soils would have been equally varied. But ploughing undoubtedly profoundly altered it by exposing soil to erosion at certain times, by disturbing soil structure, and by changing hydraulic conditions of the surface. In this context, it is interesting to note that ploughing and sowing traditionally took place in late autumn and early winter. As a result, cultivated fields remained relatively vulnerable to erosion throughout most of the rainy season, when valley-floor discharge occurred.

The effects of cultivation would, of course, also depend on the nature of discharge events, previous vegetation, and drainage-basin characteristics. Small or short-duration discharges may have been reduced in their magnitude or frequency because of slight increases in surface detention and initial permeability following ploughing. Nevertheless, large discharge events undoubtedly accomplished significant erosion and may have created arroyos. Where the original vegetation cover was quite dense, as in the cienegas, it is possible that cultivation could have doubled or even tripled flow velocities of moderate-sized events; at the same time, velocities required to erode the surface soil would have been less, and this reduction could have amounted to less than a third of that required to erode the original, vegetated surface (e.g. from 6—7 f.p.s. to 2—3 f.p.s.). Some examples of permissible flow velocities are given in Table III.9.

Livestock grazing may have had similar effects on valley-floor vegetation and soils, and these effects may have been present before those of cultivation. The tendency for livestock to congregate around dependable water-supplies, choice forage, and on flat land — conditions only satisfied consistently in valley floors — is described by Burcham (1957, pp. 191—2):

Stock were left virtually untended, which meant they were free to congregate unmolested in choice areas instead of being equally distributed over the range. During the long summer droughts forage on the hillsides would dry out early in the season while that in valleys or swales remained green; large numbers of animals would congregate on these areas of lush forage, grazing them heavily, as well as damaging both plants and soil by trampling. Dry season water supplies were limited, too, so that livestock concentrated about waterholes, to the great detriment of plant cover on immediately surrounding areas. Again, certain spots were used as rodeo grounds year after year, resulting in both local over-grazing and destruction of the plant cover through damage from the hoofs of close-herded stock; such damage resulted even though each rodeo lasted only a few days.

Such effects would have been extreme in drought years when livestock numbers increased in the vicinity of diminishing water-supplies.

The Relative Effects of Environmental Changes

To summarize, the principal environmental changes that may have affected erosiveness of flows or erodibility of materials in valley floors of coastal California during the last hundred years include (a) increases of discharge arising from increased slope runoff, (b) local increases in valley-floor gradients, (c) various flow-concentration changes, and (d) removal of valley-floor vegetation. In this section we attempt to evaluate their relative importance.

The Manning equation (p. 17) allows preliminary discussion of this comparison in terms of velocity, slope, hydraulic radius, surface roughness, and discharge. There are several problems associated with using the Manning

Table III.9   *Permissible Velocities for*
                               *Vegetation-Lined Channels**

| | | Permissible Velocity (f.p.s.) | |
Vegetation Cover	Slope (%)	Erosion-Resistant Soils	Easily Eroded Soils
Bermuda grass	Up to 5	8	6
Buffalo grass Kentucky bluegrass Smooth brome Blue gramma	Up to 5	7	5
Lespedeza sericea Weeping lovegrass Yellow bluestem Kudzu Alfalfa Crabgrass	Up to 5	3·5	2·5
Common lespedeza Sudan grass	Up to 5	3·5	2·5

* Source: Ogrosky and Mockus, 1964.

equation in this context: all the variables are to some extent interdependent and it is a little unrealistic to assume that only one variable changes at a time; Manning's roughness coefficient is especially unstable where the channel boundary is vegetated (see p. 17); and channel cross-section shape is critical when considering changes in hydraulic radius with discharge.

The difficulties introduced by these and related problems can be partly alleviated by making some simple assumptions concerning valley-floor slope, cross-sectional dimensions, and vegetal retardance, and by allowing each of these to vary in order to identify the velocity/discharge relationships that might follow from the environmental changes. Quantitative assumptions relevant to the following analysis are based on conditions in fairly narrow reaches along the valleys of San Timoteo Creek, in Cañada de Los Alamos, and in the lower course of Cholame Creek: gradient, where it is assumed to be constant, is 0·01; the untrenched valley is assumed to have a parabolic cross-section, with a top flow width of 500 feet when flow centre depth is 5 feet and other dimensions are determined by the relationship $T = 500\sqrt{D/5}$ (where T = top flow width in feet, and D = flow centre depth in feet); vegetal retardance for most calculations is assumed to be equivalent to a dense stand of grass averaging 6 to 10 inches in height. The following calculations are based on empirical relationships established by the U.S. Soil Conservation service (Ogrosky and Mockus, 1964). The results are shown in figures III.26, III.27, and III.28.

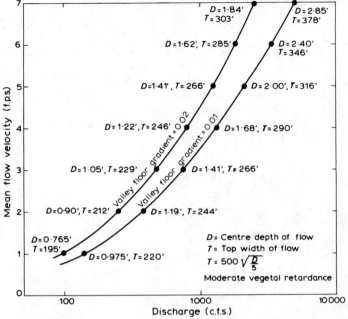

Figure III.26 Relations between discharge and mean flow velocity for two different valley-floor gradients

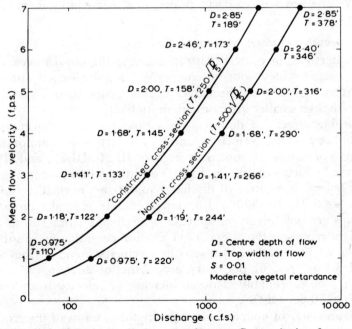

Figure III.27 Relations between discharge and mean flow velocity for two different valley-floor cross-sections

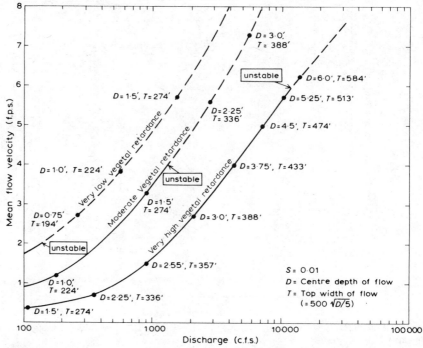

Figure III.28 Relations between discharge and mean flow velocity for different vegetal retardances

(a) Velocity and increased discharge Extensive changes in the herbaceous cover of watersheds in coastal California during the last 150 years probably caused increased valley-floor discharges. It was estimated above that in certain circumstances peak discharges during major storms may have been doubled, although smaller increases are more likely.

The possible effects of doubling peak discharge on erosiveness of flows (represented by mean velocity) under a variety of assumptions about valley-floor conditions is shown in Figures III.26, III.27, and III.28. The lowest curve in Figures III.26 and III.27 and the centre plot in Figure III.28 show the general behaviour of discharge under the 'normal' set of assumptions (i.e. $S = 0.01$, $T = 500 \sqrt{D/5}$, and moderate vegetal retardance). The relationships are non-linear: an increase of discharge from 100 to 200 c.f.s. (which might represent the effects of vegetation depletion on runoff during a given storm of moderate size) results in a velocity increase from about 0·8 f.p.s. to 1·3 f.p.s. (i.e. 62 per cent); a doubling of discharge from 2,000 to 4,000 c.f.s. would probably cause an increase of velocity from 4·9 f.p.s. to 6·4 f.p.s. (i.e. 30 per cent).

Such figures are, of course, only meaningful in terms of the erodibility of valley-floor materials. If a maximum permissible velocity of 4 f.p.s. is assumed — a reasonable value for easily erodible soils under a moderately dense cover of short grass — the valley floor would be able to tolerate discharges of about 1,300 c.f.s. without suffering serious erosion. Any general increase in discharge would probably tend to increase the frequency at which discharges greater than 1,300 c.f.s. recur and also the magnitude of very large events. Both effects would in time tend to initiate regrading of the valley floor, unless they were compensated by other phenomena such as an increase in the supply of debris from valley slopes. To double this critical discharge to 2,600 c.f.s. would raise flow velocities to 5·4 f.p.s., a value that allows the comparison between the effects of increased discharge and other environmental changes.

(b) Velocity and slope increases in longitudinal profiles Although it is most unlikely that differential sedimentation could locally double longitudinal-profile gradients in the larger valleys, this generous assumption is built into Figure III.26, which shows velocity/discharge relationships for identical valley floors sloping at 0·01 and 0·02 and suggests the effects on flow velocity of a change from the former to the latter. If permissible velocity is 4 f.p.s. (as above), then the tolerable discharge is reduced from 1,300 c.f.s. to 800 c.f.s. Similarly, to double slope with a discharge of 1,300 c.f.s. might raise mean flow velocity to 5·2 f.p.s., a value only slightly less than that obtained by doubling discharge at a constant slope. Steepening resulting from deposition by ephemeral flows is probably less effective than the graph implies because such sedimentation would probably also tend to flatten the cross-profile of the valley floor, and thus decrease the hydraulic radius of flow. Sedimentation may also have temporarily influenced vegetal retardance and erodibility by burying valley-floor vegetation with easily eroded sediments. In fact, as noted previously, the evidence for slope change by sedimentation is slender in coastal California.

(c) Velocity and concentration of flow Evidence for flow concentration by marginal valley-floor deposition is also slight, but the possible effects of such deposition deserve brief examination. For the sake of argument, the 'standard' valley floor is assumed to receive sufficient debris from valley sides to produce a parabolic cross-section 5 feet deep at a width of 250 rather than 500 feet. This is certainly a generous assumption, and assumes no deposition along the central line of the hypothetical valley floor and debris accumulated to depths of 2·4 feet at 100 feet from the central line, 9·6 feet at 200 feet, and even greater thicknesses at greater distances. As Figure III.27 shows, the discharge required to attain a permissible velocity of 4 f.p.s. is reduced from 1,300 c.f.s. to 650 c.f.s., and the velocity that would arise from a flow of 1,300 c.f.s. would be about 5·5 f.p.s.

(d) Velocity, erodibility, and the destruction of valley-floor vegetation Major alterations of valley-floor vegetation undoubtedly occurred in coastal California, and they certainly influenced erosiveness of flows and erodibility

of valley-floor materials. The functions plotted on Figure III.28 go some way towards demonstrating how relatively important these alterations might have been. The central curve represents flows under the same initial valley-floor conditions shown in Figures III.26 and III.27. The top curve demonstrates the effect of 'very low vegetal retardance', a condition equivalent to a fair to good stand of grass less than 2 inches in height (Ogrosky and Mockus, 1964). Many locations experienced more drastic vegetational changes than this, so that the plotted line is a conservative one. Ignoring contemporaneous changes in erodibility, reduced vegetal retardance might allow the initial permissible velocity of 4 f.p.s. to be attained at a discharge of 600 c.f.s.; a discharge of 1,300 c.f.s. would produce a velocity of about 5·4 f.p.s.: these changes are similar to those obtained by increasing slope or concentrating flow.

But it is inconceivable that reduction of valley-floor vegetation could have been accomplished without concurrent increases in erodibility, lowering permissible velocity to values of perhaps 2 f.p.s. or less. The potential significance of this additional effect is remarkable. According to the example modelled in Figure III.28, the vegetated valley floor once stable under discharges of 1,300 c.f.s. might, after being grazed or mown for hay, suffer erosion at discharges of about 130 c.f.s. — a reduction of an order of magnitude. Cultivation, severe trampling, and wagon trails in the valleys may have had even more serious effects.

The effects on erosion of vegetation change may have been even greater in the once well-vegetated areas near canyon heads or at naturally constricted places along valley floors. The curve for 'very high vegetal retardance' suggests that these reaches — sites that once supported meadows, cienegas, or dense, woody riparian vegetation — might have been able to accommodate very great discharges (e.g. 10,000 c.f.s.). Vegetation removal in these areas would have seriously affected even small, frequent flows: it is conceivable that such areas might have been eroded by discharges as little as 1 per cent of those under which stability had previously obtained.

Modification of valley-floor vegetation and its consequences could completely account for the initiation of most arroyos in coastal California. Increased discharge arising from livestock grazing may have contributed to entrenchment. The evidence and the need for other environmental changes are very limited. It seems probable that most arroyos in coastal California were a result of direct and indirect human activities at certain valley-floor sites and elsewhere within the entrenched drainage basins.

CONCLUSIONS

The survey of arroyos and environmental changes in coastal California leads to several general conclusions.

The distribution of arroyos in coastal California is closely related to the occurrence of fine alluvial deposits on the floors of small- or medium-sized valleys in areas of relatively high local relief. In contrast to the basin-range country of Arizona and New Mexico, the major ephemeral or intermittent streams of the large drainage basins do not appear to have been significantly entrenched in historical times. As a result, arroyos in coastal California are somewhat smaller than those in southern Arizona, although they are otherwise morphologically very similar. Quaternary cut-and-fill sequences, as represented by paired alluvial terraces adjacent to floodplains, occur in coastal California as elsewhere in the South-West.

Fine-grained alluvial deposits, which are easily eroded when wet and yet are cohesive enough to maintain steep banks and efficient, narrow channels, are an essential requirement for arroyo formation. Degradation of coarse-grained, non-cohesive materials leads to the formation of wide, shallow channel forms. Arroyos tend to widen, shallow, and disappear when they pass into such materials. The two principal sources of fine alluvial debris in headwater areas of coastal California are poorly consolidated mudstones and shales mainly in late-Tertiary formations, and unconsolidated Quaternary terrace and valley-fill sediments.

Two kinds of sites have collected such deposits and they commonly contain arroyos: (a) relatively wide reaches in generally narrow valleys and (b) the mouths of canyons where alluvial fans have been formed. In both situations, and especially in zones immediately upstream of canyons, the presence of vegetation supported by near-surface ground-water (as in cienegas) may have been fundamental in facilitating deposition of fine materials in the valley floors and in protecting the materials from removal by relatively high-velocity flows.

Short ravines, gullies, and channels have probably always existed to some extent at alluvial-fan apexes and in alluvial reaches upstream of canyons. In many cases, arroyos probably 'originated' as downstream or upstream extensions of these inherently unstable features. Although historical evidence is not conclusive, it seems probable that incipient arroyos at such locations were normally prevented from developing by vegetation, and by the ability of the relatively broad alluvial areas upstream to distribute and absorb flood flows: the creation of arroyos in historical times relates to changes in these circumstances.

There is no single date at which arroyos were initiated, and to search for one is fruitless. Rather, there is a period in which some arroyos were initiated and some channels were deepened. Some arroyos certainly existed at least in part in coastal California as early as the 1850s, and a few — such as that in the Cuyama Valley — had already attained their present dimensions by that date. But in most potentially vulnerable situations, valley floors were unentrenched and contained meadows, cienegas or swamps, and creeks a few feet wide in 1850. In some places these conditions lasted until well into the twentieth century; but in others, the first surveyors' descriptions in the 1850s, 1870s, or 1880s revealed that channels with defined banks had already been established — a situation that would not have prevailed when fine alluvial deposits were accumulating, but was probably the typical condition immediately prior to entrenchment.

Within coastal California as a whole, arroyo lengthening extended over a rather long period — from as early as 1850 in some areas to as late as the 1920s in others. Activity was especially noticeable between 1870 and 1890, and subsequently in specific years at specific places (such as 1904 in San Timoteo Canyon, 1911 in Cañada de Los Alamos). Some deepening and widening of arroyos accompanied storm periods in the late 1930s and early 1940s, and in the late 1960s and early 1970s.

The historical evidence points towards several conclusions concerning the explanation of the arroyo episode in coastal California. In the first place, there is no reason to associate arroyo cutting with secular climatic changes. The climatic records for coastal California substantiate the hypothesis that precipitation events have occurred in an essentially random manner at least since 1850.

Secondly, the floristic composition of grasslands and woodlands was extensively and radically transformed during the nineteenth century, mainly as a result of the immigration of alien culture groups and their land-use practices. Livestock-ranching played an important role in these changes in areas distant from cultivated lands. The influence of vegetation transformation on valley-floor runoff is a matter of speculation, but it seems possible that valley-floor flows were increased to some extent either in magnitude or frequency, or both.

Finally, eradication of valley-floor vegetation, and disturbance and exposure of valley-floor soils, occurred throughout coastal California in the nineteenth century as a result of cultivation and intensive use by livestock. The effects of these changes must have been considerable both on erosiveness of flows and erodibility of deposits — more so than the potential effects of any other environmental changes that might have occurred during the nineteenth century in entrenched areas. Other changes, such as increased runoff arising from livestock grazing and local concentrations of flow, may have contributed to arroyo growth; but such changes were of secondary importance.

Thus, in coastal California, it seems probable that vegetational changes, related chiefly to human land-use practices in the latter half of the nineteenth century and the early twentieth century, provided a general context within which entrenchment could proceed, and the precise loci of entrenchment and arroyo development were determined largely by the occurrence of appropriate deposits in two distinctive topographic situations.

PART IV

Concluding Remarks

The principal aim of this inquiry has been to narrow the area of speculation and uncertainty surrounding the study of arroyos and related environmental changes through examination of field and historical evidence in the context of existing explanatory hypotheses.

A major constraint on the discussion has been the fragmentary nature and varied quality of the historical record. Historical sources fall into three main categories: survey records, official statistics, and a miscellaneous collection of other relevant documents. The most detailed, comprehensive, and reliable source relating to valley-floor conditions is the surveyors' notebooks of the U.S. General Land Office, legal documents which for the most part have stood the tests of time. Other official surveys, such as those of the Southern Pacific Transportation Company and the U.S. Geological Survey, also furnish some valuable, precise data. Regional information published in official statistical reports is somewhat less reliable and useful than the survey records, with the important exception of climatic data collected by the Post Surgeon and Signal Service and the U.S. Weather Bureau. Other miscellaneous sources, including photographs, newspapers, reminiscences, and maps, are all generally less comprehensive and informative, but they commonly help to illuminate ideas suggested by field observations and the more reliable historical sources. At times it has been possible to extend arguments based on historical evidence by examining them cautiously in the light of contemporary studies (of forage yield and slope runoff, for example) and appropriate, well-established hydrological and hydraulic relationships.

To conclude, the results of the studies in southern Arizona and coastal California are briefly compared.

Morphologically, arroyos in the two areas have much in common. They are only found in fine-grained, cohesive, valley-floor sediments. They represent the most recent of several Quaternary erosion episodes (although the evidence of previous entrenchments is clear in only a few localities). Many arroyos were originally discontinuous features initiated at several locations along their valley floors. And it seems probable that some arroyos, especially those downstream of cienegas, upstream of canyons, or at alluvial-fan apexes, represent established channels that were merely lengthened, widened, and deepened in the nineteenth and twentieth centuries.

Arroyo initiation and development in southern Arizona and coastal California occurred mainly between 1850 and 1920, and especially from 1870 to 1890. It is clear that these were times of major environmental changes.

Figure IV.1 summarizes (on the model presented in Figure I.2) conclusions

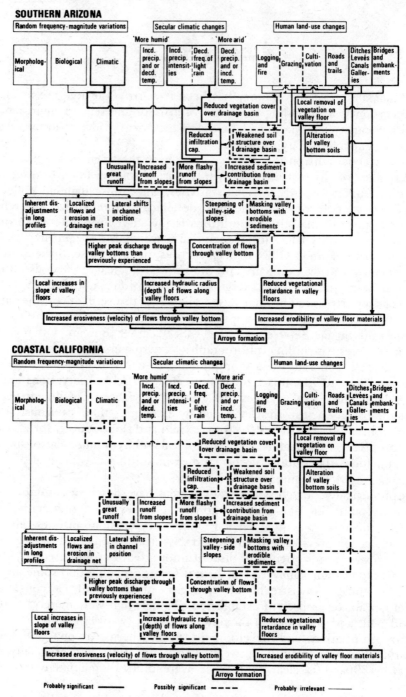

Figure IV.1 Model of arroyo formation: summary of conclusions

relating environmental changes and arroyo formation in the two study areas for the period beginning in the mid-nineteenth century. Each change and link has been classified according to whether it is considered 'probably significant', 'possibly significant', or 'probably irrelevant'. No attempt has been made to classify within these categories the relative importance of the changes or the strengths of the links.

Not only are the climates of the two areas different, but their precipitation histories in the period of arroyo formation are also distinct. Secular precipitation trends are evident in southern Arizona, and it can be argued that they have significantly influenced arroyo formation; but there is no evidence of such trends in coastal California. Both regions have experienced short-term precipitation fluctuations (e.g. droughts), but such changes appear to have been more pronounced and influential in southern Arizona than in coastal California.

Regional, secular vegetation changes are evident in both areas, but their causes and nature differ. In coastal California, major changes in floristic composition are a product of the activities of men and cattle. Significant structural changes in vegetation, wherever they occurred and whatever their ultimate effect on runoff, are also related closely to these activities. In southern Arizona, secular and short-term climatic changes may have been an important cause of vegetation change, and it can be argued that overgrazing may have been less significant as an ultimate cause of entrenchment than some have assumed. Nevertheless, regional, secular vegetation changes may have contributed towards arroyo formation in both these areas.

But great importance is attached in both areas to the transformation of valley-floor vegetation, and accompanying changes that included the creation of drainage-concentration features along valley floors (such as irrigation canals, roads, and railroad embankments) and the disturbance of valley-floor soils. It can be shown by hydraulic arguments that these changes would have profoundly modified flow conditions and could certainly have been responsible for entrenchment. Beyond doubt, drainage-concentration features provided the loci for the initiation of some arroyos.

The final conclusion from this brief comparison is perhaps the simplest and most obvious: apparently similar arroyos can be formed in different areas as a result of different combinations of initial conditions and environmental changes.

Notes

[1] The following discussion should be read with reference to Figure I.2.

[2] We are grateful to W. Earp and J. Townsend for introducing us to this 'Frail Lands' area.

[3] Sometimes referred to as Solomonsville or Solomon.

[4] The first cattle probably arrived in 1884 (Swift, 1926).

[5] Books referred to in this area are numbers: 692, 693, 703, 720, 736, 737, 766, 772, 774, 1496, 1501, 1574, 4417, 4545, 4665, 4666, 4667, and 4700. Details of authors and dates are shown on Figure II.2.

[6] A 'creek' is shown extending downstream from the cienaga on the official Cochise County map of 1904, but the significance of this is not known.

[7] Dates for this drought vary among authors. Swift (1926) said it extended from 1899 to 1904; Peterson (1950) estimated 1895–1905.

[8] H.C. Southwarth recorded a discharge of 7,548 c.f.s. in San Simon Creek in October, 1916 (Olmstead, 1919).

[9] The data in this section were kindly provided by the Southern Pacific Railroad. Documents used include: (1) map showing alignment of second section of the V.G.N.R., 10 April–15 July, 1894; (2) the same, revised March, 1905; (3) rights-of-way and track maps V-31, nos. 6, 7, 8, and 9; (4) profiles V–31, 6, 7, 8, and 9.

[10] Notebooks referred to in this section are nos. 700, 735, 744, 753, 1563, 1573, 2732, and 3832. Details of authors and dates are shown on Figure II.4.

[11] U.S. Geological Survey, 1971, *Water Resources Data for Arizona*, 1970, I, *Surface Water Records*, p. 238.

[12] Surveyors' notebooks consulted in preparing this account are nos. 913, 957, 969, 997, 1000, 1002, 1570, 2331, 2334, 3301. Details of authors and dates are shown on Figure II.5.

[13] Cochise County, Arizona Territory, by H.C. Howe (County Surveyor). Copy in Arizona Historical Society, Tucson. The map has no date but as it precedes the creation of Santa Cruz County it is prior to 1899.

[14] Personal conversations with Mr. Goodman and Mr. McCrae, residents of the Mormon settlement, St. David.

[15] Surveyors' notebooks consulted in this section are nos. 762, 763, 780, 804, 811, 845, 879, 880, 889, 935, 983, 984, 1474, 1509, 1542, 1773, 1775, 2167, 3654, 3997. Details of authors and dates are shown on Figure II.6.

[16] Railroad data from 1900 to 1928 discussed in this section were kindly provided by the Southern Pacific Transportation Company, and documents referred to are for Bridge 1033C (drawings 1–8–4, sheets 8, 9, 10).

[17] It should be emphasized that *width* data in surveyors' notebooks refer only to *section-line widths*, not to true widths. The data are therefore of greatest value for comparison at different dates to indicate general trends.

[18] There is evidence that the railroad was sometimes washed out by flooding. For example the *Arizona Daily Star* reported on 24 Sept. 1929 that a washout stranded two trains near Fairbanks.

[19] Not *all* areas in the San Pedro Valley were transformed at this time. For instance, in the south-west (the southern Huachuca Mountains and their fringing plains) and in northern Sonora vegetation changes have been slight.

[20] Unconfirmed reminiscences of Mr. Shearer, quoted by Rodgers (1965).

[21] Surveyors' notebooks referred to in this section are nos. 776, 809, 818, 821, 851, 952, 1507, 1511, 1515, 1752, 1753, 1870, 1975, 1985–7, 1997–2003, 2072, 2751, 3422, 3425, 4323. Details of authors and dates are given on Figure II.8.

[22] The 'cut down' for Sam Hughes was probably in his canal, the site of the Tucson arroyo (see below). The method of extracting undersurface flow is discussed below.

[23] In the archive of the Arizona Historical Society, Tucson.

[24] The arroyo cuts across the land owned by Dolores Gallo, Pasqual Ochoa, Jose Herreras, Deloris Rameriz, Solano Leon, and Philipe Romero shown on the Fergusson map.

[25] In the archive of the Arizona Historical Society, Tucson.

[26] In the archive of the Arizona Historical Society, Tucson.

[27] Evidence for the floods being 'new and unusual' is not given: it is by no means certain that the statement is justified.

[28] Surveyors' notebooks used in this account are nos. 841, 897, 904, 1485, and 1494. Details of authors and dates are given on Figure II.10.

[29] Mr. King, of Anvil Ranch (T.17S., R.19E.), whose family has been in Altar Valley for several generations, recollected that the arroyo developed largely along the Tucson-Altar road. The precise location of the road when entrenchment occurred need not, of course, have been the same as it was in 1886 (reported from an interview by William Miller, 1970).

[30] This traditional farming method has declined in recent years (Kelly, 1963; Papago Development Program, 1949) largely because of its unreliability, erosion, and the alternative attraction of cattle. Flood irrigation of pastures now offers more profitable possibilities (Simpson *et al.*, 1969), especially as overgrazing and overstocking are said to be problems.

[31] Charco deepening was a long-standing Papago practice according to Dobyns (pers. comm., 1970).

[32] Bryan (1929) recorded six villages or localities in Arizona and Sonora with this name or a corruption of it.

[33] Lumholtz (1912) recorded an arroyo at Ak-chin in 1909, an observation confirmed by a manuscript map in Arizona State Museum of 'Proposed Santa Rosa Reservation' by R. Aspoas and believed to be dated 1913. Bryan (1925b) also recorded one or two zones of entrenchment in the Papago country.

[34] These possibilities will be considered for southern Arizona as a whole below. See also Bryan (1929, p. 452).

[35] Thanks are due to Simon Mamake, of San Xavier, for acting as interpreter during these interviews.

[36] Similar drainage concentration is reported to have been carried out in 'Well' villages (McDowell, 1919).

[37] The following list indicates the longest records for selected gauging stations in the major entrenched valleys, and is compiled from U.S. Geological Survey (1971) data:
1. *San Simon Valley near Solomonville*
    Incomplete records for 1931 and 1932
    Complete records from May 1935
2. *San Pedro Valley at Charleston*
    Incomplete records for 1904, 1905, 1906, 1910, 1912
    Complete records for 1911, and from Sept. 1912
3. *Santa Cruz Valley at Tucson*
    Complete records from Oct. 1905
4. *Whitewater Draw near Douglas*
    Incomplete records for 1911, 1912, 1913, 1914, 1915
    Complete records for 1916–22, June 1930–3, May 1935–46, and from July 1947.

[38] e.g. *Graham County Bulletin*, 27 Feb. 1891. 'The Flood. The Gila River Never So High Before. The Heaviest Rainfall Was Below Solomonville. Mr. James Norris, one of the oldest settlers in the valley says the rise of seven years ago was then said by old native Mexicans to have been the highest ever known and the water on Tuesday was at least seven feet higher than it was then.' For other examples, see Hastings and Turner (1965, p. 42).

[39] The source of binomials and authorities is Hastings and Turner (1965), appendices A and B.

[40] The date of this report coincides with the longest and most serious drought recorded in southern Arizona (see Table II.6).

[41] Cattle were important in southern Arizona; sheep were more important in the north of the state (Haskett, 1936) and in New Mexico (Denevan, 1967).

[42] This figure compares with a report (in Griffiths, 1901) that in 1888, 40,000 cattle 'grew fat along a certain portion of the San Pedro Valley'.

[43] Such reminiscences in such a newspaper are not the most reliable of historical data.

[44] A relatively dry period towards the end of the nineteenth century is confirmed, for example, by the July data of Sellers (1960) and by the analysis of climatic records discussed in the previous section which revealed several drought periods at this time (Table II.6).

[45] In the following discussion fire has been avoided, not because of conflicting evidence concerning its effect on runoff elsewhere (e.g. Chow, 1964; Veihmeyer, 1951), but because the past and present importance of fire is unknown in southern Arizona. We have found only one reference to a serious range fire in the last hundred years — the earthquake fire of 1887 in the San Pedro Valley, which may have seriously altered vegetation (Rodgers, 1965). See also Hastings and Turner (1965, pp. 285–7).

[46] A study by Hibbert (1971) in central Arizona pointed towards an *increase* of water yield following brush control and conversion of chaparral to grass. This study is not, however, strictly applicable to changes in southern Arizona because the proportion of winter water yield is much higher in the central part of the state, and vegetation and topography are different.

[47] See channel descriptions in General Land Office Survey notebooks by J.E. Terrel, 1859, no. 272–33.

[48] U.S.G.S., Redlands 15' Quadrangle, 1899.

[49] John Goldsworthy, 1871, Book 168–5; Fred Perris, 1876, Book 169–5.

[50] Personal interview with Mr. Donald Houston, 1966.

[51] J. Perris, 1876, Book 169–5.

[52] Point 10,000 refers to the location along the arroyo 10,000 feet upstream from the mouth of Los Alamos Creek and is indicated in Figure III.9. Similar references are used in the remainder of this section.

[53] W.H. Norway, 1880, Book 164–32.

[54] B.M. Henry, 1858, Book 19–10.

[55] J.E. Freeman, 1855, Book 257–16.

[56] John Ingalls, 1871, Books 12–2 and 285–7.

[57] George Baker, 1880, Book 351–3.

[58] George Small, 1871, Book 285–4.

[59] A. McNeil, 1854, Book 13–5.

[60] H. Washington, 1858, Book 316–19.

[61] A.T. Herman, 1880, Books 13–1 and 13–4.

[62] G. Small, 1871, Book 58–2.

[63] A.W. Von Schmidt, 1853, Book 21–7; R.E.K. Whiting, 1854, Book 232–22.

[64] J.E. Freeman, 1855, Book 271–1.

[65] J.M. Gore, 1893, Books 373–4 and 373–5; 1895, Book 373–3.

[66] This last comment is based on a study of fire records in Los Angeles County from 1870 to the present held by the L.A. County Flood Control District.

[67] Where appropriate for the various methods, the following assumptions are made: (i) 'slight' compaction of soil, (ii) a small drainage area (2,000 acres), (iii) 'hilly' terrain (average slopes of 10 to 30 per cent), (iv) 'moderate' amounts of surface storage, (v) an hourly precipitation intensity of 1 inch per hour, (vi) a time of concentration of one hour, (vii) soils originally having 'moderate' infiltration rates, (viii) antecedent 21-day rainfall of 5 inches, (ix) a 24-hour maximum precipitation of 5 inches, and (x) a minimum daily temperature of 20° F.

References

ALBERTSON, M.L., and D.B. SIMONS, 1964, Fluid mechanics, in Chow, V.T. (ed.), *Handbook of Applied Hydrology* (McGraw-Hill, New York), Section 7.

ALBRITTON, C.C., JR., and K. BRYAN, 1939, Quaternary stratigraphy in the Davis Mountains, Trans-Pecos Texas, *Geol. Soc. Am. Bull.* 50, 1423–74.

ANDERSON, H.W., 1949, Flood frequencies and sedimentation from forest watersheds, *Trans. Am. Geoph. Un.* 30, 567–86.

ANDREWS, D.A., 1937, Ground water in Avra-Altar Valley, Arizona, *U.S. Geological Survey Water-Supply Paper*, 796–E, 163–80.

ANTEVS, E., 1941, Age of the Cochise culture stages, in Sayles, E.B., and E. Antevs, The Cochise Culture *Medallion Papers*, 29 Gila Pueblo, Globe, Arizona).

——— , 1952, Arroyo-cutting and filling, *J. Geol.* 60, 375–85.

——— , 1954, Climate of New Mexico during the last Glacio-Pluvial, *J. Geol.* 62, 182–91.

——— , 1955a, Geologic-climatic dating in the west, *Am. Antiquity*, 20, 317–35.

——— , 1955b, Geologic-climate method of dating, in Smiley, T.L. (ed.), *Geochronology, with special reference to Southwestern United States* (Univ. Ariz. Press, Tucson), 151–69.

——— , 1962, Late Quaternary climates in Arizona, *Am. Antiquity*, 28, 193–8.

ARIZONA BUREAU of MINES, 1969, Mineral and water resources of Arizona, *Ariz. Bur. Mines Bull.* 180.

BAILEY, R.W., 1935, Epicycles of erosion in the valleys of the Colorado Plateau Province, *J. Geol.* 43, 337–55.

BAILEY, R.W., C.W. CRADDOCK, and A.R. CROFT, 1947, Watershed management for summer flood control in Utah, *U.S. Dept. Agric. Misc. Pub.* 639.

BARNES, W.C., 1936, Herds in San Simon Valley, *American Forests*, 42, 456–7, 481.

——— , 1960, *Arizona Place Names* (Univ. of Ariz. Press, Tucson), revised and enlarged by H. Granger.

BEATTIE, G.W., 1939, *Heritage of the Valley* (San Pasqual Press, Pasadena).

BEETLE, A.A., 1947, Distribution of the native grasses of California, *Hilgardia*, 17, 309–57.

BENTLEY, J.R., and M.W. TALBOT, 1951, Efficient use of annual plants on cattle ranges in the California foothills, *U.S. Dept. Agric. Circ.* 870.

BERGER, J.M., 1898, 1901, Reports of farmer in charge of San Xavier Papago, *Ann. Repts. Dept. Int., Rept. Commissioner for Indian Affairs*.

BOLTON, H.E., 1936, *The Rim of Christendom* (Macmillan, New York).

BRYAN, K., 1920, Origin of rock tanks and charcos, *Am. J. Sci.*, 4th Ser. 50, 186–206.

——— , 1922, Erosion and sedimentation in the Papago country, Arizona, *U.S. Geological Survey Bull.* 730, 19–90.

——— , 1925a, Date of channel trenching (arroyo cutting) in the arid Southwest, *Science*, 62, 338–44.

——— , 1925b, The Papago country, Arizona, *U.S. Geological Survey Water-Supply Paper*, 449.

——— , 1926, The San Pedro Valley, Arizona, and the geographical cycle (abs.), *Bull. Geol. Soc. Am.* 37, 169–70.

——— , 1927, Channel erosion of the Rio Salado, Socorro County, New Mexico, *U.S. Geological Survey Bull.* 790, 17–19.

——— , 1928a, Historic evidence on changes in the channel of the Rio Puerco, a tributary of the Rio Grande in New Mexico, *J. Geol.* 36, 265–82.

——— , 1928b, Change in plant associations by change in ground water level, *Ecology*, 9, 474–8.

_____ , 1929, Flood-water farming, *Geog. Rev.* 19, 444—56.

_____ , 1940, Erosion in the valleys of the Southwest, *N. Mex. Quart.* 10, 227—32.

_____ , 1941, Pre-Columbian agriculture in the Southwest as conditioned by periods of al-luviation, *Ass. Am. Geog. Ann.* 31, 219—42.

_____ , 1948, Los ouelas complejas y fósiles de la altiplanicie de Mexico en relación a los cambias climaticas, *Bol. Soc. Geol. Mexicana*, 13, 1—20.

_____ , 1950, The geology and fossil vertebrates of Ventana Cave, in Haury, E.W., *The Stratigraphy and Archeology of Ventana Cave* (Univ. Ariz. Press, Tucson), 75—126.

_____ , 1954, The geology of Chaco Canyon, New Mexico in relation to the life and remains of the prehistoric peoples of Pueblo Bonito, *Smithsonian Misc. Collections*, 122.

_____ , G.E.P. SMITH, and G.A. WARING, 1934, Ground-water supplies and irrigation in San Pedro Valley, Arizona, *U.S. Geological Survey, open-file report*, 8/28/67.

BUFFINGTON, L.C., and C.H. HERBEL, 1965, Vegetational changes on a semidesert grassland range from 1858 to 1963, *Ecological Monographs*, 35, 139—64.

BULL, W.B., 1964a, Geomorphology of segmented alluvial fans in western Fresno County, California, *U.S. Geological Survey Prof. Paper*, 352-E, 89—129.

_____ , 1964b, History and causes of channel trenching in western Fresno County, California, *Am. J. Sci.* 262, 249—58.

BURCHAM, L.T., 1956, Historical backgrounds of range land use in California, *J. Range Mgt.* 9, 81—6.

_____ , 1957, *California Range Land: an historical-ecological study of the range resources of California* (Calif. Div. Forestry, Sacramento).

BUREAU of LAND MANAGEMENT, no date, Notes on the San Simon Valley.

BURNHAM, W.L., and L.C. DUTCHER, Ms., Geology and ground-water hydrology of the Redlands-Beaumont area, California, with special reference to ground-water outflow, *U.S. Geological Survey, open-file report*.

CABLE, D.R., 1967, Fire effects on semidesert grasses and shrubs, *J. Range Mgt.* 20, 170—6.

CAMPBELL, C.J., and W. GREEN, 1966, Perpetual succession of stream-channel vegetation in a semiarid region, *J. Ariz. Ac. Sci.* 5, 86—98.

CASTETTER, E.F., and W.H. BELL, 1942, *Pima and Papago Indian Agriculture*, Inter-American Studies, 1 (U. of New Mexico Press, Albuquerque).

CHOW, V.T., 1959, *Open-channel Hydraulics* (McGraw-Hill, New York).

_____ , (ed.), 1964, *Handbook of Applied Hydrology* (McGraw-Hill, New York).

CLARK, A.H., 1956, The impact of exotic invasion on the remaining New World midlatitude grasslands, in Thomas, W.L., Jr. (ed.), *Man's Role in Changing the Face of the Earth* (Univ. Chicago Press, Chicago), 737—62.

CLELAND, R.G., 1941, *Cattle on a Thousand Hills* (Huntington Library, San Marino, Calif.).

CLYMA, W., and R.J. SHAW, 1968, Natural recharge in Tucson basin, *Progressive Agric. in Arizona*, 22, 14—17.

COATES, D.R., and R.L. CUSHMAN, 1955, Geology and ground-water resources of the Douglas Basin, Arizona, *U.S. Geological Survey Prof. Paper*, 1354.

COCHRANE, D., and G.H. ORCUTT, 1949, Application of least-squares regressions to relationships containing auto-correlated error terms, *J. Am. Stat. Ass.* 44, 32—61.

COLMAN, E.A., 1953, *Vegetation and watershed management* (Ronald Press, New York).

COLTON, H.S., 1937, Some notes on the original condition of the Little Colorado River: a side light on the problems of erosion, *Mus. N. Ariz. Notes*, 10, 17—20.

COOKE, R.U., and A. WARREN, 1973, *Geomorphology in Deserts* (Batsford, London; U. California Press, San Francisco).

COOLEY, M.E., 1962, Late Pleistocene and Recent erosion and alluviation in parts of the Colorado River system, Arizona and Utah, *U.S. Geological Survey Prof. Paper*, 450-B, 48–50.

COOPERRIDER, C.K., and B.A. HENDRICKS, 1937, Soil erosion and stream flow on range and forest lands of the Upper Rio Grande watershed region in relation to land resources and human welfare, *U.S. Dept. Agric. Tech. Bull.* 567.

COTTAM, W.P., and G. STEWART, 1940, Succession as a result of grazing and of meadow desiccation by erosion since settlement in 1862, *J. Forestry*, 38, 613–26.

CRADDOCK, J.M., 1957, A simple statistical test for use in the study of climatic change, *Weather*, 12, 252–8.

CROWELL, J.C., 1950, Geology of the Hungry Valley area, southern California, *Am. Ass. Petroleum Geologists Bull.* 34, 1623–46.

——— , 1952, Geology of the Lebec Quadrangle, California, *Calif. Div. Mines Special Rept.* 24.

——— , 1954, Geology of the Ridge Basin Area, Los Angeles and Ventura Counties, in Jahns, R.H. (ed.), Geology of southern California, *Calif. Div. Mines Bull.* 170, Map Sheet no. 7.

CULLEY, M.J., 1943, Grass grows in summer or not at all, *Am. Hereford J.* 34, 8–10.

CUSOLICH, B., 1953, *Tucson* (Arizona Silhouettes, Tucson).

DE COOK, K.J., 1952, San Simon basin (ground water), Cochise County, *U.S. Geological Survey, open-file report*, 59–68.

DE LA TORRE, A.C., 1970, Streamflow in the Upper Santa Cruz Basin, Santa Cruz and Pima counties, Arizona, *U.S. Geological Survey Water-Supply Paper*, 1939-A.

DELLENBAUGH, F.S., 1912, Cross-cutting and retrograding of stream beds, *Science*, 35, 656–8.

DENEVAN, W.M., 1967, Livestock numbers in nineteenth-century New Mexico, and the problem of gullying in the Southwest, *Ann. Ass. Am. Geog.* 57, 691–703.

DOBYNS, H.F., 1951, Blunders with *bolsas*, *Human Organization*, 10, 25–32.

——— , 1962, *Pioneering Christians among the Indians of Tucson* (ed. Estudios Andinos, Lima).

DODGE, R.E., 1902, Arroyo formation (abs.), *Am. Geologist*, 29, 322.

——— , 1910, The formation of arroyos in adobe filled valleys in the southwestern United States (abs.), *Brit. Ass. Advanc. Sci. Rept.* 79, 531–2.

DORROH, J.H., JR., 1960, Meteorological characteristics of the Southwest as related to water yields, in Warnock, B.H. and J.L. Gardner, *Water yield in relation to environment in the Southwestern United States* (A.A.A.S., Alpine, Texas), 47–50.

DUCE, J.T., 1918, The effect of cattle on the erosion of canyon bottoms, *Science*, 47, 450–2.

DUTTON, C.E., 1882, Tertiary history of the Grand Canyon district, *U.S. Geological Survey Mono.* 2.

EATON, J.E., 1939, Ridge Basin, California, *Am. Ass. Petroleum Geologists Bull.* 23, 517–58.

ELOY SOIL CONSERVATION DISTRICT, 1969, Long-range program for resource conservation and development of the Eloy Soil Conservation District, MS., 19-6-69.

EMMETT, W.W., 1974, Channel aggradation in western United States as indicated by observations at Vigil Network sites, paper presented to the *International Symposium on Geomorphic Processes in Arid Environments*, Israel.

ENGLISH, W.A., 1915, Geology and oil prospects of Cuyama Valley, California, *U.S. Geological Survey Bull.* 621, 191–215.

FRICK, C., 1921, Extinct vertebrate fauna of the badlands of Bautista Creek and San Timoteo Cañon, Southern California, *Univ. Calif. Pub. in Geol.* 12, 277–425.

GOODRIDGE, J.D., 1969, A probability model of climatic cycles, *Aldine Soc. Papers in Hydrology*, 1.

GRAY, H.L. 1934, Long-period fluctuations of some meteorological elements in relation to California forest-fire problems, *Monthly Weather Review*, 62, 231—5.

GREEN, C.R., and W.D. SELLERS, 1964, *Arizona Climate* (Univ. Ariz. Press, Tucson).

GREGORY, H.E., 1917, Geology of the Navajo country, *U.S. Geological Survey Prof. Paper*, 93.

——, and R.C. MOORE, 1931, The Kaiparowits Region, *U.S. Geological Survey Prof. Paper*, 164.

GRIFFITHS, D., 1901, Range improvement in Arizona, *U.S. Dept. Agric., Bureau of Plant Industry Bull.*, 4.

GROVE, G.T., 1962, Rillito Creek, Flood Plain Study, *Tucson City Planning Office*, Report.

HACK, J.T., 1939, Late Quaternary history of several valleys of northern Arizona, a preliminary announcement, *Mus. Northern Ariz. Notes*, 11, 63—73.

HACKENBERG, R.A., 1962, Economic alternatives in arid lands: a case study of the Pima and Papago Indians, *Ethnology*, 1, 186—96.

HARRIS, D.R., 1966, Recent plant invasions in the arid and semi-arid Southwest of the United States, *Ann. Ass. Am. Geog.* 56, 408—22.

HASKETT, B., 1935, Early history of the cattle industry in Arizona, *Ariz. Historical Rev.* 6, 3—42.

——, 1936, History of the sheep industry in Arizona, *Ariz. Historical Rev.* 7, 3—49.

HASTINGS, J.R., 1958—9, Vegetation change and arroyo cutting in southeastern Arizona during the past century: an historical review, in *Arid Lands Colloquia*, Univ. of Ariz., 24—39.

——, 1959, Vegetation change and arroyo cutting in southeastern Arizona, *J. Arizona Ac. Sci.* 1, 60—7.

——, and R.M. TURNER, 1965, *The Changing Mile: An ecological study of vegetation change with time in the lower mile of an arid and semiarid region* (Univ. Ariz. Press, Tucson).

HAURY, E.H. 1950, *The Stratigraphy and Archaeology of Ventana Cave, Arizona* (Univ. Ariz. Press, Tucson, and Univ. New Mexico Press).

HAYNES, C.V., JR., 1968, Geochronology of late-Quaternary alluvium, in Morrison, R.B., and H.E. Wright, Jr. (eds.), *Means of Correlation of Quaternary Successions* (Univ. Utah Press, Salt Lake City), 591—615.

HENDRY, G.W., 1931, The adobe brick as a historical source, *Agricultural History*, 5 110—27.

——, and M.K. BELLUE, 1925, The plant content of adobe bricks, *Calif. Hist. Soc. Quart.* 4 361—73.

HIBBERT, A.R., 1971, Increases in streamflow after converting chaparral to grass, *Water Resources Res.* 7, 71—80.

HINTON, R.J., 1878, *The Handbook of Arizona* (Am. News Co., New York), republished by Arizona Silhouettes, Tucson, 1954.

HOEL, P.G., 1966, *Elementary Statistics* (Wiley, New York).

HOOVER, J.W., 1929, The Indian country of southern Arizona, *Geog. Rev.* 19, 38—60.

HOUGH, W., 1906, Pueblo environments, *Am. Ass. Adv. Sci. Proc.* 55, 447—54.

HOYT, W.G., *et al.*, 1936, Studies in the relations of rainfall and runoff in the United States, *U.S. Geological Survey Water-Supply Paper*, 772.

HUMPHREY, R.R., 1958, The desert grassland, *Botanical Review*, 24.

HUNTINGTON, E., 1914, The climatic factor as illustrated in arid America, *Carnegie Inst. Washington Pub.* 192.

JORDAN, G.L., and M.L. MAYNARD, 1970, The San Simon watershed — historical review, *Progressive Agriculture in Arizona*, 22, 10—13.

JUDSON, S., 1952, Arroyos, *Scientific Am.* 187, 71—6.

KELLY, W.H., 1963, The Papago Indians of Arizona, a population and economic study, *MS*. Bur. Ethnic Res., Anthropology Dept., Univ. of Ariz.

KENNAN, G., 1917, *The Salton Sea: an account of Harriman's fight with the Colorado River* (Macmillan, New York).

KINCAID, D.R., H.B. OSBORN, and J.L. GARDNER, 1966, Use of unit-source watersheds for hydrologic investigations in the semiarid Southwest, *Water Resources Res.* 2, 381–92.

KINCAID, D.R., and G. WILLIAMS, 1966, Rainfall effects on soil surface characteristics following range improvement treatments, *Range Mgt*. 19, 346–51.

KINCER, J.B., 1933, Is our climate changing? *Monthly Weather Rev*. 61, 251–9.

——— , 1941, Climate and weather data from the United States, in *Climate and Man* (U.S. Dept. Agric., U.S.Govt. Printing Office, Wash.), 685–99.

KNECHTEL, M.M., 1938, Geology and ground-water resources of the valley of the Gila River and San Simon Creek, Graham County, Arizona, *U.S. Geological Survey Water-Supply Paper*, 796-F, 181–222.

LAMARCHE, V.C., 1966, An 800-year history of stream erosion as indicated by botanical evidence, *U.S. Geological Survey Prof. Paper*, 550–D, 83–6.

LANTOW, J.L., and E.L. FLORY, 1940, Fluctuating forage production, *Soil Conservation*, 6, 137–44.

LEE, W.T., 1905, Notes on the underground water of San Pedro Valley, Arizona, in Newell, F.H., 58th Congress, 3rd session, *House of Representatives Document* 28, 165–70.

LEOPOLD, A., 1921, A plea for recognition of artificial works in forest erosion and control policy, *J. Forestry*, 19, 267–73.

LEOPOLD, L.B., 1951a, Rainfall frequency: an aspect of climatic variation, *Trans. Am. Geoph. Un*., 32, 347–57.

——— , 1951b, Vegetation of southwestern watersheds in the nineteenth century, *Geog. Rev*. 61, 295–316.

——— , W.E. EMMETT, and R.M. MYRICK, 1966, Channel and hillslope processes in a semiarid area, New Mexico, *U.S. Geological Survey Prof. Paper*, 352–G, 193–253.

——— , and J.P. MILLER, 1954, A postglacial chronology for some alluvial valleys in Wyoming, *U.S. Geological Survey Water-Supply Paper*, 1261.

——— , and J.P. MILLER, 1956, Ephemeral streams, hydraulic factors and their relationship to the drainage net, *U.S. Geological Survey Prof. Paper*, 282A, 1–37.

——— , and C.I. SNYDER, 1951, Alluvial fills near Gallup, New Mexico, *U.S. Geological Survey Water-Supply Paper*, 1110–A, 1–19.

LEWIS, D.D., 1963, Desert floods – a report on Southern Arizona floods of September, 1962, *Ariz. State Land Dept., Water Resources Rept*. 13.

LEWIS, P., 1960, The use of moving averages in the analysis of time series, *Weather*, 15, 121–6.

LULL, H.W., 1964, Ecological and silvicultural aspects, Section 6, in Chow, V.T. (ed.), *Handbook of Applied Hydrology* (McGraw-Hill, New York), 1–30.

LUMHOLTZ, C., 1912, *New Trails in Mexico* (Scribners, New York).

LUSBY, G.C., 1964, Causes of variations in runoff and sediment yield from small drainage basins in western Colorado, *U.S. Dept. Agric. Miscellaneous Pub*. 970, 94–8.

——— , 1970, Hydrologic and biotic effects of grazing versus nongrazing near Grand Junction, Colorado, *U.S. Geological Survey Prof. Paper*, 700–B, 232–36.

LYNCH, H.B., 1931, *Rainfall and stream run-off in southern California since 1769* (Metropolitan Water Dist. of S. Calif., Los Angeles).

——— , 1948, Pacific Coast rainfall – wide fluctuations in a hundred years! , *Western Construction News*, 76–80.

MCCLINTOCK, J.H., 1921, *Mormon Settlement in Arizona* (Manufacturing Stationers, Phoenix, Ariz).

MCDONALD, J.E., 1956, Variability of precipitation in an arid region: a survey of characteristics for Arizona, *Univ. of Ariz., Inst. Atmospheric Physics, Tech. Rept.* 1.

MCDOWELL, M., 1920, Report on the Papago Indians, Arizona, App. N., *in Reports of the Dept. Interior* for the fiscal year ended 30 June, 1919, 2, *Indian Affairs Territories*, Washington, D.C.

MARTIN, P.S., 1964, *The Last 10,000 Years: A fossil pollen record of the American Southwest* (Univ. Ariz. Press, Tucson).

_____ , J. SCHOENWETTER, and B.C. ARMS, 1961, *Palynology and pre-history, the last 10,000 years* (Geochronology Labs., Univ. of Ariz., processed).

MEINZER, O.E., and F.C. KELTON, 1913, Geology and water resources of Sulphur Spring Valley, Arizona, *U.S. Geological Survey Water-Supply Paper*, 320.

MELTON, M.A., 1965, The geomorphic and paleoclimatic significance of alluvial deposits in southern Arizona, *J. Geol.* 73, 1–38.

MILLER, J.P., and F. WENDORF, 1958, Alluvial chronology of the Tesuque Valley, New Mexico, *J. Geol.* 66, 177–94.

MONKHOUSE, F.J., and H.R. WILKINSON, 1963, *Maps and Diagrams* (Methuen, London).

NELSON, E.W., 1934, The influence of precipitation and grazing upon black grama grass range, *U.S. Dept. Agric. Tech. Bull.*, 409.

NEWELL, F.H., 1905, Third annual report of the Reclamation Service, 1903–04, 58th Congress, 3rd session, *House of Representatives Document*, 28.

NICHOL, A.A., 1952, The natural vegetation of Arizona, *U. Arizona College of Agriculture Technical Bulletin*, 127, 189–230.

ODOM, E.R., no date, Frontier Days in Old Tucson as told by Warren Allison, MS. in the Arizona Historical Society.

OGDEN, P.R., and R.O. HAWKINSON, 1970, Influence of cover, soil, and micro-relief on runoff from desert grasslands, *Am. Soc. Range Mgt., 23rd Meeting*, duplicated paper.

OGROSKY, H.O., and V. MOCKUS, 1964, Hydrology of agricultural lands, Section 21, in Chow, V.T. (ed.), *Handbook of Applied Hydrology* (McGraw-Hill, New York).

OLBERG, C.R., and F.R. SCHANCK, 1913, Special Report on Irrigation and Flood Protection, Papago Indian Reservation, Arizona, 62nd Congress, 3rd Session, *Senate Document*, 973, 62–3.

OLMSTEAD, F.H., 1919, Gila River flood control, 65th Congress, 3rd Session, *Senate Document*, 436.

OSBORN, H.B. and R.B. HICKOK, 1968, Variability of rainfall affecting runoff from a semiarid rangeland watershed, *Water Resources Res.* 4, 199–203.

_____ , and L. LANE, 1969, Precipitation-runoff relations for very small semiarid rangeland watersheds, *Water Resources Res.* 5 419–25.

PACKER, P.E., 1951, Status of research on watershed protection requirements for granitic mountain soils in southwestern Idaho, *U.S. Forest Service, Intermountain For. and Range Exp. Sta. Res. Pap.* 27.

PAPAGO DEVELOPMENT PROGRAM, 1949, *U.S. Dept. Interior, Bureau of Indian Affairs*.

PARKER, K.W., and S.C. MARTIN, 1952, The mesquite problem on southern Arizona ranges, *U.S. Dept. Agric., SW Forest and Range Expt. Sta. Circular*, 908.

PATTISON, W.D., 1957, Beginnings of the American Rectangular Land Survey System, 1784–1800. *U. Chicago Department of Geography Research Paper*, 50.

PAULHUS, J.L.H., and M.A. KOHLER, 1952, Interpolation of missing precipitation records, *Monthly Weather Rev.*, 80, 129–33.

PETERSON, H.V., 1950, The problem of gullying in western valleys, in Trask, P.D. (ed.), *Applied sedimentation* (Wiley, New York), 407–34.

—— , and F.A. BRANSON, 1962, Effects of land treatments on erosion and vegetation on range lands in parts of Arizona and New Mexico, *J. Range Mgt.* 15, 220—6.

—— , and R.F. HADLEY, 1955, Effectiveness of erosion abatement practices on semiarid rangelands in western United States, *Int. Ass. Sci. Hydrology*, 53, 182—91.

PIPER, A.M., 1959, Derivation of a master record of rainfall, paper read to Am. Geoph. Un., Pacific Southwest Region, February, 1959.

QUINN, J.H., 1957, Paired river terraces and Pleistocene glaciation, *J. Geol.* 65, 149—66.

REAGAN, A.B., 1924a, Stress aggradation through irrigation, *Pan. Am. Geol.* 42, 335—44.

—— , 1924b, Recent changes in the Plateau Region, *Science*, 60, 283—5.

REYNOLDS, H.G., 1954, Meeting drought on southern Arizona rangelands, *J. Range Mgt.* 7, 33—40.

—— , and S.C. MARTIN, 1968, Managing grass-shrub cattle ranges in the Southwest, *U.S. Dept. Agric. Forest Service, Agric. Handbook*, 162.

RICH, J.L., 1911, Recent stream trenching in the semi-arid portion of southwestern New Mexico, a result of removal of vegetation cover, *Am. J. Sci.* 32, 237—45.

RICH, L.R., 1960, Water yields from the brush and oak-woodland region of Arizona, in Warnock, B.H. and J.L. Gardner, *Water Yield in Relation to Environment in the Southwestern United States* (A.A.A.S., Alpine, Texas), 28—38.

RICHARDSON, H.L., 1945, Discussion: the significance of terraces due to climatic oscillation, *Geol. Mag.* 82, 16—18.

ROBBINS, W.W., 1940, Alien plants growing without cultivation in California, *Calif. Agric. Expt. Sta. Bull.* 637.

ROBINSON, A., 1947, *Life in California: a historical account of the origin, customs and traditions of the Indians of Alta-California* (Biobooks, Oakland, Calif.).

RODGERS, W.M., 1965, Historical land occupance of the Upper San Pedro Valley since 1870, unpublished M.A. thesis, University of Arizona.

ROWE, P.B., 1944, Soil-moisture records from burned and unburned plots in certain grazing areas of California (Discussion), *Trans. Am. Geoph. Un.* 25, 84—6.

RUSSELL, R.J., 1932, Land forms of San Gorgonio Pass, southern California, *Univ. of Calif. Pubs. in Geog.* 6, 23—121.

SAUER, C.O., 1929, Land forms in the Peninsular Range of California as developed about Warner's Hot Springs and Mesa Grande, *Univ. of Calif. Pubs. in Geog.* 3, 199—248.

SAYLES, E.B., and E. ANTEVS, 1941, The Cochise Culture, *Medallion Papers*, 29 (Gila Pueblo, Globe, Arizona).

SCHOENWETTER, J., 1962, The pollen analysis of eighteen archaeological sites in Arizona and New Mexico, Ch. 8 in Chapters in the pre-history of eastern Arizona, Fieldiana, *Anthropology*, 53.

SCHREIBER, H.A., and D.R. KINCAID, 1967, Regression models for predicting on-site runoff from short-duration convective storms, *Water Resources Res.* 3, 389—95.

SCHULMAN, E., 1942, Centuries-long tree indices of precipitation in the Southwest, *Bull. Am. Met. Soc.* 23, 148—61, 204—17.

SCHUMM, S.A., and R.F. HADLEY, 1957, Arroyos and the semiarid cycle of erosion, *Am. J. Sci.* 225, 161—74.

SCHWENNESEN, A.T., 1917, Ground water in San Simon Valley, Arizona and New Mexico, *U.S. Geological Survey Water-Supply Paper*, 425, 1—35.

SELLERS, W.D., 1960, Precipitation trends in Arizona and New Mexico, *Proc. 28th Ann. Snow Conf.*, 81—94.

SHELTON, J.S., 1966, *Geology Illustrated* (Freeman, San Francisco).

SHREVE, R.L., 1951, Vegetation of the Sonoran Desert, *Carnegie Inst. Washington Pub.* 591.

SIEGEL, S., 1956, *Nonparametric Statistics for the Behavioral Sciences* (McGraw-Hill, New York).

SIMPSON, J.R., *et al.*, 1969, Papago floodwater pastures show promise, *Progressive Agric. in Arizona*, 21, 18—19.

SMITH, G.E.P., 1910, Groundwater supply and irrigation in the Rillito Valley, *Univ. of Arizona Agric. Expt. Sta. Bull.* 64, 81—242.

SPALDING, V.M., 1909, Distribution and movement of desert plants, *Carnegie Inst. Washington Pub.* 113.

STOCKTON, C.W., and H.C. FRITTS, 1971, Conditional probability of occurrence for variations in climate based on width of annual tree-rings in Arizona, *Tree-Ring Bull.* 31, 3—24.

STOIBER, P.E., 1973, Use of the U.S. General Land Office Survey notes for investigating vegetation change in southern Arizona, unpublished M.A. dissertation, University of Arizona, Tucson.

STOREY, H.C., R.L. HOBBA, and J.M. ROSA, 1964, Hydrology of forest lands and rangelands, Section 22, in Chow V.T. (ed.), *Handbook of Applied Hydrology* (McGraw-Hill, New York).

SWIFT, T.T., 1926, Date of channel trenching in the Southwest, *Science*, 63, 70—1.

THOMAS, H.E., 1962, The meteorologic phenomenon of drought in the Southwest, *U.S. Geological Survey Prof. Paper*, 372—A.

THORNBER, J.J., 1910, The grazing ranges of Arizona, *Ariz. Agric. Expt. Sta. Bull.* 65.

THORNTHWAITE, C.W., C.F.S. SHARPE, and E.F. DOSCH, 1942, Climate and accelerated erosion in the arid and semi-arid Southwest, with special reference to the Polacca Wash Drainage basin, Arizona, *U.S. Dept. Agric. Tech. Bull.* 808.

TUAN, Y.F., 1959, Pediments in southeastern Arizona, *Univ. Calif. Pubs. in Geog.* 13.

——— , 1962, Structure, climate and basin land forms in Arizona and New Mexico, *Ann. Ass. Am. Geog.* 52, 56—68.

——— , 1966, New Mexican gullies: a critical review and some recent observations, *Ass. Am. Geog. Ann.* 56, 573—97.

TURNER, S.F., *et al.*, 1943, Ground-water resources of the Santa Cruz basin, Arizona, *U.S. Geological Survey, open-file report*.

UNDERHILL, R.M., 1939, *Social Organization of the Papago Indians* (Columbia U.P., New York).

U.S. DEPT. AGRICULTURE, 1939, Range management and agronomic practices on the San Xavier Indian Reservation, Arizona and Land classification of San Xavier Indian Reservation Arizona, *S.C.S. — Bur. Ind. Aff.*, Denver, Col.

U.S. GEOLOGICAL SURVEY, various dates, *Professional Paper*, 655, (Several studies arising from the Gila River Phreatophyte Project).

——— , 1971, *Water Resources Data for Arizona*, 1970, I, *Surface Water Records*.

U.S. WEATHER BUREAU, 1872— . *Monthly Weather Review* (pub. monthly).

——— , 1897—1906, *California Section, Monthly Climate and Crop Report* (pub. monthly).

——— , 1903, Climatology of California, *Bull. L.*

——— , 1906—9, *California Section, Climatological Service Bull.* (pub. monthly).

——— , 1914— , *California Section, Climatological Data* (pub. monthly).

——— , 1934, Climatic summary of the United States, including Puerto Rico-Virgin Islands, *Bull. W*, secs. 16, 17, 18.

——— , 1950— , *Climatological Data, National Summary* (pub. monthly).

——— , 1952— , *Local Climatological Data* (pub. annually for official stations).

——— , 1956, Substation history, Arizona, *Key to Meteorological Records Documentation No. 1.1.*

——— , 1958, Substation history, California, *Key to Meteorological Records Documentation No. 1.1.*

—— , 1960, Generalised estimates of probable maximum precipitation for the United States west of the 105 meridian, *Tech. Paper*, 38.

UPSON, J.E., and G.F. WORTS, JR., 1951, Ground water in the Cuyama Valley, California, *U.S. Geological Survey Water-Supply Paper*, 1110–B.

VEIHMEYER, F.J., 1950, Soil moisture, runoff, erosion: long-term comparative studies on vegetated and denuded plots in typical brush areas of California, *Calif. Agric.* 11–13.

—— , 1951, Hydrology of range lands as affected by the presence or absence of brush vegetation, *Int. Ass. Sci. Hyd.* 3, 226–34.

—— , 1953, Use of water by native vegetation versus grasses and forbs on watersheds, *Trans. Am. Geoph. Un.* 34, 201–12.

—— , and C.N. JOHNSON, 1944, Soil moisture records from burned and unburned plots in certain grazing areas of California, *Trans. Am. Geoph Un.* 25, 72–88.

VISHER, S.S., 1920, Climate and geology (abstract), *Science*, 51, 522–3.

WHITE, N.D., and D. CHILDERS, 1967, Hydrologic conditions in the Douglas Basin, Cochise County, Arizona, *Arizona State Land Dept., Water Resources Report*, 30.

WHITE, N.D., W.G. MATLOCK, and H.C. SCHWALEN, 1966, An appraisal of the ground-water resources of Avra and Altar valleys, Pima County, Arizona, *Arizona State Land Dept., Water Resources Report*, 25.

WOODWARD, S., 1969, Vegetation of the Murray Springs area, Cochise County, Arizona, unpublished M.A. dissertation, University of Arizona, Tucson.

WOOLLEY, R.R., 1946, Cloudburst floods in Utah, 1850–1938, *U.S. Geological Survey Water-Supply Paper*, 994.

—— , and J.C. ALTER, 1938, Precipitation and vegetation, *Trans. Am. Geoph. Un.* 19, 604–7.

WYNNE, F., 1926, The west fork of the Gila River, *Science*, 64, 16–17.

YORK, J.C., and W.A. DICK-PEDDIE, 1969, Vegetation changes in southern New Mexico during the past hundred years, in McGinnies, W.G., and B.J. Goldman (eds.), *Arid Lands in Perspective* (Univ. Ariz. Press, Tucson), 155–65.

INDEX